Perspectives on Labour Law

D1335460

This is an accessible but thought-provoking introduction to labour law. It is suitable for those coming to the subject for the first time, and it will also be of interest to more advanced students, including postgraduates, who need to think about the subject's broader themes.

The academic literature on labour law makes considerable use of human rights arguments and of economic analysis. Both of these approaches provide valuable insights into the underlying policy of the law but they can be rather off-putting for students who do not know the international human rights instruments, or who have no background in economics. This book introduces these wider perspectives on labour law and then applies them to a selection of topics, including anti-discrimination law, dismissal, working time, pay, consultation and collective bargaining, trade union membership and industrial action.

A. C. L. Davies is Fellow and Tutor in Law at Brasenose College, Oxford where she teaches Labour Law and Public Law.

The Law in Context Series

Editors: William Twining (University College, London) and
Christopher McCrudden (Lincoln College, Oxford)

Since 1970 the Law in Context series has been in the forefront of the movement to broaden the study of law. It has been a vehicle for the publication of innovative scholarly books that treat law and legal phenomena critically in their social, political, and economic contexts from a variety of perspectives. The series particularly aims to publish scholarly legal writing that brings fresh perspectives to bear on new and existing areas of law taught in universities. A contextual approach involves treating legal subjects broadly, using materials from other social sciences, and from any other discipline that helps to explain the operation in practice of the subject under discussion. It is hoped that this orientation is at once more stimulating and more realistic than the bare exposition of legal rules. The series includes original books that have a different emphasis from traditional legal textbooks, while maintaining the same high standards of scholarship. They are written primarily for undergraduate and graduate students of law and of other disciplines, but most also appeal to a wider readership. In the past, most books in the series have focused on English law, but recent publications include books on European law, globalization, transnational legal processes, and comparative law.

Books in the Series

Ashworth: *Sentencing and Criminal Justice*
Barton & Douglas: *Law and Parenthood*
Bell: *French Legal Cultures*
Bercusson: *European Labour Law*
Birkinshaw: *European Public Law*
Birkinshaw: *Freedom of Information: The Law, the Practice and the Ideal*
Cane: *Atiyah's Accidents, Compensation and the Law*
Collins: *The Law of Contract*
Cranston: *Consumers and the Law*
Cranston: *Legal Foundations of the Welfare State*
Davies: *Perspectives on Labour Law*
Davies & Freedland: *Labour Law: Text and Materials*
de Sousa Santos: *Toward a New Legal Common Sense*
Detmold: *Courts and Administrators: A study in Jurisprudence*
Diduck: *Law's Families*
Doggett: *Marriage, Wife-Beating and the Law in Victorian England*
Dummett & Nicol: *Subjects, Citizens, Aliens and Others: Nationality and Immigration Law*
Elworthy & Holder: *Environmental Protection: Text and Materials*
Fortin: *Children's Rights and the Developing Law*
Glover-Thomas: *Reconstructing Mental Health Law and Policy*
Gobert & Punch: *Rethinking Corporate Crime*
Goodrich: *Languages of Law*
Hadden: *Company Law and Capitalism*
Harlow & Rawlings: *Law and Administration: Text and Materials*
Harris: *An Introduction to Law*
Harris: *Remedies, Contract and Tort*

For my parents

Perspectives on Labour Law

A. C. L. Davies

Fellow and Tutor in Law, Brasenose College, University of Oxford

CAMBRIDGE
UNIVERSITY PRESS

PUBLISHED BY THE PRESS SYNDICATE OF THE UNIVERSITY OF CAMBRIDGE
The Pitt Building, Trumpington Street, Cambridge, United Kingdom

CAMBRIDGE UNIVERSITY PRESS
The Edinburgh Building, Cambridge CB2 2RU, UK
40 West 20th Street, New York, NY 10011-4211, USA
477 Williamstown Road, Port Melbourne, VIC 3207, Australia
Ruiz de Alarcón 13, 28014 Madrid, Spain
Dock House, The Waterfront, Cape Town 8001, South Africa

http://www.cambridge.org

First published 2004

Printed in the United Kingdom at the University Press, Cambridge

Typefaces Minion 9.75/12.5 pt, and Frutiger   *System* LaTeX 2_ε [T B]

A catalogue record for this book is available from the British Library

Library of Congress Cataloguing in Publication data

ISBN 0 521 60523 7 paperback

Contents

Preface

For many students, the first few weeks of a course in labour law can seem rather daunting. Many of the subject's main principles are derived from statute, rather than case law, so there is less room for the kind of detailed case analysis familiar from core subjects like contract and tort. And policy discussions play a much greater role in labour law than they do in, say, land law or trusts. When writing about anti-discrimination law, for example, labour lawyers think about whether positive discrimination should be permitted, or whether employers should be allowed to say that 'market forces' led them to pay men more than they pay women doing equal work.

The subject's emphasis on legislation and on policy arguments is confusing enough. But life gets even more difficult when we look at the way in which labour lawyers construct their policy arguments. In what Hugh Collins has termed the 'productive disintegration' of labour law, writers now draw on a wide range of other disciplines and approaches in order to make sense of the law.[1] As chapter 1 will show, labour lawyers have traditionally used industrial relations, a branch of sociology, as a frame of reference. But this discipline has been joined by various kinds of economic analysis, arguments from social justice, and the discourse of fundamental human rights.

This array of perspectives on labour law is what gives the subject its fascination. But for newcomers it can seem bewildering. Each perspective has its own methodology and its own set of internal problems. To understand a piece of labour law writing which draws on economic arguments, it is necessary to understand how economists think: the methods they use and the assumptions they make. To understand a piece of labour law writing which draws on human rights arguments, it is helpful to understand some of the more theoretical debates about what it means to say that someone has a 'right'. And all this must be done whilst students are trying to absorb the basic rules and principles of a large and highly complex body of law.

This book is here to help. Its aim is to introduce two of the main perspectives used in the analysis of labour law today – human rights and economics – and to show how they play out in some of the key areas of the law. It will not be argued

---

1 H. Collins, 'The productive disintegration of labour law' (1997) 26 *ILJ* 295.

that either perspective is 'correct', or preferable to the other. Each perspective offers different insights. If we work from a single perspective, there is a danger that we will blind ourselves to initiatives which do not fit with our view of the world. Collins argues that this is what happened to many labour lawyers in the 1960s and 1970s who continued to analyse the law using an outdated sociological model.[2] Equally, however, it is important to remember that the perspectives themselves are far from being one-dimensional. There are different schools of thought in economics and in the literature on human rights. There is no single 'economists' view' on the national minimum wage, for example. So we need to develop a nuanced understanding of the perspectives themselves.

Part I of this book introduces the two perspectives. Chapter 1 offers a brief history of labour law from 1945 to the present, showing how labour lawyers' arguments have changed over time. At first, the subject was dominated by sociological analysis. But as government policies changed, particularly from the 1970s onwards, rights and economics became increasingly relevant to labour lawyers' thinking. Indeed, since 1997, the government has explicitly sought to strike a balance between workers' rights and business efficiency. Chapter 2 introduces the economics perspective. It explains economists' methodology and identifies two competing schools of thought: neoclassical economics, which tends to be hostile to labour law, and new institutional economics, which suggests that legal regulation can be beneficial. Chapter 3 introduces the rights perspective. It explains the historical development of international human rights law and discusses some of the complex issues which arise when we try to interpret rights and to apply them to particular situations. Chapter 4 looks at the way in which labour law is created and applied: at the layers of international, regional and domestic regulation which make up the subject. This is essential because labour law cannot be understood as a purely 'domestic' subject. The UK is not immune to international and regional trends. And the rights and economics arguments play out in different ways at the different levels, often leading to conflicts between them. Part II of the book applies the insights of rights theorists and economists to a selection of topics in labour law. The aim is to provide an accessible introduction to each topic, and to demonstrate the interplay between the rights and economics perspectives. The book concludes with a postscript which revisits the arguments of Part I and explores the future prospects of labour law.

This book is intended to be read at least twice. The first time you read it, use it as an introduction to the basic principles of labour law and to the policy arguments surrounding the subject. Once you have studied labour law in detail and looked at the cases and statutes for yourself, I hope you will return to this book, perhaps as part of your revision. The second time you read it, try to use it to develop your own perspective on labour law, and to think about how you might defend that perspective against the arguments of others. Each chapter concludes with suggestions for further reading, and questions to consider while you do the reading. Part of the point of the

2 Above n. 1.

further reading is to give you more detail about the law, and a more in-depth account of the perspectives, than can be given in a relatively short introductory book. But do not be surprised if some of the reading challenges the arguments described in the relevant chapter. One writer might argue that one of the perspectives used does not offer any valid insights into the law. Another writer might argue that two of the perspectives need to be combined in order to understand the law properly. Yet another writer might argue that the law is best explained and developed using an entirely different approach not considered in this book at all. This might seem a bit unsettling at first. But if you persevere, you will find that the further reading gives you a much richer understanding of labour law.

Anne Davies
Oxford
December 2003

Acknowledgements

The relative slimness of this volume has not prevented me from incurring a number of debts of gratitude during the course of its development. I would like to thank Susan Newbould for first stimulating my interest in labour law. I am grateful to my fellow labour lawyers in Oxford, both past and present, for their support and intellectual companionship: Diamond Ashiagbor, Alan Bogg, Paul Davies, Sandra Fredman, Mark Freedland, and Chris McCrudden. Brasenose College granted me an invaluable term's sabbatical towards the end of the project, and I would like to thank my colleagues, particularly Bill Swadling and Arianna Pretto, for protecting me from interruptions. Excellent research assistance was provided by Amir Fuchs. I owe a particular debt to successive generations of Oxford students, who have been the unwitting guinea-pigs for this book, for their sharpness and enthusiasm.

The series editors for Law in Context, Chris McCrudden and William Twining, offered wise advice during the development of the proposal and helpful comments on drafts. Responsibility for errors is, of course, my own. I am indebted to the editorial staff of Cambridge University Press for their professionalism and efficiency in seeing the book through to publication.

And finally, my biggest debt of gratitude is, as always, to my parents, to whom this book is dedicated, for their unstinting love and support.

Table of statutes

Table of statutory instruments

Table of conventions and foreign legislation

Foreign legislation
France

United States

Table of cases

Abbreviations

JIEL	Journal of International Economic Law
LQR	Law Quarterly Review
MLR	Modern Law Review
PL	Public Law
UNTS	United Nations Treaty Series

Others

ACAS	Advisory, Conciliation and Arbitration Service
CAC	Central Arbitration Committee
CAP	Common Agricultural Policy
CBI	Confederation of British Industry
CEDAW	Convention on the Elimination of All Discrimination Against Women
CEEP	European Centre of Enterprises with Public Participation and of Enterprises of General Economic Interest
CRC	Convention on the Rights of the Child
CRE	Commission for Racial Equality
DTI	Department of Trade and Industry
EAT	Employment Appeal Tribunal
ECHR	European Convention on Human Rights (European Convention for the Protection of Human Rights and Fundamental Freedoms)
ECtHR	European Court of Human Rights
ECJ	European Court of Justice
EES	European Employment Strategy
EOC	Equal Opportunities Commission
ESC	European Social Charter
ETUC	European Trade Union Confederation
EWC	European Works Council
GATT	General Agreement on Tariffs and Trade
ICCPR	International Covenant on Civil and Political Rights
ICERD	International Convention on the Elimination of All Forms of Racial Discrimination
ICESCR	International Covenant on Economic, Social and Cultural Rights
ILO	International Labour Organisation
SMP	Statutory Maternity Pay
SNB	Special Negotiating Body
SPP	Statutory Paternity Pay
TUC	Trades Union Congress
UDHR	United Nations Universal Declaration of Human Rights
UNICE	Union of Industrial and Employers' Confederations of Europe
WERS	Workplace Employee Relations Survey
WTO	World Trade Organization

Part I

1

A brief history of labour law

Labour lawyers today commonly think about their subject using ideas about workers' rights, economic efficiency for firms or for the market as a whole, or social justice for workers. These ideas are not new. But they did not play a major role in the early history of labour law. In the 1950s, labour lawyers used sociology to make sense of their subject. This chapter will explain how rights and economics – the two key perspectives to be used in this book – started to feature more commonly in labour lawyers' thinking in the 1970s, and attained the central place they have today.[1] It will also demonstrate the importance of using more than one perspective to understand the law.

Collective laissez-faire – the 1950s

The work of Otto Kahn-Freund has exercised, and continues to exercise, a considerable degree of influence over labour lawyers' thinking. Writing in the 1950s, he drew heavily on industrial relations theory – a branch of sociology – in order to understand the law.[2] This was essential because anyone using a 'black-letter' approach – in other words, looking solely at the legal materials – would have acquired a wholly misleading knowledge of the relationship between employers and employees. For example, there were few legal controls on the circumstances in which employees could be dismissed. At common law, the contract of employment could be terminated if the employer gave notice. The courts did not inquire into whether or not the employer had a good reason for the dismissal. And there was no statutory intervention in this area until 1971. But this did not necessarily mean that in practice, employers had an unfettered power to dismiss their employees. Where trade unions were present in a workplace, they were often able to use their collective strength to protect individual employees against arbitrary dismissal.

Drawing on sociology, Kahn-Freund developed a sophisticated theory of labour law called 'collective *laissez-faire*'. Kahn-Freund's insight was that in Britain, the law

---

1 See, generally, H. Collins, 'The productive disintegration of labour law' (1997) 26 *ILJ* 295; P. Davies and M. Freedland, *Labour Legislation and Public Policy* (1993).
2 See O. Kahn-Freund, 'Legal Framework', in A. Flanders and H. A. Clegg (eds.), *The System of Industrial Relations in Great Britain: its History, Law and Institutions* (1954).

played a very minor role in industrial relations, particularly in comparison with other industrialised Western nations. There were relatively few statutes obliging employers to treat individual workers in particular ways or even to promote collective bargaining between trade unions and employers. Instead, employers and trade unions were left to regulate their own affairs. It was this policy of 'non-interference' that Kahn-Freund labelled 'collective *laissez-faire*'.

But collective *laissez-faire* did not mean that the law played no role at all. In the nineteenth and early twentieth centuries, the common law courts were hostile to the trade unions. The courts cast doubt on the legality of trade unions by declaring that their aims fell foul of the doctrine of restraint of trade.[3] And they set about developing various economic torts – conspiracy, inducing breach of contract, interfering with trade or business – which exposed strike organisers to civil liability. In the infamous *Taff Vale* case of 1901, the House of Lords held that unions could be sued in tort in their own name and held liable for the actions of their officials.[4] Collective bargaining could not easily take place under these conditions. Successive governments therefore intervened with statutes which removed the common law obstacles to collective bargaining. The Trade Union Act 1871 declared that the doctrine of restraint of trade did not apply to unions. The Trade Disputes Act 1906 protected unions from tort liability and provided that strike organisers could not be held liable for the torts of conspiracy, interference with business or inducing breach of contract. Kahn-Freund used the term 'negative law' to describe this facilitative legislation.[5]

But collective *laissez-faire* was more than just a description of the law. Kahn-Freund also saw it as an ideal for the law to strive towards, for three main reasons. First, he argued that legal intervention was unnecessary because collective bargaining was an effective way of protecting workers. The presence of unions successfully redressed the power imbalance between workers and employers. Second, he claimed that workers' rights were more secure if they were acquired through collective bargaining rather than through constitutional or legislative guarantees. He believed that if the government had not granted the rights in the first place, it could not take them away. Third, he thought that collective *laissez-faire* was more flexible than legislation because it allowed unions and employers to decide things for themselves and to respond to changing circumstances.

The demise of collective laissez-faire – the 1960s and 1970s

Collins has argued that the theory of collective *laissez-faire* exercised something of a stranglehold over labour law thinking through the 1960s and 1970s.[6] It took lawyers

---

3 *Hornby v Close* [1867] LR 2 QB 153.
4 *Taff Vale Railway Co v Amalgamated Society of Railway Servants* [1901] AC 426 (HL).
5 Above n. 2, at 44.
6 Collins, above n. 1. Cf. Lord Wedderburn, 'Collective bargaining or legal enactment: the 1999 Act and trade union recognition' (2000) 29 *ILJ* 1.

some time to realise that they needed to change their theory to accommodate new developments in legislation and public policy. Governments became increasingly interested in promoting workers' rights, and managing the economy more actively. They also wanted to reduce the level of strike action, partly for economic reasons and partly because strikes came to be seen as a problem in their own right.

Promoting workers' rights

In the 1960s and 1970s, people began to question the fairness of a system which relied almost entirely on collective bargaining to protect workers. In the eyes of its critics, collective bargaining suffered from two major flaws. First, it did not cover all industries or workplaces. In 1967, it was estimated that 50% of manual workers and 30% of white collar workers were union members.[7] Although these figures are much higher than their modern equivalents, they still suggest that many workers were not protected by collective bargaining. Second, collective bargaining did not necessarily promote the interests of all sectors of the workforce. In 1951, only 27% of women workers were union members, compared with 56% of men.[8] Unions naturally focused on protecting the majority of their members. This led them to ignore or even to attack women's claims for better treatment at work, particularly in the area of equal pay.

One major statutory response to the first of these concerns was the unfair dismissal legislation, introduced in 1971.[9] The legislation (which will be discussed in more detail in chapter 9) sought to regulate the circumstances in which an employer could dismiss an employee. The employer had to have a reason for the dismissal and had to act reasonably in making the decision to dismiss. This was a radical departure from the common law, which did not inquire into the employer's reasons at all. Advocates of the legislation pointed to the unfairness of the common law position. Although unions did much to prevent arbitrary behaviour by employers, not all employees were protected by collective representation.

The concern that unions might not protect all sections of the workforce was addressed in the anti-discrimination legislation. The Equal Pay Act 1970 (which came into force in 1975) established the basic principle that women who were doing the same work as men should receive the same pay and other benefits under their contracts of employment. An important further step came with the enactment of the Sex Discrimination Act 1975 (SDA 1975), which tackled the many other respects in which employers might discriminate: in recruitment, training, promotion and so on. It also attacked discrimination by unions against members and applicants for membership. Parliament's first attempt to tackle race discrimination, the Race Relations Act 1968, made little impact. Responsibility for enforcing the Act was given to a statutory body, the Race Relations Board, but its powers were limited. The Act's

---

7 Davies and Freedland, above n. 1, at 46.
8 Davies and Freedland, above n. 1, at 46.
9 Industrial Relations Act 1971, ss. 22–32.

weaknesses were addressed by the Race Relations Act 1976, which contained very similar provisions to those set out in the SDA 1975. Individuals were given a right to bring proceedings under the 1976 Act, and the new statutory body, the Commission for Racial Equality, had much stronger enforcement powers than the old Board.

The anti-discrimination legislation was obviously a significant move away from collective *laissez-faire*: the idea that unions and employers should be left to determine employees' terms and conditions for themselves. It was argued that some rights were so fundamental that they should be protected for all employees, regardless of employers' or unions' attitudes and regardless of whether employees were covered by collective bargaining. Indeed, the legislation challenged some established industrial relations practices. For example, it was common prior to the SDA 1975 for unions to agree that part-time workers should be dismissed before full-time workers when a firm had to make some workers redundant. In *Clarke v Eley (IMI) Kynoch*,[10] this was held to be discriminatory because the majority of part-time workers are female.

The advocates of collective *laissez-faire* sought to modify their theory in order to incorporate the unfair dismissal and anti-discrimination legislation. They argued that the legislation created a 'floor of rights' on which collective bargaining could build. As Wedderburn explains:

> The statutory 'floor of rights' now extends into many facets of employment law ... but it does not normally prevent the erection of superior conditions by way of collective bargaining. It was meant to be a floor not a ceiling.[11]

In some ways, this is a useful method of analysis. To use the example given by Wedderburn himself, unions have often been able to negotiate more generous redundancy payments for employees than those provided for in legislation. But Collins has strongly criticised the 'floor of rights' argument, claiming that labour lawyers' determination to cling on to the collective *laissez-faire* analysis blinded them to the true significance of the new developments.[12] There are certainly some problems with the 'floor of rights' idea. First, for those workers not protected by collective bargaining, the floor is indeed a ceiling. Second, as Davies and Freedland argue, it has not always been the case that the aims of legislation have coincided with those of collective bargaining.[13] As explained above, unions were slow to take up the anti-discrimination agenda, and some of the practices they agreed with employers had a discriminatory effect. The government's intervention could be seen as a way of regulating the unions, not just supporting their activities. We could therefore view the legislation of the late 1960s and the 1970s as the beginning of a shift away from collective *laissez-faire*. Either way, this period marks the emergence of workers' rights as a central concern of modern labour law.

10   [1983] ICR 165.
11   Lord Wedderburn, *The Worker and the Law* (3rd edn., 1986), p. 6.
12   Above n. 1.
13   Above n. 1, at 383–4.

Managing the economy

During the 1960s and 1970s, collective *laissez-faire* came under attack from another direction. Successive governments began to take a more active role in managing the economy. Their main goal was to ensure that the UK had a favourable balance of trade: in other words, that the value of the products exported by the UK exceeded the value of the products imported by the UK. This was thought to be a sign of a prosperous economy. But the level of inflation was very high during this period. This meant that UK products were expensive and could not compete effectively in world markets. Since inflation was, in part, attributable to the high wage demands being made by unions, the government was bound to come under pressure to intervene more fully in industrial relations, and thus to abandon the policy of collective *laissez-faire*.

Economists differ in the ways in which they explain inflation. The 'cost-push' theory links inflation most closely to the activities of workers and unions.[14] Workers always want to get paid more, and employers always want to make more profit. From time to time, workers will succeed in persuading their employer to pay them more. This will reduce the employer's profits. So the employer passes on the cost to the consumer by raising the price of its products. This restores the employer's profits to their earlier levels. But then the whole process begins again: products are more expensive so workers start to demand further pay rises. The result is a 'price-wage spiral'. External factors can also contribute to inflation. In 1973, for example, the oil-producing countries raised the price of oil by a considerable margin. This had a knock-on effect on the price of other products and raised the cost of living generally, thus leading to further wage demands by workers.

Governments responded to spiralling inflation by trying to place limits on the wage increases unions could achieve through collective bargaining, through what were known as 'incomes policies'. One of the most extreme versions of incomes policy was that contained in Part IV of the Prices and Incomes Act 1966, which applied from August 1966 to August 1967. This allowed the government to ban an employer from paying a higher wage than that paid on 20 July 1966. It was enforced by criminal sanctions against employers, and against unions which put pressure on employers to pay more. The government used its powers to enforce a six-month pay freeze, followed by six months of 'severe restraint' in which only very limited pay increases were permitted. Compulsory incomes policies were, however, highly controversial and were used by governments as a last resort. At other times, voluntary incomes policies were pursued. In 1976–7, for example, the unions agreed to a 5% limit on pay rises in order to combat spiralling inflation, which had reached 27% in 1976. But voluntary incomes policies were never very stable. They were unpopular with grass-roots trade union members who saw their standard of living decline during periods of restraint. And democratically elected trade union leaders

---

14 Two key assumptions underlie this theory: that governments increase the supply of money in response to demand, and that the prices of goods are essentially determined by what they cost.

had to respond to their members' concerns. By 1978–9, for example, the TUC was refusing to agree to another request from the government for a 5% limit on pay rises.

It is fair to say that despite the incomes policies, no government in this period succeeded in getting inflation under control. But the incomes policies are highly significant for what they tell us about labour law. They show that governments' desire to manage the economy was so great that they did not have any qualms about intervening in the process of collective bargaining. At first, labour lawyers might have dismissed this as a temporary suspension of collective *laissez-faire*. But if the economic problems could not be resolved, it was hard to see when this 'suspension' might end.

Reducing the number of strikes

The other major problem faced by governments in the 1960s and 1970s was the high level of strike action. In 1964–6, for example, 190 working days per 1000 employees were lost because of strikes.[15] Unions were in a relatively powerful position because unemployment was low. Employers could not afford to ignore the demands of workers who could easily move to jobs elsewhere. Strikes were a cause of concern for two reasons. First, it was thought that they were contributing to the UK's economic problems. If UK firms were hit by high levels of strike action, they might not be able to deliver their products to purchasers on time. This would give them a reputation for unreliability which would harm their chances of exporting goods abroad. The balance of trade might start to tip in the wrong direction. Second, there was a growing feeling that the level of strike action was a sign that the unions were out of control. Davies and Freedland suggest that the high levels of strike action at this time produced 'a crisis of truly constitutional proportions'.[16] Those on the right of the political spectrum in particular began to argue that the trade unions were running the country, not the government.

In 1965, the Labour government set up a Royal Commission, usually known as the Donovan Commission, to investigate the strike problem.[17] Much of the evidence given to the Donovan Commission advocated a stronger role for the law in regulating industrial relations. Nevertheless, the Commission broadly adopted the collective *laissez-faire* view set out by Kahn-Freund in the 1950s: that the law should intervene as little as possible. The Commission's main recommendation was that employers and unions should change the way in which they conducted collective bargaining.[18] At that time, bargaining tended to take place between unions and employers' associations covering all the firms in a particular industry. But it was supplemented by informal bargaining between shop stewards (trade union

---

15 See the *Report of the Royal Commission on Trade Unions and Employers' Associations* (Cmnd. 3623, 1968), p. 95.
16 Above n. 1, at 242.
17 See, generally, above n. 15.
18 Above n. 15, chapter 16.

representatives for small workgroups) and managers in particular workplaces. Shop stewards often called unofficial 'wildcat' strikes to protest at managers' decisions. Unions had very little control over their behaviour. The Donovan Commission attributed the strike problem to the split between the two types of bargaining. The Commission argued that bargaining should instead take place at plant or company level. This kind of bargaining would be conducted by union leaders, taking into account the needs of all the various workgroups. It was hoped that this would put an end to supplementary bargaining by shop stewards, and hence to 'wildcat' strikes. The change was not to be brought about by law. Instead, the Commission expected employers and unions to alter their practices voluntarily. In fact, some employers and unions had already begun to bargain on this basis and the change spread rapidly.

By the time the Donovan Commission reported, in 1968, the strike problem had worsened. The Labour government accepted many of the Commission's proposals but wanted to make greater use of the law to prevent strikes.[19] For example, it wanted to require unions to ballot their members before taking strike action. The government never managed to enact its plans, in part because of opposition from the unions. It then lost the general election in 1970 and the Conservatives came to power. They believed that the only way to reassert government control over industrial relations – and thus to achieve economic progress – was to provide a comprehensive legal framework to regulate trade unions and, most importantly, strike action. The Industrial Relations Act 1971 reflected two main policies. First, it sought to reduce or eliminate unofficial action organised by shop stewards by leaving such action exposed to the full force of the common law of tort.[20] Second, trade unions were given a strong incentive to behave 'responsibly' (as the government saw it) in their use of the strike weapon. The statute listed various 'unfair industrial practices' for which unions could be held liable. This was used to ban, for example, strike action against firms not directly involved in a dispute with the union.[21] However, the government's grand scheme met with considerable resistance from the trade unions. The unions' most successful strategy was to refuse to register under the Act. Because the Act's protections were confined to registered unions, all strike action by unregistered unions was exposed to liability at common law. It might be supposed that this would have put the unions in an impossible position. But the government quickly realised that a situation in which all strike action was unprotected was unsustainable. The Act's failure was a major factor in the government's electoral defeat in 1974.

The Labour government elected in 1974 tried a new tactic. It did a deal with the unions, sometimes known as the 'Social Contract'. It promised to enact more favourable labour legislation if the unions would limit their wage demands and,

---

19 For detail see the White Paper *In Place of Strife: A Policy for Industrial Relations* (Cmnd. 3888, 1969).
20 This was the intended effect of s. 96.
21 See s. 98.

in consequence, their use of the strike weapon. The new legislation had two key features. First, it marked a return to the pre-1971 approach to regulating trade unions and strike action. It left the common law to define the wrongs committed by unions and strike organisers, but provided a set of immunities to protect them from liability.[22] Second, the legislation put in place various strategies for *supporting* collective bargaining. People sometimes describe the legislation as a return to collective *laissez-faire*, but this is not entirely accurate because it went far beyond Kahn-Freund's 'negative law'. For example, the Employment Protection Act 1975 included a 'recognition procedure' which could, under certain circumstances, lead to an employer being obliged to bargain with a particular union.[23] Although the unions welcomed these changes, they did not keep their side of the bargain. There was a wave of strike action in late 1978 and early 1979 which is sometimes referred to as the 'winter of discontent'. Yet again, a failure to control the strike problem contributed to the downfall of the government.

The history of industrial conflict law in the 1960s and 1970s tells us a lot about the changing shape of labour law. It shows the demise of collective *laissez-faire*: governments of both political persuasions were prepared to use the law much more extensively. And it reinforces the importance of the economic perspective. Although strikes were seen as a problem *per se*, governments were also motivated to intervene by the fact that they disrupted the national economy. But the two main strategies tried during this period – comprehensive legislation and the much softer 'Social Contract' – were largely unsuccessful.

Individualism and deregulation – the 1980s and early 1990s

The years 1979–97 saw successive Conservative governments adopting a novel approach to labour law. The three themes we have identified so far – promoting workers' rights, tackling the strike problem, and promoting economic growth – were ongoing concerns. But they were defined in new ways, and new strategies were adopted for addressing them. We will examine each of these themes in turn, and conclude by looking at the links between them.

Promoting workers' rights: EC law

During this period, the main source of new developments in workers' rights against their employers was EC law. The Conservative government was, as we shall see, hostile to employment protection legislation and it successfully resisted many proposals for new EC legislation. In particular, the government 'opted out' of the Protocol and Agreement on Social Policy of the Maastricht Treaty, so that the UK was not subject to the employment directives enacted under it. But in the area of sex

---

22 Trade Union and Labour Relations Act 1974, ss. 13–17, as amended; Trade Union and Labour Relations (Amendment) Act 1976.
23 See ss. 11–16.

discrimination, which had an established legal basis in what was then Article 119 of the Treaty, important developments did occur.

The Equal Pay Directive of 1975 confirmed that Article 119 included a principle of 'equal value': where a woman's work could be rated as of equal *value* to that done by a man (on a series of headings like effort, concentration and so on) she should receive equal pay.[24] This was more generous than the Equal Pay Act 1970, which only covered cases where the woman's work was the *same* as the man's or where the employer had voluntarily ranked the two jobs as equal.[25] The Commission was forced to bring infringement proceedings in the European Court of Justice (ECJ) before it could persuade the government to amend UK law.[26] But the equal value principle was finally added to UK law in the Equal Pay (Amendment) Regulations 1983.[27] As we shall see in chapter 8, the Regulations are narrowly drafted, but the courts have been able to draw on EC law in order to give them a more generous interpretation.

Protecting workers' rights: individualism

One of the key ideological commitments of the Conservative Prime Minister, Margaret Thatcher, was individualism: the idea that individual rights and interests should always prevail over collective concerns. As we have seen, labour law had long placed emphasis on the protection of the individual through trade union membership and collective bargaining. The government took a very different view, identifying two main categories of individual who might be harmed by powerful unions: those who did not wish to join a union at all, and those union members who did not agree with their leaders' policies.

Those who did not wish to join a union at all were most likely to be harmed by the 'closed shop'. This term is used to describe a workplace in which all employees are required to be members of a particular trade union. The government gradually dismantled the legal protections of the closed shop until it was made wholly unlawful in 1988. Section 11 of the Employment Act 1988 gave individuals a right, as against the employer, not to be dismissed or subjected to detrimental treatment on the grounds that they were not trade union members. This had the effect of abolishing the closed shop because employers were no longer able to get rid of employees who refused to participate in the arrangement. The closed shop is, of course, highly controversial.[28] Many trade unionists would argue that although each individual worker loses his or her freedom of choice about union membership, a strong union is the best way to protect individual interests. A union with 100% support in the workplace is bound to be in a good bargaining position. From a rights perspective, however, the closed shop is much harder to justify. Most theorists would see freedom

---

24 Directive 75/117/EC, Article 1.
25 See s. 1.
26 Case 61/81 *Commission v UK* [1982] ICR 578.
27 SI 1983/1794.
28 See chapter 11.

of association as protecting people's choices: individuals should be able to choose which organisations to join and organisations should be allowed to choose whom to admit. The idea of an enforced association is hard to square with a right framed in these terms.

The second category of workers who, in the government's view, might be adversely affected by trade union power were those union members who disagreed with their leaders' policies. The Employment Act 1988, s. 3, gave individuals the right not to be 'unjustifiably disciplined' by their union. This prevented unions from taking any disciplinary action against members who refused to take part in a strike. The government argued that this protected the individual's freedom of choice. But trade unionists saw this right as yet another misguided attack on collective strength. It was claimed that individuals would ultimately lose out because unions would be weakened if they could not force all their members to take strike action.

The government's preferred interpretation of workers' rights was therefore very different from that advanced during the 1960s and 1970s, and from that adopted by the EC. It sought to use workers' rights to protect individuals from the collective strength of trade unions, rather than to protect them from the power of their employers.

Tackling strikes

Those theorists who take a more sceptical view of the government's promotion of individual rights would argue that its policies were all part of another, broader aim of reducing the power of the trade unions. The government adopted two main strategies to tackle the strike problem. One was to dismantle the laws of the 1970s which offered positive support for collective bargaining. For example, in 1980, the recognition procedure in the Employment Protection Act 1975 was abolished.[29] This left a union without any legal remedies where it had a high level of support in a particular workplace but the employer nevertheless refused to recognise it for collective bargaining. The second, and most important, strategy was to narrow the circumstances in which strike action would be protected from liability in tort.

Several examples could be given of this second strategy, but for reasons of space we will consider just one. The Trade Disputes Act 1906, s. 4, had granted trade unions complete immunity from liability in tort.[30] This was designed to ensure that employers could only sue strike organisers (although they too had some immunity) and would have no chance of getting at union funds in legal actions. The Employment Act 1982 took away the unions' blanket immunity and subjected them to the immunity rules governing strike organisers instead.[31] The statute did set a limit on the amount of damages which could be awarded against a union, but it was

---

29 Employment Act 1980, s. 19.
30 This had been repealed by the Industrial Relations Act 1971 but was re-enacted in s. 14 of the Trade Union and Labour Relations Act 1974.
31 Sections 15–16.

more common for employers to seek an injunction to stop the action. If the union breached the injunction it was exposed to unlimited fines for contempt of court. In 1990, s. 6 of the Employment Act broadened the range of officials for whose actions the union could be held liable. These provisions were intended by the government as an attack on the 'privileged position' of trade unions. The government portrayed the immunities as putting the unions 'above the law', and argued that an increase in liability would encourage unions to behave more responsibly.

In a Green Paper published in 1991, the government claimed that its attempt to reduce the power of the unions had succeeded.[32] The level of strike action was significantly lower and, it was suggested, Britain had become an attractive location for foreign firms. These arguments are, however, fiercely disputed. The level of unemployment rose substantially during the 1980s. This tends to reduce the incidence of strikes because workers are grateful to have a job at all. Moreover, union membership declined, in part because there were fewer and fewer jobs in manufacturing industries, the unions' traditional stronghold. These economic factors must also have played a part in reducing strike levels: indeed, some would say that they are the main explanation for the change.

Reducing burdens on business

In the late 1980s, the rhetoric of tackling the strike problem began to give way to a much broader set of ideas, sometimes labelled 'deregulation'. The government began to portray laws which regulated the conduct of firms – on matters such as health and safety, environmental protection, or employment – as 'burdens on business'.[33] The government argued that, as far as possible, these burdens ought to be removed, because they imposed costs on businesses and made them less competitive. Moreover, in the late 1980s, the government became increasingly focused on the need to create jobs to combat the problem of high unemployment.[34] It was argued that employers would be more willing to take on additional workers if they could do so cheaply: in other words, without having to provide them with costly legal rights. This provided another reason for reducing the level of regulation.

There are many examples of the deregulatory trend. One strategy was to repeal existing protective statutes. In 1993, the government abolished the Wages Councils.[35] These were bodies which set a minimum wage for workers in a particular trade. Although the Wages Councils had never set particularly high rates of pay, they did provide some protection for workers in the lowest-paying industries. But the government argued that they stifled competition between firms and priced workers out of jobs.

---

32 Department of Employment, *Industrial Relations in the 1990s: Proposals for Further Reform of Industrial Relations and Trade Union Law* (Cm. 1602, 1991).
33 Department of Trade and Industry, *Burdens on Business: Report of a Scrutiny of Administrative and Legislative Requirements* (1985).
34 Department of Employment, *Employment for the 1990s* (Cm. 540, 1988).
35 Trade Union Reform and Employment Rights Act 1993, s. 35.

Another strategy was to restrict access to employment rights. So, in 1979, the 'qualifying period' (the time an employee had to work before he or she could bring a claim) for unfair dismissal was raised from six months to one year,[36] and in 1985 it was raised again to two years.[37] This was presented as a measure to increase flexibility in the labour market and to create jobs. It was felt that employers would be more willing to take on new workers if they had a relatively long period in which they could dismiss those workers without fear of legal action. But this move deprived a substantial number of workers of the law's protection.

A third strategy was to ignore changes in the workplace which a more regulation-minded government might have chosen to control. For example, during this period, many employers started to arrange for their staff to have self-employed status, rather than employee status. This saved money for employers because, as we shall see in chapter 5, self-employed workers have hardly any employment rights. Many labour lawyers see this as a form of 'cheating' which the government should have controlled. But since the government's own policy was to reduce labour costs, it was hardly going to stop employers who had found a way of doing this for themselves.

Conclusion

Although it is possible to identify distinctive strands of reasoning in the Conservative policies of the 1980s, they are all linked to some extent. The government's unwillingness to promote workers' rights against their employers was linked to its desire to deregulate the employment market. The government's interest in individual rights against trade unions could not be entirely separated from its attack on the unions: it was thought that trade union members were moderate and would undermine their leaders' radical policies. And the attack on collective bargaining and strike action was linked to deregulation because it provided another way of giving employers greater freedom to make decisions for themselves. All three strands were held together by the government's overall economic policy of promoting a free market. Thus, although the use made of rights and economics arguments in this period was radically different from the use made of such arguments in the 1960s and 1970s, they retained their status as essential tools of analysis for the labour lawyer.

'The third way' – 1997-present

The Labour government elected in 1997 appears to have brought a new approach to labour law. It has abandoned some of the Conservative policies of the 1980s: perhaps most significantly, it is no longer openly hostile to EC legislation on labour issues. It remains concerned with our two familiar themes: workers' rights and a prosperous economy. But it claims to have rejected the 1980s thesis that workers' rights are always a burden on business. Rights are seen instead as *promoting* economic success. This

---

36 Unfair Dismissal (Variation of Qualifying Period) Order 1979 (SI 1979/959).
37 Unfair Dismissal (Variation of Qualifying Period) Order 1985 (SI 1985/782).

notion of striking a balance between apparently conflicting policies is sometimes labelled 'the third way'.[38] Later chapters will explore recent legislation in detail. Here we will focus on the thinking behind the government's various initiatives, as set out in the White Paper *Fairness at Work*.[39] The initiatives can usefully be divided into three groups: individual rights proposed by the government itself; individual rights derived from EC law; and changes to the law on trade unions.

The government has implemented various changes to the rights of individual workers. For example, a national minimum wage has been introduced which guarantees a certain hourly rate to virtually all workers.[40] This change is described in a chapter in *Fairness at Work* entitled 'New Rights for Individuals',[41] and one of the main justifications given is the fairness argument that it will prevent the exploitation of individual workers. But economic arguments also play an important role. The government is concerned to attract firms to invest in the UK and to create jobs. In an era of globalisation, firms can locate themselves virtually anywhere in the world. The UK is not an attractive destination in terms of cost, because wage levels are very high, particularly when compared with those in developing countries. The government argues that the UK should compete instead on the basis of its ability to produce high-quality, technologically advanced goods and services. And – as we shall see in chapter 2 – it claims that workers will contribute more to the realisation of this vision of the economy if their rights are respected.

The second set of rights discussed in *Fairness at Work* are those derived from EC law. The Labour government is less hostile to EC developments. Soon after coming into power, it signed the Protocol and Agreement on Social Policy of the Maastricht Treaty, which the Conservatives had refused to do. The Directives agreed by the other Member States by this route – such as the Parental Leave Directive and the Part-Time Workers Directive – were extended to the UK and implemented.[42] Again, the government's rhetoric when announcing these changes has reflected 'third way' ideas. They have been presented not just as advances in workers' rights, but also as advances in the competitiveness of the UK economy. In relation to the Parental Leave Directive, for example, the government suggested that if it was easier for parents to balance work and family life, more parents would choose to work, and employers would benefit from having a wider pool of talent from which to select their employees.[43] Interestingly, however, the 'deregulation' approach still has its place: the government expressed particular concern that small businesses might find some aspects of the Directive burdensome.[44]

---

38 See, generally, A. Giddens, *The Third Way* (1998).
39 Department of Trade and Industry, *Fairness at Work* (Cm. 3968, 1998).
40 National Minimum Wage Act 1998.
41 Above n. 39, para. 3.2.
42 Directive 96/34/EC (extended to the UK by Directive 97/75/EC) and Directive 97/81/EC (extended to the UK by Directive 98/23/EC) respectively.
43 Above n. 39, paras. 5.1–5.3.
44 Above n. 39, para. 5.26.

Finally, the government has made some changes to the law on trade unions. Perhaps the most important of these is the introduction of a statutory 'recognition procedure'.[45] Put simply, this means that when a union can show that it has the support of a significant proportion of a particular workgroup, the employer can be legally obliged to recognise the union for collective bargaining on pay, hours and holidays. The procedure is designed to maximise opportunities for the employer and the union to reach a voluntary agreement, but there is a possibility of compulsion as a last resort. The government concedes that the main justification for the procedure is 'to offer greater protection and security at work for the vulnerable'.[46] Nevertheless, firms' self-interest will also be served: 'Businesses and other organisations are unlikely to establish a successful partnership for change and competitiveness while overriding the wishes of a substantial group of employees.'[47]

The 'third way' raises some very interesting issues for labour law. Why should we believe the 'third way' economic arguments instead of the 'deregulation' ones? Will firms which follow the government's prescription to compete on quality instead of cost be more successful than those which do not? And are there any rights which cannot, or should not, be justified in economic terms? Chapters 2 and 3 will explore these issues in greater detail.

Modern approaches to labour law

Before we turn our attention more fully to rights arguments and economic arguments, it is worth pausing to consider some of the other perspectives we might use to analyse labour law. Although these will not be the main focus of this book, we will draw on them occasionally when they have a particular insight to offer. We will consider three: sociology, social justice, and the Rule of Law.

Sociology is, of course, the labour lawyer's traditional source of inspiration. In the 1950s, industrial relations theory was used in a very particular way to support Kahn-Freund's collective *laissez-faire* arguments. Nowadays, sociological insights do not add up to a single theory. But they do offer a valuable perspective on all aspects of labour law. This is because policy proposals should always be based on an accurate understanding of what is going on in the workplace, derived from empirical research. For example, some have suggested that the new statutory recognition procedure has not had much impact because very few cases have progressed to the later stages of the procedure. Others have claimed a substantial indirect impact for the procedure because there was a rise in the number of employers opting to recognise a union voluntarily before the new law came into force. To get to the bottom of this debate – and therefore to decide whether or not the procedure is in need of reform – we need the insights which detailed empirical research could offer.

---

45 Trade Union and Labour Relations (Consolidation) Act 1992, Sch. A1, inserted by the Employment Relations Act 1999.
46 Above n. 39, para. 4.11.
47 Above n. 39, para. 4.12.

A social justice perspective focuses on the role played by labour law in 'setting the distribution of wealth and power in society'.[48] As Collins points out, labour lawyers applying the traditional collective *laissez-faire* analysis saw trade unions as the means of achieving social justice.[49] By bargaining with employers, they would ensure that workers received adequate wages and fair conditions of employment. Low-paid workers got the blame for their own predicament: it was up to them to join unions and resolve the problem through collective bargaining. Nowadays, the picture is rather different. Although social justice is not as distinctive a mode of analysis as rights or economics, labour lawyers are prepared to consider the law's role in distributing wealth. The National Minimum Wage Act 1998, which sets a minimum rate of pay for virtually all workers, is the most obvious example of recent legislation which implements social justice ideas.

The Rule of Law offers a method of analysing any branch of the law. There are many different versions of the Rule of Law, but the most relevant for present purposes is that advanced by Raz.[50] He argues that the law should be drafted so as to allow people to plan their lives around it. Among other things, laws should be publicly available, so that people can find out about them; they should be clear, so that people can understand them; and they should be stable, so that people's plans are not disrupted by frequent changes. Compliance with these goals is, of course, a matter of degree, but even so, labour law does not always score highly on clarity or stability. For example, a quick glance at the balloting requirements in the Trade Union and Labour Relations (Consolidation) Act 1992 shows that they are highly complex. A union which was trying to comply with them might well fail. The clarity of these rules could be greatly improved.

There are at least five perspectives we can take on labour law: rights, economics, sociology, social justice and the Rule of Law. And within each of these, there are variations. We have already seen that economic arguments can be used to criticise or to support improvements in workers' rights. This range of approaches might make the subject seem rather daunting. But the use of several different types of analysis should give us a more rounded understanding of the law. And it makes the subject much more interesting.

Further reading

For a detailed account of the development of labour law from the 1950s to the early 1990s, see P. Davies and M. Freedland, *Labour Legislation and Public Policy* (1993). This book is worth reading in full if you have time. Chapters 1 and 11 summarise the book's argument. To learn about the early history of labour law, see D. Brodie, *A History of British Labour Law* (2003).

---

48 Collins, above n. 1, at 306.
49 Collins, above n. 1.
50 J. Raz, 'The Rule of Law and its Virtue' (1977) 93 *LQR* 195.

Otto Kahn-Freund's classic statement of collective *laissez-faire* can be found in chapter 2 of A. Flanders and H.A. Clegg (eds.), *The System of Industrial Relations in Great Britain: its History, Law and Institutions* (1954). The full title of the Donovan Report is the *Report of the Royal Commission on Trade Unions and Employers' Associations* (Cmnd. 3623, 1968). Chapters 1–4 are particularly useful for their defence of collective *laissez-faire* and for the snapshot they offer of industrial relations in the late 1960s. You should think particularly carefully about the place of law in a system of collective *laissez-faire*. What roles did the law play? How important was the law? Did Kahn-Freund underestimate its importance? Can you trace the influence of rights arguments or economics arguments before the 1970s? Davies and Freedland, cited above, chapter 1, and Brodie, also cited above, may help you to answer these questions.

The overall argument of this chapter draws heavily on H. Collins, 'The productive disintegration of labour law' (1997) 26 *ILJ* 295. His argument that labour lawyers have ignored analytical approaches other than collective *laissez-faire* is challenged by Lord Wedderburn, 'Collective bargaining or legal enactment: the 1999 Act and trade union recognition' (2000) 29 *ILJ* 1. Both articles provide a useful backdrop to the academic literature to be discussed in the rest of this book. The role of collective bargaining today will be considered in detail in chapters 10–12. Many labour lawyers remain strong advocates of collective bargaining, though they usually argue that it should be combined with effective statutory protection for workers' rights. See, for example, K.D. Ewing, 'Democratic socialism and labour law' (1995) 24 *ILJ* 103; and B. Hepple, 'The future of labour law' (1995) 24 *ILJ* 303. What role should trade unions play nowadays? Why do these writers think that the law cannot offer adequate protection for workers by itself? What should be the relationship between collective bargaining and statutory rights for workers?

Because of the piecemeal nature of Conservative legislation in the 1980s, it is difficult to pinpoint a single statement of government policy for that period. But it is believed that Mrs Thatcher was inspired by the writings of F.A. Hayek. Chapter 18 of *The Constitution of Liberty* (1960) will give you a taste of his views. The policy of the present government is best summed up in the White Paper *Fairness at Work* (Cm. 3968, 1998). If you are interested in the 'third way' more generally, you may find it helpful to look at A. Giddens, *The Third Way* (1998). In what ways does *Fairness at Work* diverge from the policies of the Conservative governments? In what ways does it continue those policies?

2

Economics perspectives on labour law

As chapter 1 explained, governments of the 1960s and 1970s became increasingly worried about the economic implications of labour law. They were concerned about the contribution unions' wage demands made to inflation, and about the impact of strikes on productivity. These concerns remained relevant in the 1980s, and a new one was added: that labour law might be contributing to high levels of unemployment. The Labour government has seen labour law in a different light: as a means of promoting productivity and competitiveness.

These developments in government policy have been paralleled by a growing interest among academic labour lawyers in the use of economics perspectives on their subject. In the 1980s, for example, the government drew heavily on the arguments of economists who favoured 'free markets', in which regulation by labour law would be kept to a minimum. Some labour lawyers responded by showing that not all economic analysis pointed in this direction: that there is also a significant school of thought which views labour law as one of the ways in which the government can help firms to become more successful. Later chapters of this book will explore the competing conclusions reached by economists on a selection of topics in labour law.

But all of this can seem rather daunting to lawyers with no background in economics. The purpose of this chapter is to demystify the subject by explaining some of the basic concepts economists use, and their application to labour issues. The first section will give a very brief account of the central core of economics: the subject's methodology and assumptions. The second section will examine microeconomics. This is the study of particular markets and of the forces of supply and demand which determine prices. The discussion will focus on the work of labour economists in studying the labour market. The impact of labour law is a matter of some controversy in economics, so in the third section of this chapter the two main schools of thought on this issue will be examined. Finally, the fourth section will consider some topics in macroeconomics – the study of national and regional economies – which are of particular relevance to labour law.

What do economists do?

As lawyers, we need to understand and respect the techniques economists use.[1] Otherwise, we will not be able to make good use of – or fair criticisms of – their arguments. 'Positive' economists produce theoretical models which predict how people will behave *assuming* certain facts to be the case.[2] They then test these models against real-world empirical evidence. Normative economists use this data to produce policy recommendations. The key to understanding economic analysis is to grasp the crucial role played by assumptions.

Economists start from the premise that resources such as labour, capital, land, time and personal income are scarce. This means that everybody must make choices. For example, workers have to choose between having more leisure time and having more income from employment.[3] Economists' key assumption is that people make these choices *rationally*. They weigh up the costs and benefits of each option and select the one which will make them richer ('maximise their wealth') or make them happier ('maximise their utility') or satisfy more of their preferences.[4] So, if a worker opts for more leisure time, an economist would infer that he or she values the benefits of leisure more highly than the extra income to be obtained from working longer hours. Moreover, economists commonly assume that people's basic preferences remain *stable over time*, so that if the economic environment changes, their behaviour will change too in response. If wages rise, the leisure-loving worker might decide to reduce his or her working time even further, because the same income can be generated in fewer hours.

One of the most profound criticisms which has been made of economics is that the key assumptions of rational and consistent behaviour are often false. Simon's famous model of 'bounded rationality' suggests that individuals do not in practice make decisions through a process of rational choice.[5] They often 'make do' with a satisfactory choice, even if in theory better options exist, and reassess their choices only occasionally when some crisis occurs. A worker who is satisfied with his or her current wage might stay in the job even though better-paying jobs are available. He or she might only start to think about these other jobs after an argument with his or her manager. Similarly, people's preferences do in practice change over time. For example, as workers get older, they are likely to take a much greater interest in what kind of pension scheme their employer offers.

---

1 Economists communicate with each other through graphs and equations, as well as prose. This book avoids both techniques because they are unfamiliar to lawyers and can be rather off-putting. The further reading at the end of this chapter does, however, introduce them. Once you have understood them, you will see that they are able to convey complex ideas much more efficiently than words. For an introduction, see R. Cooter and T. Ulen, *Law and Economics* (4th edn., 2004), chapter 2.

2 M. Friedman, *Essays in Positive Economics* (1953), pp. 3–43.

3 For more detail on workers' labour supply decisions, see chapter 6.

4 These are versions of utilitarianism, discussed in more detail in chapter 3.

5 H. Simon, 'Rationality in Psychology and Economics' (1986) 59 *Journal of Business* S209–S224.

Most economists would reject these criticisms. They acknowledge that their fundamental assumptions may not hold true in all circumstances. But they argue that the assumptions are essential to their methodology. They analyse real-world phenomena by building theoretical models. These models only work if they simplify the real world considerably. The assumptions are the means of simplification. Without the assumption that people behave rationally, it would be impossible to predict how people would respond to changes in economic circumstances. Without the assumption that preferences are stable over time, any change in people's behaviour could be attributed to a change in their preferences, rather than to their response to new economic conditions.[6] Friedman argues that economic models should be judged not on the validity of their assumptions, but on the accuracy of their predictions.[7] For example, rather than testing whether or not workers behave rationally, we should test whether or not some workers respond to a wage rise by opting to work fewer hours.

The best view is probably somewhere in between the extremes set out by Simon and Friedman. Economic models should usually be tested for their ability to predict how people will behave in the real world. But if a model is used *normatively*, to make policy recommendations, it would be foolish to ignore doubts about the empirical validity of its underlying assumptions. This applies not just to the core assumptions of rational and consistent behaviour, but to the multitude of other assumptions made by economists to simplify the world. It is important to look carefully at the assumptions being made whenever you read an economist's work. When two writers disagree, it is often because they are using different sets of assumptions.

Microeconomics

Microeconomists are concerned with markets.[8] Markets determine the prices of particular goods and services by bringing together buyers and sellers. The labour market determines the price of labour (wages) by bringing together employers (the buyers of labour) and workers (the sellers of labour). This section will introduce markets in general before turning to the special issues raised by labour markets.

Markets

Markets come in two types. Product markets are those in which goods or services are bought and sold. Factor markets are those in which the factors of production – the things needed to produce goods and services, such as land, labour and machinery – are bought and sold. Economists consider two main types of market player: firms and households. Firms are sellers in product markets and buyers in factor markets. Households are buyers in product markets and sellers in factor markets.

---

6 G. Becker, *The Economic Approach to Human Behavior* (1976), pp. 3–14.
7 Above n. 2.
8 For an introduction, see R. Cooter and T. Ulen, *Law and Economics* (4th edn., 2004), chapters 1 and 2.

The price of any particular product or factor is determined by the forces of supply and demand in the market. Generally, economists conclude that as prices go up, demand falls and supply rises. In the market for cars, firms will be willing to supply cars in larger numbers if they can get more money for them. But households will buy fewer cars as they become more expensive. In theory, the 'invisible hand' of the market will drive firms and households to what is known as the 'equilibrium' or 'market-clearing' price. This is the price at which supply and demand are equal. Households are willing to buy a certain number of cars at this price, and firms will produce exactly that number.

What determines the forces of supply and demand? Economists start with the assumption that firms want to maximise their profits. This involves doing two things: choosing the output of products that will generate the most income from sales, and choosing the combination of inputs (labour, machinery, raw materials) that will produce this output at the least possible cost. An equation called a 'production function' can be used to express all imaginable combinations of inputs and outputs for a particular firm: the different quantities of inputs the firm could use to produce different levels of output, and the different ways in which the inputs could be combined to produce a given level of output. Each firm calculates the combination of inputs and outputs which will maximise profits on the basis of two crucial factors: the prices of the inputs it is buying, and the prices it can get for the products it is selling.

Economists treat households in a similar way. They assume that households seek to maximise their pleasure, or to satisfy as many of their preferences as possible. Each household has a 'utility function', which expresses all imaginable ways in which products could be combined by the household to produce a given level of pleasure or satisfaction, and all imaginable quantities of products the household could consume in order to produce different levels of pleasure or satisfaction. How does the household decide how many products to consume, and in what combination? The household decides by looking at the prices of products and at the income it has available in order to buy them.

The best combination of inputs (for firms) or products (for households) is referred to as the 'optimal' or 'efficient' combination. The optimal combination of inputs for a firm is the one in which extra money spent on one input (another worker, for example) would yield exactly the same return as the same money spent on another input (a machine, for example). If a firm would benefit more from hiring workers than it would from buying machines, we can say that it has not reached its optimal combination of inputs. It needs to hire more workers until the return from hiring each additional worker is equal to that from hiring additional machines. What stops firms from simply wanting more and more of each input is the so-called law of diminishing marginal productivity. The value of adding extra inputs (extra workers, for example) increases up to a point and then starts to decline: instead of producing more outputs, the workers are just getting in each other's way.

A similar analysis applies to households. The optimal combination of products is the one at which extra money spent on one product would yield the same satisfaction as the same money spent on another product. If a household would gain more satisfaction from additional chocolate than it would from biscuits, it is clear that the household has not reached its optimal combination. But households do not (in theory) want more and more of each product. Most products are subject to the law of diminishing marginal utility: more chocolate makes you happier up to a point, but then it starts to make you feel sick.

Labour markets

Labour economists study the concepts of supply, demand and prices in labour markets. The labour market is a factor market in which workers offer their services for sale and firms are buyers. But it has several special features. First, the supply of labour raises complex issues. Workers cannot supply their labour without supplying themselves, so they care about more than just the wage they will get for the job. They also consider matters such as job security and the safety of the working environment. Moreover, workers' decisions about how much labour to supply are closely tied up with how much money they want to have available to spend as consumers, and with the career decisions of other members of their household. Second, employers might have subjective preferences about who they employ. An employer who discriminates against women may pay them less than men even though they are equally productive workers. Employers are unlikely to differentiate between other factors of production – machines or raw materials – in quite the same way. Third, workers often join together in trade unions to sell their labour as a group. As we shall see, the impact of unions on the labour market is a highly controversial issue.[9]

Economists find much to study in the issue of labour supply. They begin at the most basic level, with the individual's labour supply decision: whether to work at all, and if so, for how many hours. At any given wage, the worker can achieve various different combinations of income and leisure. This is called the 'budget constraint'. The worker selects a combination in the light of his or her preferences for work or leisure: some people are more workaholic, or more leisure-loving, than others. These preferences may change (if the worker wins the lottery or decides to retire, for example) but economists assume for the purposes of argument that they remain stable over time. In chapter 6, we will see that many economists reject the idea of having any legal control over how many hours people can work because they regard it as an unwarranted interference with individuals' preferences.

Obviously, the amount of labour an individual chooses to supply is influenced by changes in the wage rate. On the one hand, if the wage rate rises, the individual can earn the same amount of money in less time, so he or she might opt to work fewer hours (the 'income effect'). On the other hand, for each hour of leisure the individual takes, he or she is sacrificing a larger chunk of income, so he or she might decide to work more hours (the 'substitution effect'). Which of these effects dominates depends on the individual's preferences. Individuals may be more or less

9 See chapters 10–12.

responsive to changes in the wage rate: in technical terms, individual labour supply may be more or less 'wage elastic'.

It is also helpful to think about the labour supply decision not just as an individual choice, but as a decision made in the context of a household.[10] Within each household, there is a need to decide how individual members should divide their time between paid work, work in the household (cooking, childcare and so on), and consumption (enjoying the goods the household has produced). The rational household will allocate family members to the tasks they are best at: those in which they have a 'comparative advantage'. If, for example, unpaid leave to care for children is available to both parents, it makes sense for the parent who earns less to take the leave. The parent who earns more has a comparative advantage in labour market work.

The demand for labour, like the demand for all the other factors of production, is *derived* from the demand for the firm's products. The firm wants employees for the contribution they make to production, rather than for their own sake. Labour is subject to the law of diminishing marginal productivity. For example, a manufacturing firm will benefit from hiring workers up to the point at which all its machines are fully operational. There is nothing to be gained by hiring any more workers because they will not contribute anything further to productivity.

Various factors may cause a firm's demand for labour to change. The most obvious is a change in the demand for the firm's products: if demand increases, the demand for labour will also increase. Another is a change in the price of the other factors of production. If the price of machinery falls, the demand for labour may be affected in one of two ways. If the machines can be used to replace workers, the demand for labour will decrease. But if the machines need workers to operate them, the demand for labour will increase.

The demand for labour may be more or less *elastic*. This means that employers may be more or less sensitive to changes in the wage rate. Elasticity depends on a variety of factors. One is the elasticity of demand for the firm's products, for the obvious reason that the demand for labour is derived from the demand for products. Another is the proportion of the firm's costs which is accounted for by labour: firms are more likely to respond to wage changes where wage costs make up a substantial proportion of their total costs. A further factor is the extent to which other inputs can be substituted for labour. If the firm could potentially replace workers with machines, a change in the wage rate might prompt it to buy new machines. Elasticity is an important concept in the analysis of labour law because legal regulation often increases employers' costs. If demand is highly elastic, an increase in regulation is more likely to prompt employers to take action to offset the increase in their costs. If demand is inelastic, an increase in regulation is less likely to worry the employer.

The forces of supply and demand combine in the market in order to determine the wage rate. In a perfectly competitive market, the wage rate will be fixed at a level

---

10 G. Becker, 'A Theory of the Allocation of Time' (1965) 75 *Economic Journal* 493.

at which workers are willing to supply exactly the number of hours that employers want to buy. Individual firms in this market will simply offer the equilibrium wage: they can hire as many units of labour as they want at this price. If they offer a lower wage, no-one will be willing to work for them. It is unnecessary for them to offer a higher wage, since they can obtain all the labour they need at the equilibrium rate.

The operation of the labour market is, of course, affected to a very great extent by labour law. An obvious example is the introduction of a minimum wage. This interferes directly with the normal process of wage determination in the market by setting a floor below which wages cannot fall. It usually requires employers to pay some workers a higher wage than they would have received if the law had not intervened. Similarly, if the law allows strong trade unions to exist, they may be able to bargain with employers for higher wages than their members would otherwise have achieved by the operation of market forces. These and other examples will be considered in detail in later chapters.

Labour law: two schools of thought

So far, we have been looking at the relatively uncontroversial questions of what labour economists study and how they go about it. But just as lawyers disagree about the merits of a recent judgment or a new piece of legislation, economists disagree about the impact of different aspects of labour law on the labour market. Very broadly, we can divide economists into two camps: 'neoclassical' and 'new institutional'. They differ as to the goals they are pursuing (what their ideal labour market would look like) and as to the assumptions they use in their analysis. Those in the neoclassical camp tend to be hostile to legal intervention; those in the new institutional camp argue that labour law can benefit workers, firms, and the economy as a whole.

To understand these two schools of thought, it is helpful to begin by looking at the context in which they are writing. The main challenge facing the UK economy today is globalisation.[11] This term can mean many things, but for our purposes it refers to the process by which goods and services can be produced on a global scale without regard for national borders. Globalisation is made possible by advances in transport, telecommunications and information technology. For example, a car sold in the UK might be made up of components manufactured in several different countries and assembled in Germany. The components can be ordered in an instant by email. Or a telephone call to a British bank might be answered by a call centre worker in India. Because customer records are stored on computer, there is no need for the worker to be at the customer's local branch. In developed countries like the UK, globalisation is often seen as a threat. Firms can now locate their factories or call centres anywhere in the world. And they may well decide to avoid the UK

11 See U. Beck, *What is globalization?* (2000) pp. 1–21.

because wage levels are high compared with those in developing countries. So how can the UK stay competitive?

Neoclassical economics

Neoclassical economists respond to the problem of globalisation by extolling the virtues of the free market.[12] If employers are allowed to run their businesses as they see fit, with a minimum of outside intervention, they will be able to compete on a global scale. If firms in other countries can operate more cheaply, employers will respond by finding ways to cut their own costs. And if firms are profitable, society as a whole – and the employees of those firms in particular – will reap the benefit. On this view, legal regulation is perceived as a problem because it limits the options open to employers and imposes additional costs on them which may make them uncompetitive. Ultimately, this harms the very workers the legislation was seeking to protect.

The starting point for much economic analysis of law is the Coase theorem.[13] Coase argued that, in principle, if the law imposed a particular requirement on people in a market, it would make no difference to the outcomes of that market. If the rule led to inefficient outcomes, people would get round it by contracting with each other until an efficient outcome was reached. Imagine that the law requires employers to give employees paid holidays. This increases employers' costs by requiring them to pay workers while they are not working, and to make arrangements for other workers to do the jobs of those who are absent. The employer would not want to see its profits reduced, so it would pass the cost of this benefit on to the employees by cutting their wages. The new benefit does not change the allocation of resources in society: the employer pays the employees the same amount but it is made up of wages and paid holidays instead of just wages as before.[14] Many labour lawyers would be horrified at this outcome because it does nothing to redistribute wealth from the employer to the employees, but economists are concerned with efficiency, not redistribution.

However, a major qualification of the Coase theorem – and this is its crucial insight – is that this efficient solution can only be reached when transaction costs are zero. Transaction costs are all the costs associated with contracting out of the new legal rule: negotiating with the employees, drafting a new contract, and trying to make sure that both sides keep to their bargain, for example. In the real world, transaction costs are rarely zero. Neoclassical economists draw from this the conclusion that the government should interfere as little as possible in the labour market.

---

12 For an introduction (using examples from American law) see R.A. Posner, *Economic Analysis of Law* (5th edn., 1998), chapter 11; and (focusing on dismissal law in particular) R.A. Epstein, 'In defense of the contract at will' (1984) 51 *University of Chicago Law Review* 947.

13 R. Coase, 'The problem of social cost' (1960) 3 *Journal of Law and Economics* 1.

14 L.H. Summers, 'Some Simple Economics of Mandated Benefits' (1989) 79 *American Economic Review* 177; J. Gruber, 'The Incidence of Mandated Maternity Benefits' (1994) 84 *American Economic Review* 622.

Each new piece of legislation requires employers to bargain with their employees for an efficient outcome, and forces them to incur transaction costs. Thus, regulation is damaging to firms.

Neoclassical economists also emphasise the harm regulation can do to the overall level of employment. Even if the employer is willing to incur the transaction costs, it may not always be able to negotiate an efficient outcome with its workers. The law might impose a minimum wage which limits the employer's ability to cut pay below a certain level. Or workers might refuse to agree to a substantial reduction in their earnings. For example, workers whose children are grown up might not be prepared to pay for parental leave which would only benefit younger workers. In these cases, the employer must find another way to achieve an efficient outcome. One option is to keep the overall wage bill at the same level by making some employees redundant. Another option is to pass on some of the increase in costs to customers by increasing the price of its products. Globalisation makes this option particularly risky. An increase in the price of the firm's products might cause it to lose market share, particularly where its competitors are located in other countries and are not subject to the same legislative requirements. As the firm's fortunes decline, redundancies may eventually result. Both possibilities are obviously harmful to those workers who lose their jobs. They also damage the economy as a whole, because labour is not being allocated to employers who need it.

More generally, many neoclassical economists are strong advocates of the doctrine of freedom of contract.[15] This means that people should be allowed to enter into contracts with whomever they choose, on whatever terms they wish. The law should only interfere where there is evidence that a person has not given his or her genuine consent, for example, in cases of duress or undue influence. This provides another reason for rejecting detailed legal regulation of the employment relationship. Employers and employees should be allowed to agree on whatever terms they want. If an employee is willing to agree to a contract which does not provide for paid holidays, that must be because the employee does not value them. The law should not presume to tell people what is in their best interests.

This emphasis on freedom of contract is in stark contrast to much traditional labour law thinking. Most labour lawyers argue that individual workers are not well placed to bargain with employers, because each worker usually needs his or her job much more than the employer needs that particular worker. They argue that workers' rights should be protected either by the law or by collective bargaining because individual workers cannot bargain for protection themselves. This often leads critics to portray neoclassical economics as hostile to the interests of employees. However, its proponents would argue that their hostility is only to labour legislation, and that it stems from their concern to protect employees. This book will give serious consideration to the arguments of neoclassical economics. The claim that legal regulation may impose costs on workers themselves ought not to be ignored.

15 P.S. Atiyah, *An Introduction to the Law of Contract* (5th edn., 1995), chapter 1.

New institutional economics

Not all economists are neoclassicists. New institutional economics emerged in the 1970s in the pioneering work of Williamson, who sought to explain why the production of goods is often organised through the creation of firms rather than through a whole series of contracts in the market.[16] The new institutionalists argue that unregulated free markets often fail to achieve efficient outcomes. This is because many of the assumptions made by the neoclassicists – that everyone has perfect information, for example – do not apply in the real world. The new institutionalists suggest that markets may need to be regulated – often through law – in order to overcome these 'market failures'.

New institutional economists reject the solution to the problems of globalisation proffered by their neoclassical colleagues.[17] They argue that no amount of cost-cutting will ever enable the UK to compete with developing countries. Because of the high cost of living in the UK, workers would simply refuse to work at wage levels which would beat those of developing countries. Thus, according to the new institutionalists, the UK should give up trying to produce those goods which can be manufactured just as well and more cheaply elsewhere. Instead, the UK should attempt to compete on some other basis than price.

One of the UK's strengths is that its workers are (in global terms) relatively well educated and well trained. So one possible basis for competition would be to concentrate on products which require skills and expertise. This might be true of the manufacturing of particular kinds of goods, but it is more likely to be true of the provision of services. Some services are technically complex and cannot be produced by unskilled workers: legal advice is a good example of this. Others, such as software development, require continuous updating to keep pace with an ever-changing market. Skilled workers are required to suggest and develop new ideas, and to respond to customer demand.

This approach to competitiveness has important implications for the firm's relationship with its workers. If the firm is producing technically advanced services, its workers must be well trained. The firm may have to pay for some of this training so it will need workers who are likely to stay in its employment over the longer term. Otherwise the firm will not be able to recoup its training costs. If the firm is trying to innovate, it will need to be able to communicate successfully with its workers. Their suggestions, based on their detailed knowledge of production processes and customer needs, may be an invaluable source of new developments. And if the firm is focused on the quality of its products, it needs workers who are committed to the firm and therefore willing to work to a very high standard.

16 For an introduction, see O.E. Williamson, 'Transaction-cost economics: the governance of contractual relations' (1979) XXII *Journal of Law and Economics* 233.
17 For a good introduction, see S. Deakin and F. Wilkinson, 'Rights vs efficiency: the economic case for transnational labour standards' (1994) 23 *ILJ* 289; 'Labour law and economic theory: a reappraisal', in H. Collins *et al.*, *Legal Regulation of the Employment Relation* (2000).

New institutionalists argue that the law can help to create this kind of relationship between a firm and its workers. One of the reasons why many workers leave their jobs is that they find it impossible to combine work with family responsibilities. The law may be able to address this problem by requiring firms to allow parents to work from home or to provide them with time off work to deal with family problems. These measures would encourage parents to stay in work and would help firms to recoup their training costs. Similarly, a firm might miss out on its employees' ideas for innovations if it never talks to them. But if the law requires the firm to set up a works council or to recognise a trade union, the law might provide a forum in which the employees are able to discuss their ideas with management.[18]

An obvious response to the new institutionalists' approach is to point out that if a measure is beneficial to firms, they will adopt it anyway without the need for the law to make it compulsory. If a firm does not adopt the measure, this must be evidence that managers have weighed up the costs and benefits and decided that the costs are greater than the benefits. But the new institutionalists reject the neoclassical view that the market always achieves the most efficient outcomes when left to its own devices. They offer a different interpretation of the Coase theorem.[19] They argue that unregulated markets suffer from various kinds of problems which mean that transaction costs *in the markets themselves* are often very high. Employers and employees may find that it is too expensive to reach an efficient outcome on their own. This suggests that there may be a role for legal regulation where it promotes efficient outcomes.

To understand this argument, it is helpful to look at some of the 'market failures' which might generate transaction costs.[20] One problem is that the employer and employee do not have equal bargaining power.[21] In general, the employee needs the job more than the employer needs him or her, because there are plenty of other potential employees in the market. This enables the employer to behave opportunistically: ignoring longer-term goals in pursuit of short-term savings or profits. For example, the employer might promise the employee a bonus for achieving a particular target, and then dismiss the employee shortly before the payment becomes due in order to save money. But this is bad for the employer in the longer term because other workers will be less inclined to trust the employer and will not feel motivated by promises of bonus payments. The law can help to prevent this opportunistic behaviour by providing the employee with a degree of job security: in other words, by making it unlawful for the employer to dismiss people unless certain conditions

18 See J. Rogers and W. Streeck, 'Workplace representation overseas: the works councils story', in R.B. Freeman (ed.), *Working Under Different Rules* (1994).
19 See Deakin and Wilkinson (2000), above n. 17, pp. 34–8.
20 Another problem is information asymmetry: see, for example, P. Aghion and B. Hermalin, 'Legal restrictions on private contracts can enhance efficiency' (1990) 6 *Journal of Law, Economics and Organization* 381.
21 As we shall see in chapter 9, this does not mean that the employee always does what the employer wants. Employees may behave opportunistically too.

are met.[22] The examples we considered above – about training and consultation – are also situations in which the employer might decide not to pursue long-term efficiency because of the short-term costs. Thus, the law may sometimes be able to improve on the solutions generated by markets.

Even if these arguments are accepted, there is a second problem with the new institutional approach. This problem is acknowledged by many new institutionalists themselves. It is that the benefits they identify from legal regulation will not manifest themselves in every case. Our parental leave example is a good illustration of this. A firm is most likely to be worried about retaining its employees where it has to provide them with a high level of training to meet its particular needs. But if the firm's requirement is for workers with a widely available, more general skill, it will be less worried about retention. If someone leaves, the firm can hire a replacement, and he or she will be able to start work with very little training of any kind. This means that the benefits of compulsory parental leave in helping firms to retain workers will be evident in some firms and non-existent in others. Most of the time, then, the new institutionalists will be arguing that regulation should be adopted when it benefits a majority of firms, and will not be claiming that it benefits all firms.

At this point, many new institutionalists concede that economic arguments cannot provide the whole justification for legal regulation of a particular area. Imagine that it has been calculated that the provision of parental leave will benefit 70% of firms but impose a cost on the remaining 30%. This suggests that parental leave should be made compulsory, but it does leave a nagging doubt about the position of the minority of firms which will not benefit. If the firms have some common characteristic – that they are all small businesses, for example – it might be possible to draft an exception which would take them outside the scope of the new legislation. But if they are all quite different, this will not be possible. Therefore, it may be helpful to employ a rights argument alongside the economic analysis. As we shall see, parental leave can be viewed as an important right for working parents and for working mothers in particular. By helping them to balance work and family life, it broadens the range of life choices which are available to them. When parental leave is viewed in these terms, there is a good reason to make it compulsory even if it does not benefit all firms. The new institutionalists' argument supplies the justification for imposing parental leave on the firms which do benefit; the rights argument supplies the justification for the firms which do not. The relationship between rights and economics arguments will be explored more fully in the next chapter.

Macroeconomics

As well as having an impact on particular firms operating in particular markets, labour law also has an impact on the nation's economy as a whole, and it is this

---

22 See, generally, C.F. Büchtemann, 'Introduction: employment security and labor markets', in C.F. Büchtemann (ed.), *Employment Security and Labor Market Behavior* (1993).

which makes it interesting to macroeconomists. Indeed, when the government is contemplating changes to labour law, it is often motivated by macroeconomic considerations as well as concerns for the well-being of particular firms and employees. We will examine two topics: productivity and unemployment.

Productivity

To measure productivity, economists work out what the output of the economy is (its gross domestic product), and divide it by the inputs which have been used to generate it (raw materials, machinery, and workers). Labour productivity is a measure of output divided by the number of worker hours needed to generate that output. The productivity ratio tells us how many units of output we can obtain from one unit of input (one worker hour, for example). Productivity has increased when we are able to obtain more output from the same level of input. The general trend is for productivity to increase over time.

Rising productivity is regarded by economists as a sign of a healthy economy, for two reasons. First, it is the source of improvements in everyone's standard of living. Standards of living improve when the real wage rate rises. This occurs whenever there is an increase in the demand for labour. As demand increases more rapidly than supply, employers will have to offer more money in order to attract more workers into the labour market. What prompts this increase in the demand for labour? The answer is rising productivity. Firms will employ more workers as the value of what they can produce increases relative to the cost of employing them. So output rises, income rises, and the standard of living improves.

The second advantage associated with rising productivity is that it helps to combat inflation. Inflation describes the situation in which prices rise inordinately across the economy as a whole. Both product prices and the price of labour (wages) are affected, because workers expect their wages to keep pace with the cost of living. If inflation is allowed to spiral out of control, a serious economic crisis will result. There is an important debate within economics about the precise causes of inflation, but this need not concern us here. The crucial point for our purposes is that if the wage rate does rise, inflation will not occur if that rise is offset by an increase in productivity. Imagine that a worker earns £5 an hour and produces five units of output. If the wage rate increases to £6 an hour, labour costs will rise. If labour costs rise, product prices will increase, and an inflationary spiral may begin. But if the worker's productivity increases to six units of output per hour, the rise in wages to £6 per hour is offset by the productivity increase. Labour costs remain unchanged and there is no inflationary pressure as a result of the pay rise.

Since productivity increases are a good thing, it is not surprising to find that governments are keen to encourage workers and firms to improve their productivity. One strategy is through education and training. Other things being equal, a more highly trained workforce is more productive than one with less training. Thus, if the government provides a high-quality school system and subsidises vocational training courses at colleges, these measures will help to produce a trained workforce which will make firms more productive. Another strategy is to use labour law to bring about improvements in productivity. The two schools of thought in economics are usually divided about the best way of doing this. Let us take unfair dismissal law as an example. Some neoclassical economists would argue that employers should be allowed to dismiss employees 'at will': whenever they want and for whatever reason, or for no reason at all. The constant threat of dismissal hanging over all employees will encourage them to work hard and to be productive. Most new institutional economists would argue that unfair dismissal laws, which only allow employers to dismiss employees if certain conditions are satisfied, are a better way of improving productivity. They argue that workers will be more productive if they feel secure in their jobs. Whichever of these views is correct, they are both pursuing the same goal of improved productivity, because of the economic benefits it brings.

Unemployment

Since labour law is, on the whole, concerned with those who are in work, it may seem rather odd to consider those who do not have a job. But labour law may influence the level of unemployment. Many neoclassical economists believe that labour law creates unemployment by increasing the labour costs faced by employers. Others, mainly in the new institutional camp, argue that labour law can be used to reduce or mitigate unemployment. It is therefore useful for labour lawyers to understand how unemployment is measured and how economists explain it.

In August 2003, the unemployment rate in the UK was 5%.[23] People count as unemployed if they want to work, are available to work, and are actively seeking employment.[24] This means that the unemployment count does not include all those people who do not have a job. Some people do not want to work: for example, a person might have given up his or her job in order to care for a sick relative. Some people are unavailable for work: those in prison, for example. And some are not seeking work: those 'discouraged workers' who have tried for some time to get a job but have given up because they have not had any success. These various groups of people explain the gap between the unemployment rate of 5% and the employment rate of 74.5% for people of working age. It can be argued that the official unemployment statistics underestimate the true rate of unemployment in various ways. The 'discouraged workers' should perhaps be included because they would take a job if they could get one. Economists regard some unemployment in the economy – of between 4% and 6% – as a good sign.[25] If the unemployment rate is too low, inflation may result as employers increase wages in order to recruit and retain scarce workers.

A look at the various different types of unemployment identified by economists will help to explain why it occurs. One major type of unemployment is frictional

---

23 Source: National Statistics, *Labour Force Survey* (2003).
24 The UK uses the ILO's definition of unemployment.
25 For discussion, see J. Stiglitz, 'Reflections on the natural rate hypothesis' (1997) 11 *Journal of Economic Perspectives* 3.

unemployment. The labour market never clears: in other words, at any one point in time, employers will be trying to fill some vacancies and jobseekers will be looking for work. Some unemployment is inevitable even if the number of job vacancies exactly matches the number of people seeking work. Search unemployment is an important kind of frictional unemployment. It occurs when individuals spend time looking around for the best job offer and employers spend time looking for the best candidate to fill a vacancy. Another type of frictional unemployment is wait unemployment, in which workers are temporarily laid off but expect to be able to resume their jobs at a later date. Agricultural workers may be unemployed at various times during the year because of the seasonal nature of their jobs.

A second major type of unemployment is structural unemployment. This occurs when there is a mismatch between those seeking work and the job vacancies which are available. One problem might be that the unemployed workers are all in the North West while the vacancies are all in the South East. Another problem might be that the vacancies are all in information technology firms while the unemployed workers are trained in car manufacturing. These mismatches can be overcome if the jobseekers are willing to relocate and retrain, but it can take some time for the situation to be resolved. Structural unemployment is much longer-lived than frictional unemployment. In August 2003, of the unemployed aged 25–49, 12% had been unemployed for two years or more.[26] Many of those experiencing long-term unemployment are the victims of structural change. A final type of unemployment is demand-deficient or cyclical unemployment. This occurs when there is a downturn in the economy. As demand for their products falls, firms will need to reduce their labour costs. This could be done either by cutting the wages of all workers or by making some workers redundant. The redundancy solution – which creates unemployment – is more common in practice. Workers are often reluctant to accept cuts in wages unless the firm is facing bankruptcy. It is easier to make a few workers redundant than to alienate the entire workforce.

Most governments make it their policy to keep unemployment as low as possible. Various strategies can be used to achieve this. For example, the provision of Job Centres helps to reduce frictional unemployment by giving employers a means of advertising vacancies and jobseekers a way of finding out what jobs are available. The provision of training programmes may help to reduce structural unemployment by enabling those who are displaced by the demise of one industry to acquire new skills in order to work in another. Some people argue that labour law may also be used to help mitigate the problem of redundancy. A legal obligation to give the workers notice of impending redundancies may help to reduce structural unemployment by giving those workers the chance to look for a new job or to take training courses. Strong anti-discrimination laws may also be needed to ensure that the burden of unemployment does not fall unduly harshly on some groups in society. This is a particular problem in the UK at present. Statistics from 2002 show that the

26 Above n. 23.

unemployment rate was 5% in the majority white population, but for members of the ethnic minorities the rate was 12%.[27] However, neoclassical economists argue that too much legal intervention in the labour market may contribute to the redundancy problem. New labour laws may increase employers' costs and may lead to redundancies where the employer cannot pass those costs on to workers through wage cuts. This argument will be a common theme in later chapters.

The role of economics perspectives

Economics teaches us to examine legal regulation for the effect it has on the ability of workers and firms to maximise their wealth or utility. Like lawyers, economists disagree quite radically about the advantages and disadvantages of particular pieces of legislation. Economics should not be expected to provide us with a set of straightforward answers. Nor should we treat economic analysis as the only valid insight into the problems of labour law. Even the most hard-line neoclassical theorist would agree that public policy does sometimes need to act on considerations other than efficiency. Arguments from social justice or human rights must also be taken into account and might well outweigh such considerations. Nevertheless, economics plays a vital role in helping us to understand the costs and benefits of our policy choices.

Further reading

Later chapters will cover specific topics – discrimination, trade unions and so on – in more detail, so this chapter's further reading will explore economics more generally.

The classic statement of the methodology of economics is M. Friedman, *Essays in Positive Economics* (1953), pp. 3–43. You may also find it helpful to look at G. Becker, *The Economic Approach to Human Behavior* (1976), pp. 3–14; and J. Coleman, *Markets, Morals and the Law* (1988), pp. 95–132. M. Blaug, *The Methodology of Economics: or, How Economists Explain* (1980), pp. 112–34, gives a helpful account of the distinction between positive and normative economics. But does the standard methodology oversimplify things? H. Simon, 'Rationality in psychology and economics' (1986) 59 *Journal of Business* S209–S224, argues that individuals do not act rationally in the sense used by economists. Instead, they 'make do' with a satisfactory decision drawing on the information that is readily available to them. Could economists adapt their methodology to incorporate Simon's insight? Or does Simon undermine the whole basis of the discipline?

But Simon is by no means the most radical critic of economics. Many theorists argue that the discipline cannot offer any valid insights into how society should be run. Mark Kelman, writing from the perspective of critical legal studies, rejects

27 A. Smith, 'The new ethnicity classification in the Labour Force Survey' (2002) *Labour Market Trends* 657.

economics on the grounds that it makes a claim to neutrality which is wholly mis-leading: M. Kelman, *A Guide to Critical Legal Studies* (1987), chapters 4 and 5. But does economics have a single political agenda? Where does new institutional eco-nomics fit into Kelman's analysis? Duncan Kennedy attacks the rationality assump-tion even more vigorously than Simon, arguing that individuals often do not know what is best for them: D. Kennedy, 'Distributive and paternalist motives in contract and tort law' (1982) 41 *Maryland Law Review* 563. He argues for more paternalism in public policy, but does the government really know best? Finally, Dworkin argues that economics is flawed because it pays too much attention to the happiness of society as a whole and ignores the rights of individuals: R. Dworkin, 'Is wealth a value?' (1980) 9 *Journal of Legal Studies* 191. The relationship between rights and economics will be discussed further in chapter 3.

For the purposes of explanation, this chapter divided economists into two camps: neoclassical and new institutional. For an introduction to neoclassical theories, see R.A. Posner, *Economic Analysis of Law* (5th edn., 1998), chapter 11; and (in the context of dismissal laws in particular) R.A. Epstein, 'In defense of the contract at will' (1984) 51 *University of Chicago Law Review* 947. For an introduction to new institutionalism, see S. Deakin and F. Wilkinson, 'Rights vs efficiency: the economic case for transnational labour standards' (1994) 23 *ILJ* 289, and 'Labour law and economic theory: a reappraisal', in H. Collins *et al.*, *Legal Regulation of the Employment Relation* (2000). But how different do you think the two camps really are? For example, can the new institutionalists afford to ignore the costs of the laws they are advocating? The government's White Paper, *Fairness at Work* (Cm. 3968, 1998) draws on both neoclassical and new institutional arguments. Do you find the government's attempt at reconciliation convincing?

The conflict between neoclassical economics and the traditional ideology of labour law is not difficult to grasp. Compare Posner or Epstein, above, with (for example) K.W. Wedderburn 'Labour law and the individual in post-industrial soci-eties', in K.W. Wedderburn *et al.*, *Labour Law in Post-Industrial Societies* (1994). But are labour lawyers any more likely to embrace the ideas of the new institutionalists? See F. von Prondzynksi, 'Labour law as business facilitator', in H. Collins *et al.*, *Legal Regulation of the Employment Relation* (2000), for discussion.

A new perspective on labour law which has not been considered in this chapter is that of 'regulatory theory'. For an introduction to this emerging approach, see H. Collins, 'Justifications and techniques of legal regulation of the employment relation', in H. Collins *et al.* (eds.), *Legal Regulation of the Employment Relation* (2000). Is this approach neoclassical or new institutional? Or does it succeed in cutting across the two schools of thought? Notice that it focuses not only on the justification for regulation but also on the *technique* of regulation. It acknowledges the important point that not all regulation achieves its goals. This is also a key feature of 'reflexive law' theories: see R. Rogowski and T. Wilthagen, 'Reflexive labour law: an introduction', in R. Rogowski and T. Wilthagen (eds.), *Reflexive Labour Law* (1994). What is the significance of this for the new institutionalists?

3

Human rights perspectives on labour law

As we saw in chapter 1, human rights perspectives on labour law first gained ground in the 1970s. Commentators began to realise that collective bargaining could not provide all the protection workers needed. In the 1980s, labour rights became highly controversial. The government was keen to uphold workers' rights in some settings but not in others. It wanted to enforce individuals' rights against trade unions (arguing that unions treated individuals unfairly) but it did not want to enforce individuals' rights against firms (because it believed in keeping the labour market as free of regulation as possible). Today, rights perspectives on labour law are very common in the literature. Many commentators use rights language in order to evaluate the current law, and in doing so, they draw heavily on international and regional standards. The Human Rights Act 1998 (HRA 1998) has given an added impetus to the rights perspective by giving greater legal effect to some human rights.

This chapter will begin with a historical introduction to the development of human rights, focusing in particular on labour rights. This will give you an overview of the international and regional human rights instruments which will be discussed throughout the book. The second section of the chapter will turn to the complex questions of interpretation surrounding human rights: who can claim a right and against whom can they bring their claim? What exactly does any given right protect? And how (if at all) can we justify interfering with a right?

A brief overview of human rights

Since much of the discussion in this book will involve detailed examination of particular human rights, it is helpful to start with an overview of international and European human rights law. We will look first at the historical development of human rights, before outlining the two main categories of rights: civil and political, and economic and social. We will also examine the important debate about the status of these two groups of rights.

Historical development

The first major attempts to identify a list of human rights came at the end of the eighteenth century in the American Bill of Rights and the French Declaration of the Rights of Man and Citizen.[1] Responding to years of repression by tyrannical rulers, the drafters of these documents sought to lay down those rights which would protect individuals' liberty in the future. They tried to ensure that majority rule in the new democratic states they were creating would not result in the oppression of minorities. But despite these developments at the national level, it was many years before human rights became an accepted part of international law. This was largely because of the emphasis placed by international law on the sovereignty of states.[2] What went on within a state was the concern of that state's government and no-one else. Over time, exceptions to this principle began to develop. One of the most significant for labour law purposes is the creation, in 1919, of the International Labour Office, the predecessor of the modern International Labour Organisation (ILO), with the task of developing international labour standards.[3] Sceptics point out that this may have been driven by the concern of some states to protect their own industries against competition from firms established in states with lower labour standards. Nevertheless, the idea that international law could have something to say about the lives of individuals was established.

The main impetus for the development of modern international human rights law was the Second World War. Hitler's rise to power demonstrated that the democratic process was not necessarily sufficient to guard against the rise of tyranny and oppression. After the war, the international community sought to draft human rights instruments with a view to ensuring that the horrors of fascism and the Holocaust could never happen again. The UN Charter states that one of the purposes of the UN is to uphold respect for human rights.[4] However, it did not prove possible to include a statement of rights in the Charter because the governments responsible for its drafting could not agree on the contents of any such statement. In 1948, the UN General Assembly adopted the Universal Declaration of Human Rights, a non-binding statement of both civil and political, and economic and social, rights.[5] This was eventually followed by two treaties (legally binding agreements between states) which are the foundation for modern international human rights law, the International Covenant on Civil and Political Rights (ICCPR)[6] and the International Covenant on Economic, Social and Cultural Rights (ICESCR),[7] both of 1966. In the field of labour law, the ILO became established after the war as a specialist agency of

1 Both date from 1789. The American Bill of Rights was ratified two years later, in 1791.
2 L. Henkin, 'International law: politics, values and functions' (Vol. IV, 1989) 216 *Collected Courses of Hague Academy of International Law* 13, at 208–26.
3 See, generally, H.G. Bartolomei de la Cruz, G. von Potobsky and L. Swepston, *The International Labour Organisation: the International Standards System and Basic Human Rights* (1996), chapter 1.
4 Article 1.
5 G.A. Resolution 217A (III), G.A.O.R., 3rd Ses., Part I, Resolutions, p. 71. See, generally, J. Morsink, *The Universal Declaration of Human Rights: Origins, Drafting and Intent* (1999).
6 (1967) 999 UNTS 171. See, generally, L. Henkin (ed.), *The International Bill of Rights: the Covenant on Civil and Political Rights* (1981).
7 (1967) 993 UNTS 3. See, generally, M.C.R. Craven, *The International Covenant on Economic, Social and Cultural Rights: A Perspective on its Development* (1995).

the UN, and continued its work of developing and enforcing international labour standards. Developments in human rights at the international level were paralleled by similar moves at the European level, where the concern to avoid a recurrence of the war and the events leading up to it was particularly acute. In 1950, the European Convention on Human Rights, a statement of civil and political rights, came into force.[8] This was followed in 1961 by a statement of economic and social rights in the shape of the European Social Charter.[9] Both instruments operate under the auspices of the Council of Europe, an organisation which is entirely separate from the EU.

In recent years, there has been a growing interest in revising and updating some of these traditional statements of human rights. Some rights as originally drafted have come to seem outdated because of changes in social attitudes. And it has been argued that there are gaps in the protection on offer: issues which were not originally addressed are now regarded as highly important. Both these factors have been particularly relevant in the case of women's rights. A concern to improve the international protection of women's rights led to the development of the Convention on the Elimination of All Forms of Discrimination Against Women (CEDAW) which entered into force in 1981.[10] In 1996, the European Social Charter (ESC) was revised.[11] The new version contains a number of changes from the original, many of which are concerned with promoting the rights of women.

Most recently, a new player has emerged on the human rights scene, in the shape of the EU. Because the EC as originally conceived was an economic union, the Treaty of Rome 1957 contained hardly any references to human rights, with the notable exception of the right of men and women to equal pay contained in Article 119. Over the years, the Community has acquired an increasingly important role in social policy and has been an important source of protection for workers' rights. It has also developed its own human rights jurisprudence with a view to ensuring that its activities do not infringe citizens' rights.[12] In 2000, the Member States proclaimed the Charter of Fundamental Rights of the European Union, a document which combines civil and political rights with a comprehensive statement of economic and social rights.[13] This is not the EU's first statement of human rights, nor is it legally binding. But it is highly significant because it is likely to form part of the new EU Constitution. It is also of interest as a very up-to-date statement of human rights.

---

8 See, generally, D.J. Harris, M. O'Boyle, and C. Warbrick, *Law of the European Convention on Human Rights* (1995).

9 See, generally, D.J. Harris, *The European Social Charter* (1984).

10 1249 UNTS 13. See A. Byrnes, 'Toward more effective enforcement of women's human rights through the use of international human rights law and procedures', and R.J. Cook, 'State accountability under the Convention on the Elimination of All Forms of Discrimination Against Women', in R.J. Cook (ed.), *Human Rights of Women* (1994).

11 The UK is a signatory to the original version but not to the revised version.

12 See, generally, P. Craig and G. de Búrca, *EU Law: Text, Cases and Materials* (3rd edn., 2003), chapter 8.

13 Hereafter 'EU Charter'. See Craig and de Búrca, above n. 12, pp. 358–63.

Types of rights

It will be apparent from the discussion above that the international community has, from an early stage, divided rights into two categories: civil and political, and economic, social and cultural. Civil and political rights focus on the individual in his or her capacity as the citizen of a liberal democracy. They protect the individual against the state, through rights not to be tortured, or subjected to an unfair trial. And they enable the individual to take part in the democratic process, through rights to freedom of expression and to vote. Economic and social rights focus on the material needs of the individual. They include rights to health care, housing, social security, a living wage, reasonable limits on working hours and so on. Some aspects of labour law do have links to citizenship: freedom to associate with others and form groups can cover both political parties and trade unions. But economic and social rights clearly have the greatest relevance to workers.

The split between civil and political rights and economic and social rights occurred largely for political reasons. In the 1960s, Communist governments argued that economic and social rights were the most important kind, whereas Western liberal democracies placed the highest value on civil and political rights. The only way to achieve agreement on rights at the international level was to separate the two types, which explains the existence of two instruments, the ICCPR and the ICESCR. Although the UN has always asserted that the two types of rights are 'indivisible' and of equal status, the debate about their relative worth continues today.

One significant difference between the two types lies in the kind of action the state must take in order to protect them. Civil and political rights can, in general, be secured by legislation which prohibits their infringement. A right not to be tortured can be protected by a ban on torture. Economic and social rights usually require positive action – and expenditure – by the state. To respect the right to health care, the state must have mechanisms in place for providing medical treatment to those who cannot afford to pay for it. This important distinction is usually recognised in the drafting of human rights instruments. For example, the ICCPR requires states 'to give effect to' civil and political rights, whereas the ICESCR imposes, for the most part, a weaker obligation to 'take steps ... with a view to achieving progressively the full realisation of the rights' it contains.[14]

Two further distinctions between the two types of rights flow from this. The first is that the realisation of economic and social rights depends on a state's level of development, whereas (in theory at least) it should be possible for even the poorest state to uphold civil and political rights. Since one of the characteristics of human rights is that they are 'universal' – applicable to everyone regardless of circumstances – this has led many commentators to question whether economic and social rights are truly worthy of the name. Against this, it can be argued that the rights never cease to apply: it is just that their content varies according to the wealth of the state.

14 Where a right does not require expenditure (such as Article 8 of the ICESCR), states are expected to give immediate effect to it.

The second distinction between the two types of right relates to their justiciability: in other words, whether they can be applied by courts. We expect courts to apply rights because they are meant to act as a limitation on what the executive and legislative branches of government are permitted to do. Civil and political rights are suitable for adjudication in court because they raise relatively straightforward questions of compliance. Economic and social rights are much more problematic because of the variability of their content. A court is not well placed to decide whether the government should allocate its resources to housing or to health care. It does not have the expertise or the democratic legitimacy to make these decisions. However, the difficulties of adjudicating on economic and social rights can be exaggerated.[15] Courts can decide cases in which the state has the resources but has chosen not to make them available. Courts can even decide cases involving scarce resources by asking whether the state has made *reasonable* efforts to promote individuals' rights.

There are at least three competing views on these categories of rights. The most radical form of scepticism would confine the term 'right' to civil and political rights, denying this status to all economic and social rights because of their vagueness and lack of universality and justiciability. It is often argued that if individuals have civil and political rights, they will be able to secure protection for their economic and social interests through the democratic process. Thus, there is no need to complicate the picture by giving these interests the status of rights. A more moderate form of scepticism would allow that economic and social rights are genuine rights, but would claim that they are less fundamental than civil and political rights. They are something to aspire to, whereas civil and political rights must be complied with. A third school of thought – that adopted by the UN itself – argues for the 'indivisibility' of human rights: the rights in both categories are human rights and have equal status. Theorists who take this view emphasise the importance of people's material needs: indeed, a person who is homeless or starving would probably value a right to shelter or food more highly than the right to vote.

Civil and political rights

The two most important civil and political rights of relevance to labour law are freedom of association and the right not to be discriminated against. Freedom of association features in the UN Universal Declaration of Human Rights (Article 23(4)), the ICCPR (Article 22), and the European Convention on Human Rights (ECHR) (Article 11). The ECHR definition is typical: 'Everyone has the right to freedom of peaceful assembly and to freedom of association with others, including the right to form and to join trade unions for the protection of his interests.' There are two important features to note about the civil and political right to freedom of

---

15 For theoretical discussion, see C. Scott and P. Macklem, 'Constitutional ropes of sand or justiciable guarantees? Social rights in a new South African Constitution' (1992) 141 *University of Pennsylvania Law Review* 1. Leading cases include *Soobramoney v Minister of Health, Kwazulu-Natal* (1998) 4 BHRC 308; *Government of the Republic of South Africa v Grootboom* (2001) 10 BHRC 84; *Minister of Health v TAC* (2002) 13 BHRC 1.

association. First, it tends to include a right to refuse to be a member of an association alongside the right to be a member. This has been an important feature of the case law of the European Court of Human Rights (ECtHR).[16] Second, the civil and political rights formulation (unlike that in economic and social rights documents) does not usually specify any consequential rights such as a right to engage in collective bargaining or a right to strike. Applicants to the ECtHR have sought to argue that the phrase 'for the protection of his interests' implicitly includes these consequential rights, but despite early indications that this interpretation would be supported, later cases have been extremely cautious.[17]

The right not to be discriminated against features in almost every human rights document, whether civil and political or economic and social. Article 26 of the ICCPR contains a strong anti-discrimination right:

> All persons are equal before the law and are entitled without any discrimination to the equal protection of the law. In this respect, the law shall prohibit any discrimination and guarantee to all persons equal and effective protection against discrimination on any ground such as race, colour, sex, language, religion, political or other opinion, national or social origin, property, birth or other status.

This is much more clearly drafted than its equivalent in the Universal Declaration, Article 7. Older human rights documents tend not to cover all the grounds of discrimination which are regarded as unacceptable in modern society. Article 21(1) of the EU Charter of Fundamental Rights is a good illustration of how the right might be updated:

> Any discrimination based on any ground such as sex, race, colour, ethnic or social origin, genetic features, language, religion or belief, political or any other opinion, membership of a national minority, property, birth, disability, age or sexual orientation shall be prohibited.

Some instruments contain a right not to be discriminated against which applies only to the human rights contained in the instrument itself. This is true of Article 2(2) of the ICESCR and Article 14 of the ECHR, so it cuts across the divide between civil and political rights and economic and social rights. Under this formulation, the victim of discrimination cannot complain unless one of his or her other rights has been violated in a discriminatory manner. For example, a person dismissed from employment as a result of discrimination would have no grounds of complaint under the ECHR because there is no right in the Convention covering dismissal. When it comes into force, Protocol 12 to the ECHR will improve the protection offered to discrimination victims by creating a free-standing right not to be discriminated against similar to those in the ICCPR or the EU Charter.

---

16 See, for example, *Young, James and Webster v UK* (1981) 4 EHRR 38.
17 See chapters 10 and 12 for more detail.

Civil and political rights instruments do contain some other rights of relevance to labour law. These include freedom of religion,[18] freedom of expression[19] and freedom of assembly.[20]

Economic and social rights

For ease of exposition, economic and social rights will be considered in two groups, 'traditional' and 'modern'. The 'modern' category will include those rights found only in the most recent instruments such as the EU Charter of Fundamental Rights and the revised ESC 1996. We will look first at those 'traditional' rights found in the older economic and social rights instruments, such as the ICESCR and the ESC 1961, as well as the recent instruments.

Like civil and political rights instruments, economic and social rights instruments protect freedom of association. But they usually specify in some detail exactly what this means. Article 8 of the ICESCR protects the right to form and join trade unions. Article 8(1)(b) protects the 'right of trade unions to establish national federations or confederations', and most significantly, Article 8(1)(d) protects 'the right to strike, provided that it is exercised in conformity with the laws of the particular country'. The ESC 1961 addresses similar issues in Articles 5 and 6, both of which have been accepted by the UK and have remained unchanged in the revised ESC 1996. Article 5 protects 'the freedom of workers and employers to form local, national or international organisations for the protection of their economic and social interests and to join those organisations'. Article 6 addresses collective bargaining in some detail. It requires governments to promote both consultation and collective bargaining, and to provide a mechanism for conciliation and voluntary arbitration to settle disputes. It also requires governments to respect 'the right of workers and employers to collective action in cases of conflicts of interest, including the right to strike, subject to obligations that might arise out of collective agreements previously entered into'. For many labour lawyers, these rights are much more significant than those in civil and political rights instruments. They acknowledge that effective trade union action requires more than just a right to be a member, and their content is much clearer.

Economic and social rights instruments usually contain a right to work. This is true of the UN Universal Declaration (Article 23(1)), the ICESCR (Article 6) and the ESC 1961 (Article 1). Although this may sound like the most important labour law right there could possibly be, it is in fact directed at the government's economic and education policies rather than at employers. Thus, Article 1 of the ESC 1961 requires signatories to promote full employment and to provide vocational guidance and training.

More significant are the rights concerning wages and working conditions. Article 23(3) of the UN Universal Declaration states that 'everyone who works has the right

18 See, for example, Article 18 of the ICCPR; Article 9 of the ECHR.
19 See, for example, Article 19 of the ICCPR; Article 10 of the ECHR.
20 See, for example, Article 21 of the ICCPR; Article 11 of the ECHR.

to just and favourable remuneration ensuring for himself and his family an existence worthy of human dignity, and supplemented, if necessary, by other means of social protection'. This is echoed in Article 7 of the ICESCR and Article 4 of the ESC 1961 (which remains unchanged in the 1996 revision). Article 23(2) of the Universal Declaration states that 'everyone, without any discrimination, has the right to equal pay for equal work'. This too is repeated in the ICESCR (Article 7) and the ESC 1961 (Article 4(3)). The UK did not accept the latter obligation because UK law did not conform to it when the ESC was ratified in 1962.

'Traditional' economic and social rights instruments usually afford workers some rights in relation to working conditions. Article 2 of the ESC 1961 addresses the right to 'just conditions of work', focusing in particular on the provision of paid holidays (accepted by the UK) and the limitation of working hours (not accepted by the UK). Article 7 of the ICESCR and Article 24 of the Universal Declaration contain similar obligations. The ICESCR (Article 7) and the ESC 1961 (Article 3) also give workers a right to safe and healthy working conditions.

The EU Charter of Fundamental Rights 2000 and the revised ESC 1996 contain versions of all the rights we have been considering so far, but they also add some new rights which we will label 'modern' economic and social rights. In the realm of individual employment rights, one of the most significant additions is the right not to be unfairly dismissed. Article 4(4) of the ESC 1961 contains an obligation to ensure that workers receive 'reasonable' notice if their employment is to be terminated, but Article 24 of the ESC 1996 goes much further, requiring states to protect the right of workers not to be arbitrarily dismissed and to ensure that any worker who is so dismissed can obtain compensation. Article 30 of the EU Charter states that 'every worker has the right to protection against unjustified dismissal'. Article 26 of the ESC 1996 protects the right to dignity at work, and applies both to sexual harassment and to other forms of bullying ('recurrent reprehensible or distinctly negative and offensive actions directed against individual workers in the workplace or in relation to work'). The EU Charter contains a general reference to working conditions which protect a worker's dignity (Article 31). This might be interpreted to cover bullying, but it does not spell out a detailed right not to be harassed.

Both instruments contain equality rights which are much broader than the 'traditional' right to equal pay. Article 23 of the EU Charter states that 'equality between men and women must be ensured in all areas, including employment, work and pay'. The Article also allows positive action to improve the position of the under-represented sex in any particular situation. Article 20 of the ESC 1996 also contains a general right to equal treatment without discrimination on grounds of sex in all aspects of the employment relationship. These generous equality rights are coupled with significant new rights for working parents, both male and female. Article 33(2) of the EU Charter provides:

> To reconcile family and professional life, everyone shall have the right to protection from dismissal for a reason connected with maternity and the right to paid maternity leave and to parental leave following the birth or adoption of a child.

The ESC 1961 was unique among 'traditional' instruments in providing a right to maternity leave (Article 8). This has been substantially amended in 1996 so that it focuses solely on protecting pregnant women and nursing mothers. Outdated references to protecting all women engaged in night work or dangerous work have been removed. Article 27 of the ESC 1996 promotes equal treatment between men and women workers with family responsibilities and those without. Signatory states are obliged to promote the provision of childcare facilities, to ensure that parental leave is available, and to ensure that workers cannot be dismissed solely on the ground of their childcare responsibilities.

Finally, the 'modern' economic and social rights instruments include rights for workers to be informed and consulted within the firm. As chapter 10 will explain, some European countries have a long tradition of 'works councils', groups of employee representatives who meet regularly with the employer to discuss a range of workplace issues. There is no equivalent tradition in the UK because of the policy of collective *laissez-faire* outlined in chapter 1. The most general right in the ESC 1996 is Article 21, which requires states to ensure that consultation takes place regularly on the financial position of the undertaking, and when necessary on important business decisions which might affect workers' interests. Article 29 offers a more specific right to consultation in the event of collective redundancies. Article 28 addresses the rights of workers' representatives, requiring that they should have the facilities they need to carry out their role and that they should be protected from discriminatory treatment. Finally, Article 22 requires states to protect the right of workers to take part in the determination and improvement of their working conditions and working environment, including health and safety issues and social facilities. The EU Charter, Article 27, contains a general right to information and consultation to be elaborated in accordance with relevant Community and national law.

International human rights instruments and domestic law

Chapter 4 will demonstrate that there is an important relationship between these various international and regional instruments and domestic law. The development of new standards at the international level may lead to changes in English law, as the government makes a commitment on the international level to bring domestic law into compliance. Or the development of new standards in English law may lead the government to put pressure on other countries to adopt the same standards so that UK firms do not suffer a competitive disadvantage in comparison with their foreign counterparts. More generally, and perhaps most importantly for our purposes, international human rights standards are often used by commentators as a set of benchmarks against which to measure domestic law. Those which have been agreed in Europe carry weight because they show what countries with similar economic and social contexts consider to be appropriate protection for workers. Those which have been agreed internationally are, arguably, even more powerful because they reflect the consensus of countries facing different economic circumstances and cultural norms. However, despite the strong rhetorical force which the label 'right' instantly grants, we must scrutinise rights arguments – whether made by governments or by commentators – with care. This is because any given right is open to a variety of different interpretations.

Interpreting rights

Our discussion of the interpretation of rights will be divided into four topics. The first two relate to the people involved: who can claim a right and against whom can the right be claimed? The second two relate to the content of the right in question: what exactly does the right protect and what weight does it carry in argument? It is impossible to provide definitive answers to these questions: the answers depend on the right we are considering and the context in which it is being applied. The identity of the right-holder might be quite different for the right not to be discriminated against and the right to strike, and the content of the right to strike might vary as between the ILO jurisprudence and the decisions of the House of Lords. But it is important to understand that these questions exist and that they need to be asked in any rights debate. This will help you to make critical use of the rights literature.

Right-holders

Most of the time, it is obvious who can claim a right. If a woman is refused a job because of her sex, she can claim that her individual right not to be discriminated against has been violated. The position is more complicated where the right is one which could belong to an individual or to a group. The right to strike is a good example. Does it belong to a group, such as a trade union, or to each worker as an individual?

The answer depends in part on the underlying basis of the right to strike: why do we give people a right to strike in the first place?[21] One view is that the right to strike is essential to support collective bargaining by trade unions. When union leaders go to the employer with their pay demands, they need to have some kind of threat in order to persuade the employer to listen to them. Strike action constitutes that threat. On this basis, strike action is a right for trade unions: for groups of workers, not individuals. On another view, however, the right to strike is an individual right to stop work in order to protest at the employer's actions. It might be based on one of a number of rights traditionally held by individuals, such as freedom of expression or the right not to be subjected to forced labour. Every person has the right to stop work regardless of whether or not he or she is participating in collective action organised by a union.

The identity of the right-holder is particularly important in the situation in which a union has organised a strike but some members do not want to take part.[22] If the

---

21 See chapter 10 for further discussion.
22 See chapter 11 for further discussion.

right belongs to individuals, they have a choice about whether or not to exercise it. It would be wrong for anyone to compel them to exercise their right to strike when they have expressed a preference for going to work. If the right belongs to the union, however, the position can be interpreted differently. In order to exercise its right to strike, the union can only act through its members. It can be argued that the strike will not be effective unless all the members take part. Therefore, the union should be permitted to compel its members to comply with the instruction to go on strike.

It is fair to say that group rights are a relatively new development in international law. Traditionally, theorists have assumed that rights would be held by individuals. This helps to explain why many labour lawyers are sceptical about human rights approaches to their subject.[23] They fear that a human rights argument will involve giving more power to individuals at the expense of trade unions. They argue that although this may seem beneficial to individuals, it harms them over the longer term. This is because strong unions are better placed than individuals to bargain with large firms. Groups of workers can balance out the employer's superior economic strength; individuals cannot do so however many rights the law gives them.

Rights against whom?

The international and regional instruments we considered earlier clearly impose obligations on the state to protect and promote the rights they contain. To comply with these obligations, the state may need to impose duties on private individuals. For example, the right not to be discriminated against requires legislation to ensure that employers, landlords, retailers and other private individuals do not commit acts of discrimination. It is not enough for the state itself to refrain from discriminating. But there is a broader debate about whether human rights themselves should be regarded as rights against everyone or as rights against the state. This debate has important practical ramifications when a state enacts a set of human rights guarantees.

The emphasis on rights as claims against the state reflects, in large measure, the historical development of human rights. Civil and political rights were a response to the emergence of national governments with real power to intervene in their citizens' actions. The state was seen as the most likely candidate to interfere with individuals' freedom of speech or to take away their right to vote. Economic and social rights are also focused on the state. The concern here was that the state might provide citizenship rights to individuals whilst leaving them in poverty and ignorance. The rights set out a model of how the state should use its wealth.

The idea that rights should in themselves be enforceable against private individuals has its origins in the modern concern with power in all its guises. Today, it is widely acknowledged that governments are not the only powerful institutions in society.[24] Indeed, other institutions – large multinational corporations, for

---

23 See, for example, K.D. Ewing, 'The Human Rights Act and labour law' (1998) 27 *ILJ* 275.
24 For discussion, see D. Oliver, *Common Values and the Public-Private Divide* (1999), pp. 31–7.

example – may wield more power than some governments. Human rights activists have therefore sought to impose the responsibility for respecting human rights on anyone who might violate them. From an employee's point of view, it does not matter whether he or she is forbidden to join a trade union by a government decree outlawing collective action or by a threat from the employer that all union members will be dismissed. Both actions violate the right to freedom of association.

Against this, it can be argued that it is unfair to subject private individuals to the obligation to comply with human rights guarantees when they are broadly framed and difficult to interpret. It is a breach of the Rule of Law requirement that individuals should be able to understand the law and use it to plan their lives.[25] The government should take responsibility for interpreting human rights and ensuring that they are given effect in the ordinary law. Individuals should be able to comply with human rights simply by acting lawfully. Any breaches of human rights by private parties should be remedied by the government.

This debate is of particular relevance to labour law because workers' rights are likely to be violated by employers, most of whom are private individuals or firms. When looking at particular human rights guarantees, particularly in domestic law, it is important to ask whether or not they can be enforced against private parties. The HRA 1998 is ambiguous about the extent to which it can be used in this way.

Scope

Perhaps the most important issue of interpretation in human rights is scope: what exactly does each human right protect? Does the right to strike protect all strikes whatever their motivation? Does the right not to be unfairly dismissed apply when the employee has been at fault? Does the right not to be discriminated against apply to discrimination on the grounds of a person's genetic features? All these questions will be discussed in detail in later chapters. For now, we will examine some general points about interpreting rights. The important message is that there are no simple answers.

A first point to note is that most international human rights instruments have a mechanism for interpretation. Often, this takes the form of a court or commission which can hear complaints from groups or individuals within signatory states who feel that their rights have been violated. The court or commission's role is to interpret the human right in question and to apply it to the case. These interpretations have considerable authority as 'official' statements of the meaning of a right in a particular instrument. For example, the European Committee on Social Rights interprets the ESC. It assesses whether states' regular reports show that they are in compliance, and hears complaints from bodies such as trade unions under the collective complaints procedure. The ECtHR has power to adjudicate individual claims that signatory states have violated Convention rights, and to award compensation. The various interpretative bodies do not exist in a vacuum: they often refer to each other's

25 J. Raz, 'The Rule of Law and its Virtue' (1977) 93 *LQR* 195.

interpretations. For example, the ECtHR sometimes refers to ESC jurisprudence when deciding cases on trade union rights.[26]

With many international instruments, it is possible to gain access to the *travaux préparatoires*: documents which explain the process of drafting and the intentions of the drafters. The *travaux* may be of use when a word or phrase is ambiguous, by giving an indication of what the drafters had in mind.[27] However, there are problems. One is that international instruments are often deliberately ambiguous because the many signatories cannot agree on a definite interpretation. The *travaux* may just show that there was a dispute about the meaning of a particular provision. Another is that when older instruments are applied to modern problems, the *travaux* may not offer any guidance. The question whether an older guarantee against discrimination should cover discrimination on the grounds of a person's genetic features is unlikely to have been dealt with in the *travaux*. Human rights instruments are usually treated as 'living' documents which can be adapted to new circumstances and are not confined to the meanings originally intended by the drafters.[28]

When interpreting a human rights guarantee, it is particularly important to have regard to the purpose being served by the right: what are we using it to protect? It is impossible to interpret human rights texts without getting into a discussion of their underlying values. Differences of opinion between those interpreting human rights – whether officially or as commentators – often stem from differences in identifying and understanding those underlying values. One basis commonly advanced for human rights is that they preserve individuals' liberty or autonomy.[29] Individuals should be able to make choices about their lives with the minimum of interference from other people, and should be able to make plans in a relatively stable and well-ordered society. Rights to freedom of expression and religion give individuals a private sphere within which they can decide, without interference, what to say and what to believe. Another possible basis for human rights is that they protect individuals' dignity.[30] Human rights are needed to ensure that each individual is treated with equal concern and respect by society. The right not to be discriminated against is an obvious example of this. It prevents us from treating individuals differently on the basis of characteristics which do not make them any less worthy of our respect.

Our particular concern in this book will be with labour rights. Many labour rights are simply fundamental human rights applied in a labour relations setting. As a result, they have the same underlying justification. The right not to be discriminated against by an employer is no different from the right not to be discriminated

26 See, for example, *Schmidt and Dahlströhm v Sweden* [1979–80] 1 EHRR 632.
27 See the Vienna Convention on the Law of Treaties (1969), 1155 UNTS 331, Articles 31 and 32.
28 See, for example, *Tyrer v UK* [1979–80] 2 EHRR 1 at 10.
29 H.L.A. Hart, 'Bentham on legal rights' in A.W.B. Simpson (ed.), *Oxford Essays in Jurisprudence: Second Series* (1973).
30 R.M. Dworkin, *A Matter of Principle* (1985), chapter 17.

against by government officials. But there are some rights which only apply in labour law. Some of the economic and social rights, like the right to a fair wage or to paid holidays, are examples of this. These rights can be justified either in a labour-specific way or in a more general way. For example, it could be argued that the right to a fair wage stems from the inequality of bargaining power which usually exists between worker and employer. The worker cannot bargain for a fair wage and therefore needs the protection of the law to prevent exploitation by the employer. That would be a labour-specific justification. A more general justification would appeal to a broader value such as dignity. Here, the argument would be that we can put a minimum value on labour. Any worker who is made to work for less is being treated as if he or she is less worthy of concern and respect than other people. His or her dignity is violated. We shall see in later chapters that our choice of justification for labour rights can have important consequences for their interpretation. In general, the choice of a broader justification enables labour lawyers to bolster their arguments with powerful ideals which have widespread support. But sometimes a labour-specific justification is preferable because ideals drawn from other spheres of activity may have unintended consequences in labour law.

The interpretation of human rights is a complex and challenging task which provokes controversy amongst and between human rights bodies, governments and commentators. When looking at competing interpretations it is important to examine the underlying justification being offered for the right in question. This is also relevant when assessing whether or not an interference with the right can be justified, and it is to this that we will now turn.

Weight

Rights carry special weight in political argument. If they had the same status as any other consideration, there would be no point in attaching the label 'right'. They could easily be overridden by other arguments. At the same time, however, it is clear that rights are not absolute. A right cannot be exercised without any regard to the costs it might be imposing on others. For each right, we need to decide to what extent interferences or exceptions can be permitted.

Let us begin by examining the role of rights in political argument. To do this, we need a general theory of how political decisions are made. Utilitarianism is a useful starting point. Utilitarianism focuses on the consequences of actions. The early utilitarians evaluated actions in terms of how much pleasure and pain they would give.[31] Thus, they argued that a particular action should be taken where it maximised pleasure and minimised pain in society. More modern versions usually

---

31 J. Bentham (1876), *An Introduction to the Principles of Morals and Legislation* (ed. J.H. Burns, H.L.A. Hart and F. Rosen, 1996), chapter 1; J. S. Mill (1863), *Utilitarianism* (ed. R. Crisp, 1998), chapter 2.

rephrase this in terms of the satisfaction of people's preferences: a particular action should be taken when it will satisfy the largest number of preferences. Utilitarians are often classified as 'act-utilitarians' or 'rule-utilitarians'. Act-utilitarians weigh up the consequences of each proposed action taken on its own.[32] Rule-utilitarians examine each proposed action in the light of general rules which have been found in the past to maximise pleasure and minimise pain.[33] Rule-utilitarianism is often regarded as more practical than act-utilitarianism because less effort needs to be put into each individual decision.[34] But it is not entirely convincing. If a rule-utilitarian insists on keeping to a rule even if it will lead to pain in a particular case, he or she is no longer a true utilitarian examining the consequences of his or her actions. If the rule-utilitarian disregards the rule, his or her approach is no different to that of an act-utilitarian who would decide each case on its merits, taking into account the general benefit to society which arises if people usually comply with rules.

A common criticism of utilitarianism is that it allows substantial harm to be caused to a few individuals provided that the general welfare is improved. Is the happiness of the many sufficient to outweigh the misery of the few? To use a classic example, imagine that a terrorist has planted a bomb somewhere in a busy city centre, and will only reveal its exact location if tortured. The torture will cause profound misery for the terrorist and for his or her torturers. Nevertheless, an act-utilitarian would probably carry out the torture, on the basis that the pain caused to the terrorist and the torturers would be outweighed by the pleasure given to those who were evacuated before the bomb went off. A rule-utilitarian might manage to avoid this solution. He or she could argue that there was a general rule that torture by the state was unacceptable, which should be upheld regardless of the circumstances. But this falls into the trap, noted above, of abandoning utilitarianism's basic focus on the consequences of actions. In any event, the critics of utilitarianism feel that there is something missing from this argument. They argue that utilitarianism should be qualified by respect for people's *rights*.

There are two main theories about the role that rights should play. On the first theory, rights should have special weight in the utilitarian calculation in that they should count for more than other kinds of interests. However, a right could be outweighed by a large number of ordinary interests. On the second theory, rights should have priority over other kinds of interests and could not be outweighed by them, however many of them there were. Dworkin is the most famous exponent of the second view:

---

32 Bentham and Mill (above n. 31) are usually regarded as act-utilitarians, though for a rule-utilitarian interpretation of Mill, see J.O. Urmston, 'The interpretation of the moral philosophy of J.S. Mill' (1953) 3 *Philosophical Quarterly* 33.

33 See, generally, B. Hooker, 'Rule-consequentialism, incoherence, fairness' (1995) 95 *Proceedings of the Aristotelian Society* 19.

34 R.M. Hare, 'Ethical Theory and Utilitarianism', in H. D. Lewis (ed.), *Contemporary British Philosophy* (fourth series) (1976).

Individual rights are political trumps[35] held by individuals. Individuals have rights when, for some reason, a collective goal is not a sufficient justification for denying them what they wish, as individuals, to have or to do, or not a sufficient justification for imposing some loss or injury upon them.[36]

These 'rights as trumps' almost always outweigh ordinary interests, save in exceptional cases when it is necessary to 'prevent a catastrophe'.[37]

However, the difference between the two theories may not be so great as it seems. Dworkin only accords 'trumps' status to fundamental rights. He accepts that other, lesser rights can be limited 'to obtain a clear and major public benefit'.[38] Thus, his approach to non-fundamental rights is exactly the same as that adopted by theorists who take the first view. So both camps accept that rights can be outweighed by ordinary interests. The only difference between them is that those who take the second view, like Dworkin, argue that there is a small category of fundamental rights to which this basic rule does not apply.

Whichever theory we adopt, we need to attribute some value or weight to the right under consideration. This is because we need to decide how many ordinary interests are needed on the other side of the scales in order to outweigh it. And if we are adopting Dworkin's view, we also need to know whether the right is in the 'fundamental' category, so that it cannot be outweighed at all. But how do we decide how important a particular right is? One factor to take into account is the underlying rationale of the right. If the right is protecting a person against a very serious form of harm – being tortured, for example – we might consider it to be more important (or more likely to be 'fundamental') than a right which is protecting a person against a lesser form of harm, such as being made to work long hours. Another factor to look at is whether any theorists or human rights organisations have come up with a helpful classification. For example, some attempt has been made by the ILO to identify fundamental labour rights.[39] It has chosen, among others, the right not to be discriminated against and the right to freedom of association and collective bargaining. It has argued that these rights represent part of the bare minimum which should be upheld by all states regardless of their circumstances. But all such classifications can be contested. We could argue, for example, that the right to a minimum wage is just as important because it safeguards workers' dignity and protects them from exploitation. In short, according weight to a particular right always involves a highly controversial value judgement.

On the other side of the scales (unless we have a Dworkinian fundamental right to uphold) there are 'ordinary interests'. What are these ordinary interests? In labour

---

35 This metaphor is from card games. A trump card is one which beats cards from other suits even though its numerical value is lower. So if Hearts are trumps, the two of Hearts will beat a high-value card like the King of Spades.

36 R. Dworkin, *Taking Rights Seriously* (2nd impression with appendix, 1978), p. xi.

37 Dworkin, above n. 36, p. 191.

38 Dworkin, above n. 36, p. 191.

39 ILO, *Declaration on Fundamental Principles and Rights at Work* (1998).

law, they are often made up of arguments about the economic impact of a particular right on the employer and on the economy. Let us take the right to equal pay as an example. This right allows a woman to claim that she is doing the same job as a man and should be paid the same wage. If her claim is successful, the employer's wage bill will obviously rise because it will be obliged to pay her the extra money paid to the man. The employer will have to increase the price of its products and may lose market share. The crucial question is whether the woman's right to equal treatment is sufficient to outweigh the potential harm to the employer. Labour lawyers are sometimes tempted to be very dismissive of employers' claims, but some caution is required because a downturn in the employer's business may affect the pay and prospects of workers as well as the employer's profits. In this case, it seems likely that the right to equal pay would prevail, because it is of considerable importance in combating discriminatory treatment. Courts and commentators continue to struggle with these issues.

The need to weigh rights against ordinary interests helps to demonstrate why labour lawyers have been so interested in the work of those economists who identify positive benefits to firms in complying with labour rights. Their arguments often suggest that a new labour right will not impose costs on employers. This means that the right can simply be enforced without weighing it against ordinary interests. However, as we saw in chapter 2, these economic arguments are controversial and may not always be able to demonstrate that a right will benefit *all* firms. It is rare to find a situation in which there are no arguments at all against a particular right. Labour lawyers may still need to be able to justify rights for their own sake and to demonstrate that they outweigh cost considerations.

Sometimes, we find that there are rights on *both* sides of the weighing scales. An obvious example is where one person's right to freedom of expression might infringe another person's right to respect for his or her privacy. Theorists in both camps agree that in this situation, one right must give way to the other. There is no other option. We simply have to make a choice about which right to protect. The utilitarian calculus is helpful here because it encourages us to make the choice which will cause the lesser amount of suffering. In labour law, there are many examples of conflicts between workers' rights and those of others. Imagine a group of police officers who wish to exercise the right to strike. Perhaps they have a powerful claim: staffing shortages are forcing them to patrol dangerous areas on their own, thus putting their lives at risk. But if the police officers are permitted to go on strike, law and order would quickly break down. Criminals would soon realise that they could act with impunity. The rights and freedoms of ordinary citizens would inevitably be violated. For this reason, it is usually regarded as legitimate for a government to ban police officers and others who provide 'essential services' from striking.[40]

40 For discussion, see G.S. Morris, *Strikes in Essential Services* (1986).

Further reading

For an account of international human rights law, see H.J. Steiner and P. Alston, *International Human Rights in Context* (2nd edn., 2000), especially chapters 1-4; or C. Tomuschat, *Human Rights: Between Idealism and Realism* (2003). For an introduction to the jurisprudential issues surrounding rights see J. Waldron, *Theories of Rights* (1984); or F.M. Kamm, 'Rights', in J.L. Coleman and S. Shapiro (eds.), *The Oxford Handbook of Jurisprudence and Philosophy of Law* (2002).

Rights theories are not without their critics. M.A. Glendon, *Rights Talk: the Impoverishment of Political Discourse* (1991), attacks rights on the grounds that they oversimplify complex debates and draw attention away from more important notions of duty and responsibility. D. Kennedy, *A Critique of Adjudication* (1997), chapters 12 and 13, argues that rights are indeterminate: they purport to offer solutions to problems but in practice they are too vague and contradictory to do so. For a summary of the critiques and a response, see C. Sunstein, 'Rights and their critics' (1995) 70 *Notre Dame Law Review* 727. What is the relationship between rights and duties? What role should rights play in political and legal discourse? And what conception of rights does Sunstein defend? Do you agree with the concessions he makes to the critics?

Economic and social rights are of particular relevance to labour law: see K.D. Ewing, 'The Human Rights Act and labour law' (1998) 27 *ILJ* 275, and 'Social rights and constitutional law' (1999) *PL* 104. You should therefore familiarise yourself with the debate about the status and enforceability of economic and social rights. Compare M. Cranston, 'Human rights: a reply to Professor Raphael', in D.D. Raphael (ed.), *Political Theory and the Rights of Man* (1967), with D. Beetham, 'What future for economic and social rights?' (1995) 43 *Political Studies* 41, and C. Fabre, 'Constitutionalising Social Rights' (1998) 6 *Journal of Political Philosophy* 263. Are economic and social rights capable of being fundamental, universal and clearly specifiable? Can they be enforced by the courts? Economic and social rights require the government to interfere with markets. What does this tell us about the likely attitude of neoclassical economists to economic and social rights? Why might neoclassical economists be more enthusiastic about civil and political rights? Revisit the readings on neoclassical economics in chapter 2 for some ideas.

Most human rights discourse in the labour law context focuses on workers' rights, not employers' rights. Employers' 'rights' are usually treated as important interests which may justify an interference with, or limitation of, workers' rights. Why do you think this is? Would it be helpful to think about employers' rights too? If so, what rights would employers have?

4

Modes of regulation

In this chapter, we will focus on the various modes of regulation in labour law: in other words, on the various different ways in which labour law is created and applied. You might think that this topic is too straightforward to merit a chapter to itself. Surely labour law is created by Parliament and applied by the courts? But matters are not so simple. It can no longer be argued that labour law is solely a matter for national governments. As we saw in the last chapter, some rights in the ECHR are relevant to labour law. These can now be enforced in the UK courts using the HRA 1998. Even more significantly, EU law (which takes priority over inconsistent national law) covers many aspects of employment, such as equal pay between men and women, collective consultation and the protection of atypical workers. Finally, the UK is bound in international law by ILO Conventions on important areas such as freedom of association and collective bargaining.

These various layers of regulation may come into conflict with each other. For example, the EU might propose legislation designed to promote workers' rights in a particular area – collective consultation, for example – but a UK government which was keen to reduce the regulatory burdens on businesses might be hostile to such legislation. Our discussion of rights and economics perspectives on labour law is highly relevant here: when two layers of regulation come into conflict, it is usually because they are striking a different balance between rights arguments and economics arguments. The eventual outcome will depend on matters of practical enforceability: the UK may be able to resist new EU legislation at the negotiating stage, but once it has been passed, the government must implement it or face sanctions of various kinds.

The difficulties are, however, not confined to the relationship between national law and regional or international norms. Within national law, the interaction between Parliament and the courts has long been controversial and warrants study in itself. The courts have tended to draw heavily on common law doctrines when interpreting labour law statutes, prompting critics to argue that Parliament's aims are not always implemented to the full. The second part of this chapter will consider modes of regulation *within* national law.

International and regional regulation

International and regional regulation of labour law takes place against the background of a globalising world economy.[1] Globalisation pits national governments against each other as they try to attract multinational firms to invest in their countries. Many writers believe that this will lead to a 'race to the bottom': governments will reduce their labour standards to the lowest possible level in the belief that multinationals want to locate where labour is cheap. As we saw in chapter 2, there is considerable controversy surrounding the merits of this approach. Writers who believe in preventing the 'race to the bottom' advocate the setting of minimum labour standards at the international or regional level.[2] This would mean that labour standards were no longer an area for competition between states. However, regulation at this level can be difficult to achieve. By resisting agreement, states may feel that they are able to keep a competitive advantage for themselves. Writers who are less concerned about the 'race to the bottom' may be suspicious of international or regional organisations. They argue that such organisations are dominated by powerful countries which already have high labour standards. These countries use the rhetoric of human rights to impose their own standards on the rest of the world. But their real motivation is 'protectionist': a desire to take away the legitimate competitive advantage of countries with lower labour standards in order to protect their own industries.

The International Labour Organisation

The International Labour Organisation (ILO) was established in 1919 as part of the international community's response to the First World War. In the wake of the Second World War, its role was reaffirmed and expanded, and it became one of the UN's specialised agencies, with the remit of promoting social justice and labour rights.[3] The UK is one of its 175 member states. The ILO's main method of operation is to agree detailed conventions on different aspects of labour law. Member states may choose whether or not to ratify these conventions. Once a state has ratified a convention, the ILO monitors its compliance with the obligations it imposes, but as we shall see, the ILO has virtually no powers of enforcement. Given the ILO's remit, it is hardly surprising to find that it is heavily focused on workers' rights. We will look first at the interaction between rights and economics arguments within

---

1 The discussion will focus on the ILO, ECHR and EU. Space precludes a full discussion of other parts of the international human rights regime, such as the ICCPR/ICESCR, or of the ESC at the regional level.

2 For a good introduction to the debate, see E. Lee, 'Globalization and labour standards: a review of issues' (1997) *ILR* 173.

3 For further detail about the structure and functions of the ILO, see H.G. Bartolomei de la Cruz, G. von Potobsky and L. Swepston, *The International Labour Organisation: the International Standards System and Basic Human Rights* (1996). The ILO website is a useful source of ILO documents and background information: http://www.ilo.org.

the ILO itself, before turning to an examination of the ILO's relationship with UK governments.

Globalisation is often regarded as having created an 'identity crisis' for the ILO.[4] Its emphasis on detailed labour standards began to seem irrelevant in a climate of competition between states to attract multinational firms. And its inability to enforce its conventions became an embarrassment when new international organisations concerned with trade, particularly the World Trade Organization (WTO) were shown to have a much greater degree of effectiveness. The ILO responded in 1998 with the *Declaration of Fundamental Principles and Rights at Work*. This provides that all ILO member states, regardless of which conventions they have ratified, are bound to uphold four fundamental rights: freedom of association and collective bargaining, freedom from forced labour, freedom from child labour, and the right not to be discriminated against. The Declaration gave a new impetus to the ILO's activities by encouraging it to focus on a limited group of rights, instead of trying to promote hundreds of detailed conventions. On the one hand, the Declaration can be regarded as enhancing the 'rights' orientation of the ILO. Whereas before, the ILO was clearly focused on workers' rights, the Declaration emphasises the overlap between workers' rights and fundamental human rights. The ILO has gained legitimacy by emphasising (relatively) uncontroversial rights and by tapping into the powerful rhetoric of human rights. On the other hand, some elements of the Declaration reflect the view that international organisations like the ILO may be used to protect powerful countries from legitimate competition. Thus, the Declaration provides that:

labour standards should not be used for protectionist trade purposes, and that nothing in this Declaration and its follow-up shall be invoked or otherwise used for such purposes; in addition, the comparative advantage of any country should in no way be called into question by this Declaration and its follow-up.[5]

This limits the ILO's ability to pursue the rights in the Declaration where they might impose costs on a country and make it less attractive as a location for multinationals. Many rights commentators have been highly critical of the way in which free trade economics arguments have been allowed to intrude into the Declaration.[6] But perhaps it would not have been possible to reach agreement on the Declaration without acknowledging those arguments.

Despite the mixed message contained in the Declaration, the ILO remains strongly rights-orientated. This has led to conflicts with successive UK governments which have tended to focus on economics arguments of various kinds. Perhaps the

---

4 See B.A. Langille, 'The ILO and the New Economy: recent developments' (1999) 15 *International Journal of Comparative Labour Law and Industrial Relations* 229.

5 ILO, *Declaration of Fundamental Principles and Rights at Work* (1998), para. 5.

6 See, for example, Langille, above n. 4.

best illustration of this is in the area of freedom of association.[7] The ILO has long held the view that freedom of association is a fundamental right, and in 1950 a special Freedom of Association Committee was established to investigate alleged violations.[8] The UK has ratified both Convention 87 on Freedom of Association and Protection of the Right to Organise (1948) and Convention 98 on the Right to Organise and Collective Bargaining (1949), but it has been the subject of some 80 complaints to the Freedom of Association Committee and remains in breach of some aspects of the two Conventions.

Article 1(1) of Convention 98 provides that 'workers shall enjoy adequate protection against acts of anti-union discrimination in respect of their employment'. UK law contains provisions which protect employees at all stages of the employment relationship: hiring, dismissal, and during employment itself.[9] As chapter 11 will explain, these provisions may be criticised in a number of respects. But for now, we will concentrate on one particular problem. In the 1980s, many employers decided that they did not want to recognise trade unions for collective bargaining any more. In order to bring about this change, they offered extra pay to workers who were willing to sign so-called 'personal contracts' which were not negotiated by a trade union. Workers who refused to sign did not receive the extra pay. This could be regarded as a form of discrimination against trade union members. But it did not count as such in law. Under the Trade Union and Labour Relations (Consolidation) Act 1992 (TULRCA 1992), s. 146(1), an employee has the right not to be subjected to any detrimental treatment by the employer for the purpose of:

(a) preventing or deterring him from being or seeking to become a member of an independent trade union, or penalising him for doing so,
(b) preventing or deterring him from taking part in the activities of an independent trade union at an appropriate time, or penalising him for doing so . . .

Although this appears to offer strong protection to employees, it must be read in conjunction with s. 148(3).[10] This requires the tribunal to find that, where an employer wishes to 'further a change in his relationship with all or any class of his employees', this should be construed as his purpose even if he has also acted for a purpose which would be prohibited by s. 146. The tribunal may only depart from this interpretation where 'it considers that no reasonable employer would act or fail

---

7 See, generally, T. Novitz, 'Freedom of association and "fairness at work" – an assessment of the impact and relevance of ILO Convention No. 87 on its fiftieth anniversary' (1998) 27 *ILJ* 169; 'International promise and domestic pragmatism: to what extent will the Employment Relations Act 1999 implement international labour standards relating to freedom of association?' (2000) 63 *MLR* 379.
8 For further detail on the Committee's work, see the ILO website (n. 3 above) and L. Swepston, 'Human rights law and freedom of association: development through ILO supervision' (1998) 137 *ILR* 169.
9 TULRCA 1992, ss. 146, 152–3.
10 This provision is sometimes referred to as the 'Ullswater amendment' because it was proposed by Viscount Ullswater in the House of Lords.

to act in the way concerned' in order to change his relationship with his employees.[11] Since employers who wanted to derecognise unions were changing the relationship with their employees, they were protected by s. 148(3) against a finding that they had discriminated against trade unionists.[12]

In a case brought by the TUC against the UK government,[13] the ILO Freedom of Association Committee was quick to point out the difficulties with s. 148(3). The provision 'limits considerably the margin of appreciation of a tribunal in examining whether a given employer's action does prevent or deter a worker from being or becoming a member of a trade union'.[14] The tribunal is not permitted to assess whether the employer's legitimate purpose is predominant: the legitimate purpose must be accepted even if the employer's main purpose is an anti-union one. As the Committee explained, a worker's discrimination claim is only likely to be successful in 'extraordinary circumstances'.[15] The Committee therefore found the government to be in breach of Convention 98.

However, the ILO's promotion of workers' rights does not readily translate into compliance on the part of member states.[16] One of the common criticisms of the ILO is that it is good at setting standards but in a weak position to enforce them. Under Article 22 of the Constitution, member states must submit an annual report which explains how they are implementing the conventions they have ratified. If a state is failing to comply, another state may make a complaint or a trade union may make a representation to that effect.[17] The Governing Body refers complaints to a Commission of Inquiry where appropriate.[18] The Commission publishes its report and the Committee of Experts on the Application of Conventions and Recommendations follows up on implementation of the Commission's recommendations. Representations are reviewed by the Governing Body, which may decide to publish the representation along with any response received from the relevant government, or to appoint an ad hoc committee to investigate the matter further.[19] Freedom of association cases are dealt with by the Freedom of Association Committee, which also publishes its reports. The ILO does not have powers of enforcement, such as the ability to levy fines against governments.[20] All it can do is to persuade governments to comply. Phrases like 'moral suasion' or 'the mobilisation of shame' are

---

11 TULRCA 1992, s. 148(3).
12 *Associated Newspapers Ltd v Wilson* [1995] 2 AC 454 (HL).
13 ILO Freedom of Association Committee, Case 1730, Report No. 294.
14 Above n. 13, at para. 199.
15 Above n. 13, at para. 199.
16 For a more detailed account of the enforcement of ILO standards, see F. Maupain, 'The settlement of disputes within the International Labour Office' (2000) 2 *JIEL* 273.
17 ILO Constitution, Articles 26 and 24 respectively.
18 See ILO Constitution, Articles 26–9.
19 ILO Constitution, Article 25.
20 Under ILO Constitution, Article 33, the 'Governing Body may recommend to the Conference such action as it may deem wise and expedient to secure compliance' with the recommendations of a Commission of Inquiry. This has been used only once, in 2000, to address the problem of forced labour in Burma/Myanmar.

commonly used to describe the ILO's approach to enforcement. A truly recalcitrant government could simply ignore the ILO's views. And since states are under no obligation to ratify ILO Conventions in the first place, they could simply withdraw ratification if they were in breach.

Moreover, ILO Conventions cannot be enforced in the domestic courts because English law takes a 'dualist' approach to international law.[21] International law and domestic law are viewed as two separate spheres. International law governs the relations between states, whereas domestic law governs the relationship between states and citizens. A citizen may not bring an action in domestic law to challenge a breach of international law.[22] This means that the only sanctions available against the UK government for a breach of an ILO Convention are those imposed by the ILO itself.

The saga of TULRCA 1992, s 148(3) is now drawing to a close. The government has announced its intention to repeal the offending provision.[23] But this is not in response to pressure from the ILO. Instead, it reflects the fact that s. 148(3) was also condemned by the ECtHR as a breach of the freedom of association guarantee in Article 11 of the Convention. Thus, although the ILO 'layer' of regulation is strongly rights-based, its success in pushing English law in this direction is limited. ILO standards probably have some indirect influence because they are widely used by commentators, trade unions and others in criticising the law and suggesting new policy developments, but the extent of this influence is difficult to measure.

The European Convention on Human Rights

The ECHR was adopted in 1950. Until recently, it had similar status to ILO legislation – it bound the government in international law but had limited consequences in domestic law – though successive governments have had a fairly good record of complying with judgments of the ECtHR.[24] The HRA 1998, which came into force in October 2000, empowered the UK courts to decide various types of cases involving Convention rights. However, although this has enhanced the practical possibilities of enforcement, the impact of the Convention on labour law is likely to be relatively limited. As a statement of civil and political rights, few of the substantive rights it contains are of relevance in the workplace, and those which do apply tend to be narrowly defined.[25]

---

21 I. Brownlie, *Principles of Public International Law* (6th edn., 2003), chapter 2.
22 Where a statute is ambiguous, a court may refer to international obligations in order to resolve the ambiguity, applying the presumption that Parliament does not intend to legislate in breach of such obligations: *Salomon v Customs and Excise Commissioners* [1967] 2 QB 116 at 143–4, per Diplock LJ.
23 Department of Trade and Industry (DTI), *Review of the Employment Relations Act 1999* (2003), pp. 61–6.
24 See R.R. Churchill and J.R. Young, 'Compliance with judgments of the European Court of Human Rights and decisions of the Committee of Ministers: the experience of the United Kingdom, 1975–1987: (1991) 62 *British Yearbook of International Law* 283.
25 See, generally, K. D. Ewing, 'The Human Rights Act and labour law' (1998) 27 *ILJ* 275.

Employees have achieved some notable victories before the ECtHR. In *Lustig-Prean and Beckett v UK*, the Court found a breach of Article 8 (right to respect for private and family life) when the claimant was dismissed from the armed forces on grounds of homosexuality after a highly detailed investigation into his private life.[26] In response to this and other decisions, the government put a stop to the policy of excluding gays and lesbians from the armed forces. In *Wilson v UK*, the Court found that Article 11 (freedom of association) was violated by TULRCA 1992, s. 148(3) and related provisions which allowed employers to offer workers a pay rise if they accepted contracts which had not been negotiated by a trade union.[27] The government is proposing to amend the law in order to comply with this decision.[28]

However, one of the criticisms commonly levelled at the Convention is that the rights it contains tend to be narrowly defined.[29] Article 9, which protects everyone's freedom of thought, conscience and religion, provides a good illustration of this. The Article includes a right to manifest one's religion or belief. This often takes the form of attending religious worship. In the employment sphere, a conflict may arise when a person is under a religious obligation to attend worship during his or her working hours. In *Stedman v UK*, the applicant was asked by her employer to accept a contractual variation which would require her to work on Sundays.[30] She refused to accept the variation because it interfered with her religious obligations. The European Commission on Human Rights[31] rejected her case as manifestly inadmissible. The Commission refused to acknowledge any connection between her refusal to work on Sundays and her religious beliefs, holding that she had been dismissed 'for failing to agree to work certain hours rather than for her religious belief as such'.[32] Moreover, the Commission emphasised the fact that she was free to resign and seek alternative employment which did not involve Sunday working. This decision shows a clear reluctance to impose any obligations on the state – and thus indirectly on employers – to accommodate religious worship. Although the decision is not explicitly (or even implicitly) motivated by economic considerations, it has the effect of prioritising them through its emphasis on freedom of contract. The employer is permitted to offer a contract which organises working time as it sees fit, and the employee is free to 'take it or leave it'. This minimises cost to the employer by imposing no requirement to respect employees' religious beliefs, and instead imposes all the cost on the employee. Moreover, the option of finding another job may not be readily available in practice: in times of high unemployment, jobs may

---

26 [1999] 29 EHRR 548.
27 [2002] 35 EHRR 20.
28 DTI, above, n. 23.
29 Ewing, above n. 25, at 288–9.
30 [1997] 23 EHRR CD 168.
31 The Commission's primary role was to act as 'gatekeeper' to the Court, filtering out inadmissible claims and promoting friendly settlements. Protocol 11 to the ECHR replaced the Commission and Court structure with a single Court which makes its own admissibility decisions. The Commission ceased to exist in 1999.
32 [1997] 23 EHRR CD 168 at 169.

be scarce, and in some sectors, it may be impossible to find a job which does not require some Sunday working.

The potential impact of the ECHR is even further reduced by the fact that Convention rights rarely 'trump' other considerations. Most of the rights which are relevant to labour law are *qualified*: states may justify interferences with the rights on certain grounds.[33] Article 9(2) is typical:

> Freedom to manifest one's religion or beliefs shall be subject only to such limitations as are prescribed by law and are necessary in a democratic society in the interests of public safety, for the protection of public order, health or morals, or for the protection of the rights and freedoms of others.

In the employment sphere, the reference to 'the rights and freedoms of others' could be used to bring in the employer's contractual and property interests as reasons for limiting workers' religious freedoms. The phrase 'necessary in a democratic society' has been interpreted by the ECtHR as requiring the use of a proportionality test,[34] a stringent form of review in which the harm to the individual is weighed against the public authority's goals. But the effect of the proportionality test is limited by the ECtHR's use of the concept of 'margin of appreciation'.[35] The ECtHR, as a supra-national court, is not always well placed to decide exactly which interferences with rights are permissible in the various signatory states. It therefore allows them some discretion to make their own decisions on issues of particular controversy. The concept of 'margin of appreciation' has no place in the HRA 1998, because UK courts can be taken to have an understanding of conditions in the UK.[36] However, the courts have expressed the view that public authorities may in some circumstances be better placed to decide sensitive issues than courts. The concept of 'deference' has been used in some cases to allow public authorities a degree of discretion.[37] This means that the government may have less to fear from the ECtHR or the domestic courts than the proportionality test would at first sight imply.

However, despite the limitations on the substantive content of Convention rights, they are at least enforceable by claimants in English law, thanks to the HRA 1998. Section 6 of the Act creates a cause of action against public bodies, stating that '[i]t is unlawful for a public authority to act in a way which is incompatible with a Convention right'. The Act divides public bodies into 'pure' and 'hybrid' bodies. A person employed by a 'pure' public authority would be able to rely directly on s. 6. But those employed by 'hybrid' bodies or by private employers (the majority of employees) are only able to use the Act if it has so-called *horizontal* effect. The key provision is s. 6(3)(a) of the Act, which extends the definition of 'public authority'

---

33 Ewing, above n. 25, at 289.
34 See, for example, *Olsson v Sweden* [1989] 11 EHRR 259 at 285.
35 See *Handyside v UK* [1979–80] 1 EHRR 737 at 753–4.
36 See, for example, *Brown v Stott* [2003] 1 AC 681 at 703, per Lord Bingham.
37 Above n. 36.

to include courts or tribunals. This means that the courts themselves are obliged to act compatibly with Convention rights.

The cases can be divided into two groups: those which fall to be decided at common law, and those which fall to be decided by the application of statutory provisions. In common law cases involving private parties, the courts have held that they are under a duty to develop the common law in the light of the Convention. However, this does not appear to extend to creating a new cause of action where none existed before, because this would amount to extending s. 6 to private parties. Dame Elizabeth Butler-Sloss P put the point clearly in *Venables v NGN*:

> That obligation on the court does not seem to me to encompass the creation of a free-standing cause of action based directly upon the articles of the convention . . . The duty on the court, in my view, is to act compatibly with convention rights in adjudicating upon existing common law causes of action, and that includes a positive as well as a negative obligation.[38]

Thus, in common law cases the HRA 1998 has some horizontal effect, at least where the law can be developed incrementally to accommodate it. The second group of cases involves statutory interpretation. This group has particular significance for labour law because most cases involve statute law rather than common law. Section 3(1) of the HRA 1998 governs statutory interpretation: 'So far as it is possible to do so, primary legislation and subordinate legislation must be read and given effect in a way which is compatible with the Convention rights.' Significantly, this section does not contain any language which would suggest that it is confined to cases involving public authorities. The view that it should be employed in 'horizontal' cases is reinforced by the s. 6 obligation on the courts to act compatibly with the Convention. Thus, all labour law statutes must now be regarded as subject to ss. 3 and 4, even in a case between an employee and a private employer.

The relationship between the domestic courts and the ECtHR is governed by s. 2. This obliges the domestic courts to 'take into account' any relevant jurisprudence of the ECtHR: in other words, they must consider it but need not follow it. It seems unlikely that the domestic courts would offer a lower degree of protection to a Convention right than that afforded by the ECtHR, because this would force the claimant to pursue his or her case to Strasbourg in order to obtain a remedy. A more realistic possibility is that the domestic courts might offer a higher level of protection to certain rights. However, as we shall see in the second part of this chapter, this may not occur in labour law because the courts have a tendency to favour employers over unions and workers.

Like the ILO, the ECHR is a rights-focused layer of regulation. Unlike the ILO, it has a direct impact in English law through the HRA 1998. But this does not necessarily mean that it will bring about a major shift towards rights thinking in

---

38 [2001] 1 All ER 908 at 918.

labour law. Much will depend on how the relevant rights, and their limitations, are construed.

The European Union

The EU is a fascinating case-study of the interplay between rights and economics. As the early nomenclature indicates, the European Economic Community was an organisation with economic aims. Over time, the social policy agenda has become increasingly important and EU law has begun to protect a wider range of workers' rights.[39] This has led to clashes with UK governments of both political persuasions because of the high value they have placed on the countervailing economic concerns of flexibility and business competitiveness. Paradoxically, from a rights perspective, it can be argued that the EU's rights agenda is too heavily influenced by economic arguments, and that rights are all too often sacrificed to 'market forces'. A complex picture also emerges in the area of enforcement: the doctrine of supremacy indicates that all conflicts must be resolved in favour of EU law, but in practice, national governments have a substantial degree of discretion in their implementation of EU provisions.

When the Treaty of Rome was signed in 1957, the only significant labour law provision it contained was Article 119 (now Article 141), giving a right to equal pay between men and women. The French government had pressed for the inclusion of this provision because France already had equal pay laws. It was feared that French products would be undercut by cheaper products from other Member States in which women were paid less than men.[40] Thus, the rationale for the EEC's initial foray into social policy was an economic one. Over time, the EU's competence in the field of labour law has expanded considerably to include equal pay between men and women,[41] health and safety, working conditions, termination of employment, information and consultation, collective representation, and equality between men and women as regards working conditions,[42] though pay, freedom of association and the right to strike are specifically excluded.[43]

As the EU's competence has expanded, increasing emphasis has been placed on the rights dimension of labour law. The EU Charter of Fundamental Rights, agreed by the Member States in 2000, is the most recent example of this new emphasis.[44] The Charter is not at present legally enforceable although it is expected that it will be incorporated into the Treaties at some point in the future. The new emphasis on rights stems from two main factors. First, there has for some time been a concern

---

39 For excellent discussions of the historical development of EU social policy, see C. Barnard, 'EC Social Policy' in P.P. Craig and G. de Búrca (eds.), *The Evolution of EU Law* (1999); S. Fredman, 'Social Law in the European Union' in P.P. Craig and C. Harlow (eds.), *Lawmaking in the European Union* (1998).
40 Barnard, above n. 39, p. 481.
41 Article 141 EC.
42 All contained in Article 137 EC.
43 Article 137(5) EC.
44 See, generally, B. Hepple, 'The EU Charter of Fundamental Rights' (2001) 30 *ILJ* 225.

that the rights which are well protected by the constitutions of the Member States are not explicitly protected in the Treaties and could therefore be overridden by EU legislation. The validity of any such legislation could not be challenged in the national courts because of the doctrine of supremacy (that EU law takes priority over national law, even national constitutional law) espoused by the ECJ.[45] The ECJ itself has developed a doctrine of fundamental rights in response to these concerns.[46] The Charter represents an attempt to put this approach on a firmer legal basis. Second, there has been a growing realisation that the EU is not popular among ordinary citizens. The EU is widely perceived to favour businesses over individuals and to promote free market ideology over social concerns. Measures like the Charter can be seen as part of an attempt to raise awareness among citizens of the benefits of EU membership.[47]

Another important development has been the introduction and use of 'social dialogue' as a legislative technique. Most directives are agreed after a complex procedure involving the Council (made up of representatives of the Member States) and the European Parliament.[48] Before the legislative process begins, however, the Commission must consult the representatives of management and labour, often referred to as the 'social partners'.[49] If the social partners so desire, they may decide to regulate the area themselves by reaching an agreement under Article 139 EC. This agreement may be enacted as a directive by the Council,[50] or implemented by further agreements between trade unions and employers' associations within each Member State.[51] The social dialogue can be regarded as a novel way of promoting 'grass-roots' participation in the legislative process, and of ensuring that new legislation is responsive to the needs of those who will have to implement it.[52] But it has been criticised as undemocratic, particularly because it bypasses the European Parliament.

Despite – or perhaps because of – these recent developments, it is difficult to pinpoint the current perspective of EU law. Many rights theorists argue that the EU

---

45 Case 6/64 *Costa v ENEL* [1964] ECR 585. See, generally, P. Craig and G. de Búrca, *EU Law: Text, Cases and Materials* (3rd edn., 2003), chapter 7.

46 Case 11/70 *Internationale Handelsgesellschaft* [1970] ECR 1125. For discussion, see B. de Witte, 'The past and future role of the European Court of Justice in the protection of human rights', in P. Alston (ed.), *The EU and Human Rights* (1999).

47 See, for example, P. Alston and J.H.H. Weiler, 'An "ever closer union" in need of a human rights policy: the European Union and human rights', in P. Alston (ed.), *The EU and Human Rights* (1999), pp. 14–8.

48 See Articles 137 and 251 EC.

49 Article 138 EC. The social partners are (on the labour side) the European Trade Union Confederation (ETUC), and (on the management side) the European Centre of Enterprises with Public Participation and of Enterprises of General Economic Interest (CEEP) and the Union of Industrial and Employers' Confederations of Europe (UNICE).

50 Examples include Directive 99/70/EC on Fixed-Term Work, and Directive 97/81/EC on Part-Time Work.

51 The only example of this so far is the *Framework Agreement on Telework*, 16 July 2002.

52 For discussion, see B. Bercusson, 'Democratic legitimacy and European labour law' (1999) 28 *ILJ* 153.

remains primarily an economic institution. It makes concessions to workers' rights only when they are unlikely to impose substantial costs on businesses. This argument is commonly made in relation to Article 141, on equal pay.[53] Imagine a situation in which an employer wishes to expand its business by recruiting new employees.[54] There is a shortage of suitable recruits, so the employer offers to pay the new recruits more than it is paying its existing workforce. It so happens that the existing workforce is predominantly female whereas the new recruits are predominantly male. The situation is one of indirect pay discrimination, in which the employer's policy appears to be neutral as between men and women but in practice puts women at a disadvantage.[55] Under ILO Convention 100, differences in pay between men and women may only be justified where they correspond to differences in the work to be performed.[56] But under EU law, differences in pay may be justified where the employer is responding to the forces of supply and demand in the market, provided that the employer is paying no more than is absolutely necessary to attract the new recruits.[57] It can be argued that firms' profitability would be severely affected if they could not offer the market rate, or if they were required to increase the pay of existing employees to match the market rate. However, critics point out markets may themselves be discriminatory. They suggest that the willingness of women to accept and remain in lower paying jobs may be due to discrimination rather than coincidence.[58] If EU law were genuinely committed to the protection of workers' rights, it would force employers to correct market discrimination instead of allowing them to reflect it.

However, this view of EU law has not been shared by UK governments in recent years. They have argued that EU law is overly protective of workers' rights and takes insufficient account of the needs of businesses. The Conservative governments of 1979–97 expressed open hostility to new EU legislation.[59] They vetoed measures which required the unanimous approval of the Member States, and refused to be bound by the Social Chapter signed by the other Member States in Maastricht in 1992, which extended the EC's competence in the field of social policy. Since 1997, the Labour government has adopted a more conciliatory tone and has signed up to the Social Chapter.[60] But the government remains sceptical about the value of some new EU measures despite its commitment to economic arguments which promote labour rights. For example, the government opposed the Framework Directive on Informing and Consulting Employees,[61] arguing that it would impose an

---

53 See, for example, S. Fredman, 'European Community discrimination law: a critique' (1992) 21 *ILJ* 119 at 130–2.
54 See *Rainey v Greater Glasgow Health Board* [1987] IRLR 26 (HL); Case C-127/92 *Enderby v Frenchay HA* [1993] IRLR 591 (ECJ).
55 See chapter 7 for further discussion of this concept.
56 Article 3(3).
57 Case C-127/92 *Enderby v Frenchay HA* [1993] IRLR 591 (ECJ).
58 Fredman, above n. 53.
59 See P. Davies and M. Freedland, *Labour Legislation and Public Policy* (1993), pp. 576–99.
60 See DTI, *Fairness at Work* (Cm. 3968, 1998), p. 9.
61 Directive 2002/14/EC.

unnecessary burden on businesses.[62] When opposition failed, the government sought to limit the obligations the Directive would impose. For example, as Bercusson explains, the original draft stated that an employer's decision could not take effect until after it had consulted its employees.[63] This provided a strong sanction for a failure to consult. The UK government successfully argued that this provision should be struck out in favour of a discretion on the part of Member States to prescribe an appropriate penalty for failure to consult.[64]

This brings us to an important general point about the nature of EU labour legislation: its inherent flexibility. Most such legislation takes the form of directives. Article 249 EC states that 'a directive shall be binding, as to the result to be achieved, upon each Member State to which it is addressed, but shall leave to the national authorities the choice of form and methods'. Thus, by definition, directives leave Member States a discretion as to how they are to be implemented. This makes it much easier to secure agreement on new proposals, and gives Member States an opportunity to ensure that directives mesh properly with pre-existing national law. However, the danger is that this flexibility can be abused by Member States to undermine new directives by implementing them in a minimalist way. For example, the Directive on Fixed-Term Work gives Member States various options for preventing the abuse of successive fixed-term contracts.[65] One is to limit the duration of successive fixed-term contracts. The UK has placed a maximum limit of four years on such contracts, which contrasts with, for example, two years in Germany.[66] Thus, the flexible nature of directives means that the EU has less power to set norms for Member States than it might seem to have at first sight.

Obvious failures to implement directives may be addressed through enforcement proceedings brought by the Commission.[67] For example, the UK government initially implemented the Collective Redundancies Directive so that it applied only to workplaces in which a trade union was recognised.[68] The government argued that compulsory consultation in other workplaces would be contrary to the UK's tradition of *voluntary* trade union recognition.[69] In enforcement proceedings, the ECJ held that the UK had failed to implement the Directive properly because it had not provided consultation rights to all workers.[70] However, the effectiveness of enforcement proceedings is inevitably limited by the fact that the Commission has finite resources for investigating alleged breaches and bringing cases before the Court.

62 DTI, above n. 60, p. 22.
63 B. Bercusson, 'The European social model comes to Britain' (2002) 31 *ILJ* 209 at 239–40.
64 Directive 2002/14/EC, Article 8.
65 Directive 99/70/EC, clause 5.
66 M. Weiss, 'The Framework Agreement on Fixed-Term Work: a German point of view' (1999) 15 *International Journal of Comparative Labour Law and Industrial Relations* 97.
67 See Article 226 EC.
68 Then Directive 75/129/EEC, originally implemented by the Employment Protection Act 1975, Part IV.
69 P. Davies, 'A challenge to single channel' (1994) 23 *ILJ* 272.
70 Case C-383/92 *Commission v UK* [1994] IRLR 412.

The weaknesses of Commission enforcement are mitigated somewhat by the possibility that individual litigants might invoke EU law in the national courts. Articles of the Treaty may have both horizontal and vertical direct effect (provided that certain conditions are met),[71] so individuals may base their case directly upon an Article whether they are employed by the state or by a private firm. Directives have vertical but not horizontal direct effect,[72] so they can only be relied upon by public sector employees. However, under the *Marleasing* case, directives may be used as a guide to the interpretation of national law even in a case between two private parties.[73] Finally, where the state's failure to implement a directive has caused harm to an individual, he or she may be able to claim damages against the government under the *Francovich* case.[74]

In the labour law context, the inability of individuals in private sector employment to base their case on a directive has proved to be highly problematic. For example, the UK legislation implementing the Collective Redundancies Directive requires the employer to consult when it 'proposes' redundancies,[75] whereas the Directive uses the term 'contemplate'.[76] It is widely believed that UK law is incompatible with the Directive because 'contemplate' refers to a much earlier stage in the employer's thought process than does 'propose'. But when this issue arises in a case against a private firm, the individual employee cannot rely on the wording of the Directive. He or she must instead persuade the court to use the Directive as a guide to the construction of the English provisions. The obligation to interpret national law compatibly with a directive only applies 'insofar as it is possible to do so'.[77] In the case of redundancy consultation, the prevailing view in the courts is that the two terms are so different that compatible construction is impossible.[78] The national provisions are therefore applied even though they are incompatible with EU law.

What role for national law?

It seems appropriate to conclude our discussion of modes of regulation by considering whether there are any issues on which the UK government can enact what it pleases, unconstrained by the ILO, the ECHR or the EU.[79] In fact there are three main areas of discretion. The first is pay. The EU has no competence on this matter[80]

---

71 Craig and de Búrca, above n. 45, pp. 182–9.
72 Craig and de Búrca, above n. 45, pp. 202–11.
73 Case C-106/89 *Marleasing SA v La Comercial Internacional de Alimentacion SA* [1990] ECR I-4135. See Craig and de Búrca, above n. 45, pp. 211–20.
74 Cases C-6 and 9/90 *Francovich and Bonifaci v Italy* [1991] ECR I-5357. See Craig and de Búrca, above n. 45, pp. 257–71.
75 TULRCA 1992, s. 188(1).
76 Directive 98/59/EC, Article 2(1).
77 Case C-106/89 *Marleasing SA v La Comercial Internacionale de Alimentacion SA* [1990] ECR I-4135 at 4159.
78 *MSF v Refuge Assurance plc* [2002] IRLR 324.
79 Of course, it is not inconceivable that the government could withdraw from these institutions, but this remote possibility will be disregarded for the purposes of the present discussion.
80 Article 137(5) EC.

and the ECHR contains no relevant provisions. ILO Convention 26, the Minimum Wage-Fixing Machinery Convention (1928), was initially ratified by the UK but was denounced in 1985. The second area of discretion is the law regarding termination of employment. Although the EU has competence in this area,[81] it has not yet exercised its powers. The ECHR may have some indirect relevance – where the manner in which dismissal takes place constitutes a violation of privacy rights, for example[82] – but it would not apply in the vast majority of dismissal cases. And the UK has not ratified ILO Convention 158, the Termination of Employment Convention (1982). Third, and perhaps most surprisingly, the government is relatively unconstrained in the regulation of collective bargaining and the right to strike. Article 137(5) EC specifically excludes the EU from these areas. Article 11 of the ECHR contains a right to freedom of association, but the ECtHR has refused to extend this to include a right to bargain with the employer or to take industrial action.[83] Although the UK has ratified ILO Conventions 87 and 98, it has not ratified Convention 154 on Collective Bargaining (1981). Moreover, as the discussion above explained, the practical enforceability of ILO standards is limited.

Purely national regulation of workers' rights is still possible in these areas. But large chunks of labour law are shared with international or regional regimes: for example, freedom of association with the ECHR, and sex and race discrimination with the EU. The aim of this discussion is not to make a point about sovereignty. Rather, it is to make the point that the law is often the result of a compromise struck between the government and an international or regional regime. Compromises are necessary because a different interpretation of rights and economics arguments is likely to hold sway at each level of regulation. The shape of those compromises will depend on the relative power of the government and the other levels of regulation. A rounded understanding of labour law must be alive to the conflicts and tensions inherent in multi-layered regulation.

Modes of regulation within national law

Each layer of regulation – the ILO, the ECHR and the EU – is, of course, made up of different institutions. At the national level, labour law is made up of statutes and statutory instruments proposed by the government and approved by Parliament, case law developed by the courts and, in some instances, by negotiations between employers and workers.[84] These institutions may come into conflict because of the different ways in which they strike a balance between rights arguments and economics arguments. The balance struck by governments depends on their political

---

81   Article 137(1)(d) EC.
82   *Lustig-Prean and Beckett v UK* [1999] 29 EHRR 548.
83   See chapters 10 and 12 for discussion.
84   A similar analysis could be performed for the ILO, ECHR and EU, but there is insufficient space to do so here. The further reading at the end of this chapter will give you some ideas as to what such an analysis might contain.

complexion and on the social and economic circumstances they face. The changing shape of labour law over the last century and into the present day was considered in chapter 1. The outcome of negotiations between employers and workers depends heavily on their relative bargaining positions. The role of such negotiations will be considered in later chapters. Our focus here will be on the courts. Labour law only fully acquired the status of a subject in its own right in the second half of the twentieth century. It is made up, in part, of elements of tort, contract and public law. Not surprisingly, the courts have drawn heavily on techniques from these more familiar subjects in employment cases. This approach has been criticised by many labour lawyers. They argue that the courts favour employers against employees, and employers or individual union members against trade unions. In other words, the courts favour neoclassical economics arguments over workers' rights.

Parliament has delegated to the courts the task of defining 'employee', one of the central organising concepts of labour law.[85] Since an employee is a person who works under a contract of employment, the courts have gone about this task using familiar methods from the law of contract. For example, in *Express and Echo Publications Ltd v Tanton*, the court found that a term entitling Mr Tanton to use a substitute instead of performing the work himself was inherently inconsistent with the existence of a contract of employment.[86] This meant that Mr Tanton was an independent contractor, beyond the scope of employment protection laws. The court stressed that the correct approach was to focus on the contract document:

> Of course, it is important that the industrial tribunal should be alert in this area of the law to look at the reality of any obligations. If the obligation is a sham, it will want to say so. But to concentrate on what actually occurred may not elucidate the full terms of the contract. If a term is not enforced, that does not justify a conclusion that such a term is not part of the agreement.[87]

As a matter of contract law, this is entirely correct. The 'parol evidence rule' states that where the parties have put their contract in writing, the document should, on the whole, be treated as the sole source of the terms of the contract.[88] But labour lawyers have argued that the decision works to the disadvantage of employees. Contracts of employment are usually drafted by employers or their legal advisers and offered to employees on a 'take-it-or-leave-it' basis. Employers may be tempted to insert terms which are inconsistent with a contract of employment in order to ensure that individuals do not acquire employee status and all the employment rights this would bring. The narrow notion of a 'sham' term in *Tanton* does not offer much protection to employees in this situation.

---

85 Employment Rights Act 1996 (ERA 1996), s. 230(1).
86 [1999] IRLR 367 (CA).
87 [1999] IRLR 367 at 369 (CA), per Peter Gibson LJ.
88 *Jacobs v Batavia and General Plantations Trust Ltd* [1924] 2 Ch 329. For the many exceptions to the rule, see G.H. Treitel, *The Law of Contract* (11th edn., 2003), pp. 192–201.

The courts have also drawn on the techniques of public law in employment cases.[89] In unfair dismissal, the Employment Tribunal must decide whether the employer acted 'reasonably' in dismissing the employee.[90] This test was interpreted by the Employment Appeal Tribunal (EAT) in *Iceland Frozen Foods Ltd v Jones* to require an assessment of whether the conduct of the employer was within a 'band of reasonable responses' to the situation.[91] The notion of a 'band of reasonable responses' emphasises the fact that more than one course of action might be reasonable and indicates that tribunals should only interfere in extreme cases. It is similar to the *Wednesbury* formula in public law, which allows courts to review the decisions of public authorities only where they are 'so unreasonable that no reasonable [authority]' would have made them.[92] In public law, this approach was justified by the argument that judges were not well-placed to second-guess the decisions of politicians and skilled administrators. Whatever the merits of this argument in public law, labour lawyers have argued that it is indefensible in the employment sphere. Employment Tribunals consist of two lay members (one with union experience and one with employer experience) in addition to a legally qualified chairman. It is claimed that tribunals do have the experience which would be required for a more searching review of the employer's conduct.

The courts' use of public law techniques has had radically different results in cases brought by individuals against trade unions.[93] The courts have taken the view that the individual is in a vulnerable position when faced with the collective strength of the union. They have therefore used public law principles designed to prevent the abuse of power when interpreting the contract of membership between the union and the individual. For example, in *Esterman v NALGO*, the union instructed its members not to volunteer to help with local government elections as part of a dispute with local authority employers.[94] The claimant disobeyed the instruction and was threatened with disciplinary proceedings. The court took the unusual step of granting an injunction to prevent the union from hearing the disciplinary proceedings on the grounds that no reasonable union acting in good faith could have found that the complainant was unfit to be a member of the union. Instead of asking whether the union was in breach of contract, the court asked the public law question of whether the union had acted rationally. Decisions like *Esterman* have the merit of protecting individual union members against unfairness. Such protection was particularly important when closed shops were lawful, because individuals working in closed shops who were expelled from their unions would also lose their jobs.[95]

---

89 For discussion, see P.L. Davies and M.R. Freedland, 'The impact of public law on labour law 1972–1997' (1997) 26 *ILJ* 311.
90 ERA 1996, s. 98(4).
91 [1983] ICR 17 at 24–5 (EAT), per Browne-Wilkinson J.
92 *Associated Provincial Picture Houses v Wednesbury Corporation* [1948] 1 KB 223 at 228–30, per Lord Greene MR.
93 There is now extensive statutory regulation of this area. See chapter 11 for detail.
94 [1974] ICR 625.
95 See chapter 11 for a fuller discussion of the closed shop.

But labour lawyers have criticised the courts for denying unions the autonomy to set and apply their own rules, arguably a key element of a right to freedom of association.[96]

There is much debate as to the motivation behind these decisions. On one view, they are simply technical applications of rules from other areas of law which happen not to fit very well with the underlying themes of labour law. On another view, it can be argued that the courts are (consciously or unconsciously) inclined to favour employers.[97] A belief in the liberty of the individual makes the courts unsympathetic towards the collective power of trade unions. And a belief in freedom of contract makes the courts unsympathetic towards attempts to regulate the contract of employment by granting statutory rights to workers. These traditional concerns of the common law are closely related to those of neoclassical economics, discussed in chapter 2.

If the courts do have a tendency to favour employers, this is likely to bring them into conflict with other layers of regulation. For example, they may be reluctant to use ILO standards in their decisions, or they may construe the rights in the ECHR narrowly. They may also come into conflict with the government when it passes legislation based on rights or new institutional economics arguments. Later chapters will consider a number of important judicial decisions in labour law. As you examine these decisions, you need to decide whether or not labour lawyers' criticisms of the courts are valid.

Further reading

S. Deakin and G.S. Morris, *Labour Law* (3rd edn., 2001), chapter 2; or H. Collins, K.D. Ewing and A. McColgan, *Labour Law: Text and Materials* (2001), chapter 1, give an account of the sources and institutions of labour law. For introductory accounts of the roles of the ILO, ECHR and EU, see, respectively: H.G. Bartolomei de la Cruz, G. von Potobsky and L. Swepston, *The International Labour Organisation: the International Standards System and Basic Human Rights* (1996); D.J. Harris, M. O'Boyle, and C. Warbrick, *Law of the European Convention on Human Rights* (1995), especially chapters 1 and 12; and B. Bercusson, *European Labour Law* (1996), especially chapters 1 and 2.

What factors influence whether or not English law is brought into compliance with international human rights obligations? Consider (among others): the legal status of international human rights instruments, the moral legitimacy of particular instruments, the extent to which they take account of concerns about costs, government policy, the role of complaints mechanisms, and the role of trade unions and other campaigning organisations. For discussion in relation to the ILO, see

---

96 ILO Convention 87, *Freedom of Association and Protection of the Right to Organise* (1948), Article 3.
97 See, for example, J.A.G. Griffith, *The Politics of the Judiciary* (5th edn., 1997), especially chapter 3.

T. Novitz, 'Freedom of association and "fairness at work" – an assessment of the impact and relevance of ILO Convention No. 87 on its fiftieth anniversary' (1998) 27 *ILJ* 169; 'International promise and domestic pragmatism: to what extent will the Employment Relations Act 1999 implement international labour standards relating to freedom of association?' (2000) 63 *MLR* 379. On the ECHR, see R.R. Churchill and J.R. Young, 'Compliance with judgments of the European Court of Human Rights and decisions of the Committee of Ministers: the experience of the United Kingdom, 1975–1987' (1991) 62 *British Yearbook of International Law* 283; K.D. Ewing, 'The Human Rights Act and labour law' (1998) 27 *ILJ* 275. On EU law, see A. McColgan, 'Family-friendly frolics? The Maternity and Parental Leave etc. Regulations 1999' (2000) 29 *ILJ* 125; 'The Fixed-Term Employees (Prevention of Less Favourable Treatment) Regulations 2002: Fiddling While Rome Burns?' (2003) 32 *ILJ* 194.

Some modes of regulation were excluded from the discussion in this chapter for reasons of space, but you should also think about what influence they might have. Have a look at H.J. Steiner and P. Alston, *International Human Rights in Context* (2nd edn., 2000), pp. 305–20 on the ICESCR, and chapter 9 on the ICCPR. On the latter see also D. Fottrell, 'Reinforcing the Human Rights Act – the role of the International Covenant on Civil and Political Rights' (2002) *PL* 485. On the ESC, see K.D. Ewing, 'Social rights and human rights: Britain and the Social Charter – the Conservative legacy' (2000) 2 *EHRLR* 91; 'The Council of Europe's Social Charter of 18 October 1961: Britain and the 15th cycle of supervision' (2001) 30 *ILJ* 409.

Within domestic law, you should think about the role of the courts in interpreting labour legislation. For general discussion of this topic, see P.L. Davies and M.R. Freedland, 'The impact of public law on labour law 1972–1997' (1997) 26 *ILJ* 311; and S. Anderman, 'The interpretation of protective employment statutes and contracts of employment' (2000) 29 *ILJ* 223. Why do the courts approach labour law cases in the way that they do? Is it due to political bias, or are there other plausible explanations? What strategies can the legislature adopt to ensure that the courts give full effect to provisions which are intended to protect workers?

Part II

5

Who is protected by employment law?

This chapter will be an important testing-ground for your views on the various theoretical positions we have explored so far. Its topic is: who is protected by employment law? You might expect that the whole workforce would be protected, but in fact this is not the case. The law divides people into three groups – employees, workers, and the self-employed – and offers them different levels of protection. Employees are the traditional subjects of employment law, so they get all the available rights. Self-employed people are thought to be capable of looking after themselves, so with a few exceptions they are not given any rights at all. This twofold classification has come to seem problematic in recent years because of the rising number of so-called 'atypical workers': people who do not fit within the law's definition of an employee but do not seem to be genuinely self-employed either. Since 1997, some legislation has used a third concept – 'worker' – to include these people. Workers do not have as many rights as employees but they are better protected than the self-employed.

From a neoclassical economics perspective, labour rights are viewed as a burden on business. If an employer is obliged by the law to confer rights on workers, it will compensate for this increase in its costs either by cutting those workers' wages or by making some of them redundant. The employer will also be reluctant to create new jobs. But if the law allows the existence of different categories of people in the workforce, some of whom have fewer rights, employers are provided with a welcome opportunity to reduce their costs. New institutional economists take a very different view. They argue that labour rights help to make workers more productive by making them feel secure in their jobs and valued by the firm. Although rights are costly, they also bring compensating economic benefits. On this view, rights should be available to everyone.

Most rights theorists would also argue that rights should be granted to all. Rights are usually formulated in universal terms: 'Everyone has the right to . . .' Technical distinctions between different categories of people in employment should not be used to deny protection to certain groups. However, there are some possible exceptions to this general rule. One is that some groups may not need the protection of the law because they are able to secure protection through their own bargaining power. A more controversial exception is to suggest that because some rights are often considered to be less fundamental than others, these less significant rights need not be granted to everyone. For example, it could be argued that all working people should have civil and political rights but that economic and social rights need only be granted to a smaller subset of people. However, it is difficult to identify a fair way to decide who should be in this privileged subset.

Typical and atypical workers

Most writers approach this topic by drawing a distinction between typical and atypical workers. This terminology is not entirely helpful. It implies that atypical workers are the exception rather than the rule, and while this is probably true today they may one day come to outnumber typical employees. And it implies that atypical workers are a single group with the same characteristics, whereas in fact workers may be atypical in a variety of different ways. But we need to begin by identifying the typical worker. He or she works:

- for a single employer;
- on an indefinite contract (i.e. one with no end date);
- at the employer's premises; and
- regularly for that employer whether or not the firm is busy.

The atypical worker is a person whose employment diverges from this norm in *one or more* respects. It is unusual to find a worker who is atypical in every respect. Let us examine some of the different types of atypical worker and the issues they face.

One type is the agency worker. The typical worker works for one employer which makes use of his or her services. The agency worker works for an employment agency, which hires out his or her services to a 'principal' or 'user'. So who employs the agency worker? In general, it is unlikely to be the user, though the user may have some legal responsibilities towards the agency worker.[1] The employer is much more likely to be the agency, though some agency workers have been found by the courts to be self-employed.[2] Often, the only way to resolve the confusion is through litigation, but this is an unpalatable option because it is costly and disruptive. Many agency workers are left uncertain as to their status and, as a result, as to the employment rights they can claim.

Another type of atypical worker is the fixed-term worker. The typical employee usually has an indefinite contract with no fixed end-point. This contract can be terminated by the employer but in doing so, the employer must comply with the requirements of unfair dismissal law.[3] The fixed-term worker is employed for a specified period of time. This may seem attractive, because at least the worker

---

1 These include a duty not to discriminate (for example, the Race Relations Act 1976 (RRA 1976), s. 7, and see *Harrods Ltd v Remick* [1997] IRLR 583 (CA)) and a duty to pay the minimum wage (National Minimum Wage Act 1998 (NMWA 1998), s. 34).
2 See *Johnson Underwood Ltd v Montgomery* [2001] IRLR 269.
3 See chapter 9.

knows when he or she must look for a new job. However, in practice, fixed-term workers may be in an uncertain position. Often, the employer will leave open the possibility that the fixed-term contract might be renewed: for example, if the firm remains busy or if a woman on maternity leave decides not to return to work. But the individual is always vulnerable to losing his or her job whenever the fixed-term contract comes to an end.

A third group of atypical workers consists of those who work at home, in contrast to typical workers who work at the employer's premises. 'Traditional' homework is a relatively low-paid and predominantly female occupation common in industries such as garment manufacturing. Women take in sewing to do at home and are paid for each garment they complete. More recently, improvements in communications technology have made it possible for many office workers to work from home, using email and the internet to keep in touch with their employer. This form of working – sometimes known as teleworking – is often popular with parents who wish to have more flexibility in combining their work with family life. One problem faced by homeworkers is that the employer may not give them equal terms and conditions with those doing similar work on the employer's premises. It may be difficult for homeworkers even to discover this because they do not meet other employees. This leads to the further problem that homeworkers may not be involved in collective activities in the workplace. For example, they are unlikely to be members of trade unions.

Perhaps the commonest group of atypical workers consists of those who work on an 'as required' basis. Typical employees expect to turn up for work regardless of whether or not the firm is busy enough to need their services. The employer takes the risk that employees may sometimes be idle during quiet periods. But those who work on an 'as required' basis must bear the risk of a shortage of work themselves. This group covers a multitude of different contractual arrangements. One subset consists of zero-hours workers, who are under contract to the employer but who are not guaranteed any particular number of hours per week. Another consists of casual workers, who are hired when they are needed. They may work for several different employers or regularly for one employer. And finally, there are 'freelance' workers who are taken on to perform some specific task. Again, they may hire themselves out to several different employers, or be dependent on the one employer for a considerable period of time. These various kinds of workers cannot predict how much they will earn each week.

Researchers have tried to determine what proportion of the UK workforce is atypical, but this is quite difficult to do. Burchell *et al.* conducted a survey in which they asked individuals what their employment status was. They estimated that 86% of the British workforce were typical employees.[4] However, one obvious problem with the survey method is that people may not classify themselves accurately. Burchell

---

4 B. Burchell, S. Deakin and S. Honey, *The Employment Status of Individuals in Non-Standard Employment* (1999).

et al. interviewed some of their respondents to find out how they were classifying themselves, and after these interviews they were only able to say with certainty that 64% were employees. Another 30% might or might not have been employees. Indeed, the tests applied by the courts to decide who is a typical employee and who is not are so ambiguous that researchers may not be able to classify people with any certainty even when presented with all the details of their employment relationship.

The Workplace Employee Relations Survey (WERS) approaches the question of employment status from a very different perspective.[5] Instead of asking what proportion of the workforce are typical employees, it focuses on what proportion of workplaces use atypical workers. Because the survey has been conducted four times between 1980 and 1998, it may also help to show changes over time.[6] The proportion of firms using homeworkers is relatively low and has stayed stable over time: 4% in 1990; 5% in 1998. But other forms of atypical work appear to have become more common. For example, the proportion of workplaces using workers on fixed-term contracts of less than one year's duration rose from 19% in 1980, to 22% in 1990, to 35% in 1998. The proportion of workplaces which had recently used agency workers was 20% in 1980 and had risen to 28% in 1998.

Economics perspectives

Writers in the neoclassical tradition identify two main benefits to employers from using atypical workers.[7] One is that the employer is able to shift the risk of a downturn in business to the workers instead of having to shoulder the risk itself. The other is that atypical workers do not qualify for many statutory employment rights, making them cheaper to hire than employees. New institutional economists question the wisdom of both these strategies. They argue that individuals will be more productive if they have secure jobs and if their rights are respected by their employer.

Employees in 'typical' jobs expect to turn up for work each day, and to get paid, regardless of whether or not the firm is busy. The employer takes the risk that the employees may not always have work to do. But some kinds of atypical work involve passing this risk on to the worker. For example, casual workers are called in by the employer *only* when the firm is busy. The employer makes a saving because it does not have to pay these workers when they are not needed. In practice, most firms cannot manage without some 'typical' employees. If the employer runs a shop, it would not make sense to send all the staff home when the shop was quiet, since customers would quickly lose patience with a shop that did not keep to its advertised opening hours. But it would make sense for the employer to have a 'core' workforce

---

5 N. Millward, A. Bryson and J. Forth, *All Change at Work?* (2000), pp. 43–8.
6 Though there are some difficulties in doing so because not all of the questions asked have been identically worded in all four studies.
7 The classic study is J. Atkinson, *Flexibility, Uncertainty and Manpower Management* (1984). See also H. Collins, 'Independent contractors and the challenge of vertical disintegration to employment protection laws' (1990) 10 *Oxford Journal of Legal Studies* 353 at 356–62.

of full-time employees, and then to supplement them with a 'periphery' of casual workers who could be brought in during busy periods.[8] This is often referred to in the literature as 'numerical flexibility', and it can generate considerable cost savings for some employers.[9]

Atypical workers are cheaper to employ not just because they work only when they are needed, but also because they do not qualify for all of the employment rights granted to employees. This links to the first advantage and is also a benefit to employers in itself. The fact that atypical workers do not qualify for unfair dismissal protection or redundancy payments allows employers to hire and fire them at will in pursuit of numerical flexibility. And their lack of rights also saves employers money. As we saw in chapter 2, neoclassical economists regard employment rights as a burden on business. The employer's labour costs are made up of the wages it must pay and the cost of providing employment rights. The employer's aim is to keep these costs as low as possible, so whenever a new employment right is introduced, the employer will either reduce the employees' pay or reduce the number of people it employs. Atypical workers are cheaper to employ because they are entitled to fewer costly rights on top of their wages. Thus, the employer can save money by converting existing employees into atypical workers. And when new labour rights are introduced by the government, it is less likely that atypical workers will qualify for them and therefore less likely that the employer will need to cut wages or make people redundant in order to absorb them.

Many writers in the neoclassical tradition would claim that the existence of atypical work is beneficial to workers as well as to employers, even though workers do not get so much legal protection. They point to two main advantages. First, they argue that an atypical job is better than no job at all.[10] Employers are more likely to create new jobs if they can do so cheaply and without making a long-term commitment. When a new casual worker is hired, for example, the employer only has to pay the person when he or she is working, does not have to grant many legal rights, and does not make any promises about how much work will be provided in the future. Second, they argue that not everyone wants a 'typical' job. Students or parents with childcare responsibilities might be glad of some extra income occasionally without having to take on a permanent job. However, not all forms of atypical work are convenient for workers. A parent needs to know when he or she is likely to be called in to work so that a babysitter can be booked, but the firm might want workers who can be called in at very short notice.

New institutional economists take a very different view on the availability of employment rights. They argue that employment rights can make a positive contribution to the profitability of firms.[11] They would therefore wish to see rights

---

8 Atkinson, above n. 7, chapter 5.
9 Atkinson, above n. 7, para. 4.4.
10 Atkinson, above n. 7, para. 3.15.
11 See, generally, S. Deakin and F. Wilkinson, 'Rights vs efficiency? The economic case for transnational labour standards' (1994) 23 *ILJ* 289.

afforded to the entire workforce – to atypical workers as well as to typical employees – unless it can be shown that a particular right would not enhance competitiveness. As we saw in chapter 2, their perception of employment rights stems from their desire to see firms competing not just on the price of their products but on their quality and innovation. There are many possible examples of how employment rights might help firms, but we will look at just two: loyalty and training.

Loyalty may seem rather woolly, but according to the new institutionalists, it is important. A loyal employee will have the firm's best interests at heart. If an important customer places an urgent order, he or she will work late to make sure that it is finished in time. If there are ways of making the production process more efficient, he or she will draw them to the attention of the management. How can a firm generate this kind of loyalty? The answer is to respect the rights and needs of its workforce. People will respond well if they are treated well.[12] When a firm takes on a typical employee, it makes a substantial commitment. It undertakes to give the employee a steady job and a regular income even when times are hard. And the employee is protected by a range of legal rights. The atypical worker, by contrast, is a commodity to be picked up when the employer is in need and to be discarded when times are hard. The atypical worker might decide to behave loyally if it seemed likely that the employer would offer a permanent job as a result. But it is more probable that he or she would simply do the minimum required to fulfil the employer's expectations.

The new institutionalists also emphasise the relationship between typical work and the provision of training. One of the major benefits of training is that employees can be taught to perform a variety of different tasks within the firm. This 'functional flexibility' enables the firm to remain productive when one part of the business is quiet, because employees can be redeployed on other duties.[13] It addresses the same problem as 'numerical flexibility', discussed above, but in a very different way. The rational employer decides whether to offer training by comparing the costs of the training with the benefits it will secure from having a more skilled person in the workforce. These benefits can be calculated by looking at how much that person's productivity will increase and how long he or she will stay with the firm. This last consideration helps to explain why it does not make sense to train atypical workers. A permanent employee might stay with the firm until retirement. A flexible worker is less predictable: he or she might leave if a permanent job became available at another firm, for example.

The obvious response to this set of arguments is to ask why firms use atypical work at all. If typical work has these benefits, then surely it would be rational for firms only to hire typical employees. The fact that they continue to use atypical workers must indicate that the benefits of worker loyalty are not sufficient to outweigh the costs of typical employment, at least for some firms and some jobs. However, writers in the

---

12 A. Fox, *Beyond Contract: Work, Power and Trust Relations* (1974), especially chapter 1.
13 Atkinson, above n. 7, para. 4.3.

new institutional tradition have a number of alternative explanations of why firms might continue to use atypical workers. First, firms may not realise the benefits of typical employment. Since atypical work is a new management 'fad', firms may try it out for some time before discovering that the typical employment they had previously been using was preferable after all. Second, firms may be more focused on short-term gains than on longer-term performance. The advantages of typical employment may take some time to manifest themselves, whereas the advantages of atypical employment, particularly the cost savings, are immediately apparent. And third, even if firms realise the importance of focusing on long-term survival and perceive the advantages of typical work, they may find it difficult to stop using atypical work because of the fear that they will be outdone by their competitors in the short-term. Although productivity will increase later on, the firm will face a difficult period of rising costs and falling sales while it makes the transition to typical employment.

These competing theories have important implications for the shape of labour law. From the neoclassical perspective, the law should not try to regulate atypical work. This would increase employers' costs and stifle job creation. From the new institutional perspective, the law should in general discourage the use of atypical workers because they are unlikely to be as productive as typical employees. An obvious way to do this would be to extend employee rights to atypical workers. But before we see how English law has responded to these arguments, we need to examine some rights perspectives.

Rights perspectives

Perhaps the best way to introduce rights perspectives on the scope of employment law is to look at the approach writers in this tradition take to the *history* of atypical work.[14] We will then examine two different ways in which rights arguments could be used: to support the granting of rights to all members of the workforce, and to support a two-tier system in which only the most fundamental rights would be guaranteed to everyone.

The strategy of protecting the workforce through minimum rights enshrined in legislation became popular in the 1970s, due to a growing realisation that not everyone was protected by collective bargaining.[15] This legislation (with the exception of the SDA 1975 and RRA 1976) granted rights to employees only. But at this stage, the choice of 'employee' as the organising concept of employment law was not particularly problematic, since atypical workers made up a tiny minority of the workforce. In the 1980s, employers began to make more use of atypical work. Since the economy was in recession, it was not surprising that employers sought

14 See, for example, S. Fredman, 'Labour law in flux: the changing composition of the workforce' (1997) 26 *ILJ* 337.
15 See chapter 1.

ways of saving money. But atypical work involved saving money by evading the law. Employers designed contracts deliberately so that individuals would be workers without rights rather than employees with rights. The evasion was at its most blatant when employers dismissed their employees and re-engaged them on an atypical basis.[16] From a rights perspective, it seems obvious that the government should have reacted to these developments by expanding the scope of employment law so that all members of the workforce were protected, thus restoring the law to the position it adopted at the beginning of the 1970s. As we shall see, however, no government has yet adopted this strategy.

The argument that all rights should be afforded to all workers starts from the premise that working people face the same or broadly similar set of issues in the workplace regardless of whether the law classifies them as typical or as atypical.[17] For example, if a person is called to a disciplinary hearing by the employer, he or she might find this situation highly intimidating and might value the presence of a union representative or other companion. And if a person's child is taken ill at school during the working day, he or she might need a reasonable amount of time off work to go and make arrangements for the care of that child. At the moment, the former right is available to workers as well as employees,[18] whereas the latter is available only to employees.[19] It is hard to see why the status of someone's contract should make this much difference.

Many commentators explain the fundamental similarity between typical and atypical workers by pointing out that both groups are (in general) *economically dependent* on the employer.[20] One manifestation of this is that both employees and workers usually rely on their main job as their source of income and could not easily manage without it if they were dismissed. But this does not fully capture the meaning of economic dependence in this context. The real question is whether these groups of people are able to negotiate with their employer: about their rate of pay or hours of work, for example. Of course, a highly skilled employee may be able to name his or her price. But for most people, jobs are offered on a 'take it or leave it' basis. This extends to employment status: it is the employer who decides whether a new recruit will be an employee or a worker. Individuals do not usually understand the significance of employee status, and even if they do, they are unlikely to have a chance to bargain about it. The only people who are not economically dependent on the employer are those who are genuinely self-employed: who run their own business and hire themselves out to a variety of customers. These are people who decide what their price is and offer it to the potential customer, and

16 For example, *Ready Mixed Concrete (South East) Ltd v Minister of Pensions and National Insurance* [1968] 2 QB 497, discussed below.
17 See, for example, B. Hepple, 'Restructuring employment rights' (1986) 15 *ILJ* 69; Collins, above n. 7; Fredman, above n. 14.
18 Employment Relations Act 1999 (ERA 1999) s. 10.
19 ERA 1996, s. 57A (inserted by ERA 1999).
20 For discussion and critique, see P. Davies and M. Freedland, 'Employees, workers, and the autonomy of labour law', in H. Collins *et al.* (eds.), *Legal Regulation of the Employment Relation* (2000).

who are able to negotiate their own terms and conditions, such as the hours they will work. The implications of this for employment law are obvious. Its protection should be granted to everyone in the economically dependent group. This excludes the self-employed, but includes *both* employees and workers.

However, adopting a rights perspective does not necessarily involve taking this radical view. As we saw in chapter 3, it is common to find that some rights are treated as more fundamental than others. It could therefore be argued that the most fundamental rights should be available to all workers, while less fundamental rights could be granted only to the smaller category of employees. Again, self-employed people would in general be expected to negotiate for their own protection.

But why would we want to draw these distinctions? Perhaps the most obvious reason is to respond to the neoclassical economists' argument that labour rights impose costs on employers. Some rights are clearly costly: the right to a minimum wage may require the employer to pay its workers more than it would otherwise have chosen to do. Other rights impose costs indirectly: if workers have a right to be consulted, managers must spend time preparing for, and taking part in, meetings with worker representatives. Moreover, for all rights, firms must devote resources to finding out what the law requires and to ensuring that they have procedures for complying. Thus, the decision to limit the number of people who qualify for certain rights offers a way of controlling the costs to be borne by firms.

The most direct way to implement this would be to divide rights into those which are costly and those which are less so. Firms could then be required to grant the less costly rights to all workers and the more costly ones only to employees. This sometimes happens at an international level when attempts are made to get developing countries to grant minimum rights to workers in their legislation. Emphasis is placed on 'low-cost' rights so that developing countries cannot rely on the argument that they cannot afford to comply. Two of the ILO's core rights are freedom of association and the right not to be discriminated against.[21] It is arguable that these rights can be achieved (in a basic sense, at least) without much expenditure.[22] For example, the government could simply ban discrimination on grounds of race, sex and so on, repeal any laws prohibiting trade unionism, and prohibit detrimental treatment of trade union members.

But there are two major problems with this approach. The first is that it is too simplistic to equate 'cheap' rights with fundamental rights. Some rights might be considered so fundamental for the protection of workers that they should be granted to all *even though* they will impose some costs on employers. The minimum wage might be an example of this. Basic considerations of dignity suggest that employers should not be able to get the benefit of labour without paying a reasonable price for it. But even if a more sophisticated distinction between fundamental

---

21 ILO, *Declaration on Fundamental Principles and Rights at Work* (1998).
22 See C. McCrudden and A.C.L. Davies, 'A perspective on trade and labor rights' (2000) 3 *JIEL* 43 at 49–52.

and non-fundamental rights is developed, a second problem remains. Why is it that individuals should have more rights just because they fall into the legal category of employee? Individuals do not, in general, choose their employment status. Employers tend to decide whether someone should be a worker or an employee, subject to the possibility that a court might see things differently. In short, an individual's status is a matter of luck. This is not a good basis on which to allocate rights.

The scope of employment law

In the 1980s, the government adopted the neoclassical economics perspective towards the scope of employment law. It allowed employers to develop new forms of atypical work and did not step in to close the legal loopholes they were exploiting. The government's policy was to reduce the burden of labour rights on businesses, so it was hardly going to interfere with employers who found ways to do this for themselves. Since 1997, the government has developed the concept of 'worker' to extend employment rights to those atypical workers who are unable to qualify for rights as employees. This has been paralleled by developments in EC law which have sought to tackle some of the specific problems faced by particular types of atypical worker. These developments suggest that the new institutional economics arguments and rights arguments have begun to have more influence. However, as we shall see, although workers are better protected than the self-employed, they do not get all the rights currently granted to employees. This suggests that neoclassical arguments about the cost of rights are still playing an important role.

Employees

According to ERA 1996, s. 230(1), an employee is 'an individual who has entered into or works under . . . a contract of employment'. The contract of employment is a common law concept. A person seeking to show that he or she is an employee must fulfil three criteria:

1. there must be 'mutuality of obligation' between the parties to the contract;
2. there must be a relationship of employer and employee; and
3. the contract must not contain any terms inconsistent with the relationship of employer and employee.

At the most basic level, a contract exists when an individual does some work and the employer pays him or her for it. However, according to Freedland, the contract of employment consists of two 'levels'.[23] One level is the basic wage-work bargain just described. The other level is a promise by the employer to provide future work,

---

23 M. Freedland, *The Personal Employment Contract* (2003) pp. 88–92. The author makes clear that this analysis is also applicable to other types of contract, such as workers' contracts.

and a promise by the employee to accept that work. This level is sometimes referred to as the 'global contract' because it links the separate wage-work bargains into an ongoing contract.

This requirement makes it difficult for casual workers to attain the status of employees. From the employer's point of view, the benefit of using casual workers is that they can be brought in when the firm is busy and laid off when it is not. This does not in general involve a promise by the employer to provide future work. Some casual workers may approach the job on a similar footing: that they are under no obligation to accept the work offered by the firm. However, other casual workers may feel that they have made a promise to accept future work. This may be because they cannot afford to live without the work, or because the employer will not contact them again if they refuse. When this occurs, the firm gains the benefit of dependent labour without having to take on the full obligations of an employer, simply by refusing to promise future work.

In *Nethermere (St Neots) Ltd v Taverna and Gardiner*, the court used the contractual device of a 'course of dealing' in order to create a global contract.[24] It held that because the employer had in practice provided work and the employees had accepted it over a long period of time, this had 'hardened into' a contract of employment. The parties' practices had become promises. This is not, however, the usual approach. Most other cases have followed *O'Kelly v Trusthouse Forte plc*, in which the court held that casual workers could not show mutuality of obligation.[25] The employer was under no obligation to offer work to a group of casual waiters, and although they might in practice accept that work for financial reasons, they had made no contractually binding promise to do so. They did not therefore count as employees.

Once claimants have overcome the hurdle of 'mutuality of obligation', they must then demonstrate the existence of an employee/employer relationship. Over the years, the courts have developed a number of tests for this. In the *Ready Mixed Concrete* case, the court held that a person was an employee if the employer *controlled* his or her work.[26] It was said that: 'control includes the power of deciding the thing to be done, the means to be employed in doing it, the time when and the place where it shall be done'.[27] In practice, however, many people who are usually thought of as employees have a substantial degree of discretion over these issues. For example, a doctor might be an employee of a hospital, but managers would not be able to tell the doctor how to treat the patients. In *Stevenson, Jordan and Harrison* the court held that an employee was someone whose work was 'integral' to the employer's business.[28] But this is also difficult to apply. The engineer who fixes the machinery in the employer's factory may seem 'integral' when the machines have broken down,

24 [1984] IRLR 240.
25 [1983] IRLR 369. See also *Clark v Oxfordshire Health Authority* [1998] IRLR 125, and *Carmichael v National Power plc* [1998] IRLR 301.
26 *Ready Mixed Concrete v Minister of Pensions* [1968] 2 QB 497.
27 [1968] 2 QB 497 at 515.
28 *Stevenson, Jordan and Harrison Ltd v MacDonald and Evans* [1952] 1 TLR 101.

but in law he or she may well be an independent contractor or even the employee of another firm.

The most modern test is the 'risk' test, set out in the case of *Market Investigations Ltd v Minister of Social Security*.[29] The court held that the question to ask was: who took the risk of profit and loss? If the employer bore the risk, the claimant would count as an employee. But if the claimant bore the risk, he or she would not count as an employee. This fits with the popular perception of the employer as the risk-taking entrepreneur and the employee as someone who simply works for a reliable wage. However, even this test may not work in all circumstances. Through employee share ownership or performance-related pay schemes, employers are increasingly encouraging employees to take a share of the risks associated with the business. These schemes may blur the apparently clear boundary between employer as risk-taker, and employee.

The final hurdle for the potential employee is to show that there are no terms in the contract which are inconsistent with an employment relationship. In a series of recent cases, the courts have stressed that an employee is someone who performs work personally for the employer. If an employee does not feel like going to work, he or she cannot simply send someone else instead. This would be a breach of contract. The courts have inferred from this that if a person does have the contractual right to send a substitute, then he or she cannot be an employee: *Express and Echo Publications Ltd v Tanton*.[30] This decision has been much criticised by commentators because it provides employers with an easy way of avoiding the obligations of the employment relationship. Since employers usually draft contracts, they can simply insert a substitution clause. However, the position has been mitigated somewhat by *MacFarlane v Glasgow CC*.[31] Here, the employees were able to provide a substitute but only from a list of names approved by the employer and only when they were unable to work for some valid reason, such as illness. The court held that this more limited substitution clause was not inconsistent with a contract of employment.

More generally, rights theorists have been highly critical of the courts' approach to the definition of 'employee' in particular.[32] Their argument is that the courts have failed to take sufficient account of the fact that workers' rights are at stake and that employers may be trying to evade their obligations. The courts do not generally construe employment status in a purposive way. In other words, they do not take into account what right a person is seeking when they are deciding what status he or she should have in law. As Fredman points out,[33] the *O'Kelly* case concerned casual waiters who had been dismissed for joining a trade union.[34] TULRCA 1992, s. 152 grants protection against dismissal on this ground only to employees. But a court

29 [1969] 2 QB 173.
30 [1999] IRLR 367.
31 [2001] IRLR 7.
32 Fredman, above n. 14.
33 Fredman, above n. 14, at 347.
34 *O'Kelly v Trusthouse Forte plc* [1983] IRLR 369.

might have been justified in construing the concept of 'employee' broadly in this case, because the right to belong to a trade union is fundamental and every effort should be made to uphold it.

Workers

'Worker' is a middle category between employee and self-employed. Labour law in fact contains two different definitions of 'worker', which we will label 'the worker definition' and 'the broad worker definition'. The broad worker definition (to be discussed in the next section) includes some self-employed people whereas the worker definition does not.

The worker definition in s. 230(3) of ERA 1996 is:

... an individual who has entered into or works under ...

(a) a contract of employment, or

(b) any other contract, whether express or implied and (if it is express) whether oral or in writing, whereby the individual undertakes to do or perform personally any work or services for another party to the contract whose status is not by virtue of the contract that of a client or customer of any profession or business undertaking carried on by the individual ...

The first point to note is that this definition includes employees in para. (a). This means that if a statute gives a right to 'workers', employees benefit from that right as well. But so do the people who fall within para. (b). Thus, if a right is granted to workers it will help more people than a right which is granted only to employees. To fall within (b), the claimant must fulfil three criteria:

1. there must be mutuality of obligation between the parties to the contract;
2. he or she must be under a duty to perform the work personally; and
3. he or she must not be running a business.

We have already met the first two criteria in our discussion of the definition of an employee. They are highly significant because they cast doubt on whether the introduction of the 'worker' concept will help as many atypical workers as the government claims. The authority for the proposition that workers need to show mutuality of obligation is *Byrne Brothers (Formwork) Ltd v Baird*.[35] As we have seen, mutuality is not usually present where a worker is employed on a casual basis, so most casual workers will not be protected by the new concept. The requirement that a worker performs the work personally is expressly set out in the statutory definition itself. This makes it difficult for individuals whose contract contains a substitution clause to establish that they are workers, although as we saw above, the courts' recent decisions indicate that a limited power of substitution is not incompatible with an obligation to perform personally.[36]

35 [2002] IRLR 96.
36 *MacFarlane v Glasgow CC* [2001] IRLR 7.

The third criterion is that a worker is someone who is not a self-employed person running his or her own business. According to *Byrne Brothers v Baird*, one of the first cases on this issue, the worker concept must be understood in the light of its purpose: to extend the protection of employment law to some of the people who would not fall under the definition of an employee. The EAT commented:

> The reason why employees are thought to need such protection is that they are in a subordinate and dependent position vis-à-vis their employers: the purpose of the [worker definition] is to extend protection to workers who are, substantively and economically, in the same position. Thus the essence of the intended distinction must be between, on the one hand, workers whose degree of dependence is essentially the same as that of employees and, on the other, contractors who have a sufficiently arm's-length and independent position to be treated as being able to look after themselves in the relevant respects.[37]

The worker concept would be deprived of all its meaning if the distinction between worker and self-employed was drawn in exactly the same way as the distinction between employee and self-employed. Equally, however, the approach cannot be entirely different since similar issues of dependence and independence arise in both situations. The EAT's solution is to use the same test for worker/self-employed as is used for employee/self-employed – whether or not the person is economically dependent on the alleged employer[38] – 'but with the boundary pushed further in the putative worker's favour'.[39] Thus, when the legal concept at issue in a case is 'worker', it will be much harder to persuade the court that the claimant is self-employed than it would be if the legal concept at issue was 'employee'.

Self-employed people

By now, it should be reasonably clear who counts as self-employed. A self-employed person runs his or her own business and takes the risk of profit and loss. He or she does not count as an employee or as a worker under the definitions we have considered so far. Indeed, he or she may be the employer of others. Self-employed people only have the chance of legislative protection when the 'broad worker definition' is used.

The 'broad worker definition'[40] is encapsulated in the following quotation:

> 'Employment' means employment under a contract of service or of apprenticeship or a contract personally to execute any work or labour.[41]

---

37 [2002] IRLR 96 at 101.
38 The test derived from the *Market Investigations* case, *Market Investigations Ltd v Minister of Social Security* [1969] 2 QB 173.
39 [2002] IRLR 96 at 101.
40 This label is used here because it locates the definition accurately in the employee-worker-self-employed spectrum. Confusingly, however, the legislation uses the terms 'employee' and 'employment'.
41 SDA 1975, s. 82(1).

This definition includes employees because they are employed under a 'contract of service'. The requirements of mutuality of obligation and of a duty to perform the work personally both still apply. But significantly, there is no exclusion for people running their own business. This means that self-employed people can fall within the broad worker definition *but only* where they perform the work personally. So a self-employed plumber who did repairs him- or herself would be a worker on this definition, but the owner of a plumbing firm who employed staff to carry out repairs would not be. This definition gives employment law its widest possible scope.

Why does it matter?

These three definitions are very important because they represent three different levels of protection in employment law. The self-employed get almost no protection, workers get some protection, and employees get all the protection the law has to offer. Litigation in this area is common as individuals strive to get into a more protected category and employers seek to avoid the legal obligations which would follow from this.

Self-employed people are, in general, outside the scope of employment law. On a practical level, it would be unfair to impose the obligations of an employer on everyone who hires a self-employed person. If I hire an electrician to fix something in my house, I do not expect to have to ensure that the electrician is observing the Working Time Regulations 1998 or being paid the national minimum wage. The self-employed person is running his or her own business and should be able to negotiate for the protections he or she needs. So the minimum wage (for example) should not be an issue because the self-employed person is able to charge a rate for the job. As we saw above, this can be reconciled even with a 'rights for all' approach because self-employed people are not being denied their rights. Instead, their rights are being enforced through their own ability to bargain for them. However, it is important to ensure that the category of self-employment is not drawn too widely to include people who are not able to protect themselves.

The only major form of protection for some self-employed persons is under the anti-discrimination legislation.[42] Statutes such as the SDA 1975 and the RRA 1976 use the 'broad worker definition' which includes those self-employed people who perform the work personally.[43] The law's policy here is to spread the protection of discrimination law – and the fundamental right to be free from discrimination – to as broad a group of people as possible. Moreover, this can be done without imposing significant obligations on others. All it means is that a householder has no right to refuse to hire a plumber on the ground that she is female, for example.

---

42 For discussion, see Davies and Freedland, above n. 20, pp. 278–81.
43 Equal Pay Act 1970 (EqPA 1970), s. 1(6)(a); SDA 1975, s. 82(1); RRA 1976, s. 78(1); DDA 1995, s. 68(1); Employment Equality (Sexual Orientation) Regulations 2003 (SI 2003/1661), reg. 2; Employment Equality (Religion or Belief) Regulations 2003 (SI 2003/1660), reg. 2.

Workers get the protection of discrimination law and some additional rights as well. The term has been used in many (though not all) pieces of legislation enacted since 1997. Workers benefit from:

- the national minimum wage;[44]
- the working time regulations;[45]
- the right to be accompanied at a disciplinary or grievance hearing;[46] and
- the right not to be discriminated against on the ground of working part-time.[47]

The use of 'worker' reflects an acknowledgement on the part of the government that a growing number of people fall outside the employee definition without being genuinely self-employed, and that these people deserve some protection. Under the Employment Relations Act 1999 (ERA 1999), s. 23, the government took the power to extend to workers any of the rights which are currently available only to employees. This provision has not yet been invoked.

Employees are traditionally the subject of employment law and remain the best-protected group. They get all the rights afforded to workers and the self-employed, and a very large number of other rights as well. These additional rights include:

- the right not to be discriminated against on grounds of trade union membership;[48]
- the right not to be discriminated against on the ground of having a fixed-term contract;[49]
- redundancy payments;[50]
- protection against unfair dismissal;[51]
- maternity leave, paternity leave, and parental leave;[52]
- emergency leave to deal with family crises;[53]
- the right to request flexible working;[54] and
- the right to a written statement of terms and conditions of employment.[55]

Some of these rights are only available after the employee has worked for the employer continuously for a specified period of time. The right to a written statement of terms and conditions is available only after one month,[56] presumably to minimise the bureaucracy which must be complied with for very short-term

44 NMWA 1998, ss. 1 and 54(3).
45 Working Time Regulations 1998 (SI 1998/1833) (WTR 1998), reg. 2(1).
46 ERA 1999, s. 10.
47 Part-time Workers (Prevention of Less Favourable Treatment) Regulations 2000 (SI 2000/1551), reg. 1(2).
48 TULRCA 1992, ss. 146, 152–3.
49 Fixed-Term Employees (Prevention of Less Favourable Treatment) Regulations 2002 (SI 2002/2034).
50 ERA 1996, s. 135.
51 ERA 1996, s. 94.
52 ERA 1996, ss. 71–5 (inserted by ERA 1999 and amended by the Employment Act 2002 (EA 2002)); ERA 1996, ss. 80A–E (inserted by EA 2002); ERA 1996, ss. 76–80 (inserted by ERA 1999).
53 ERA 1996, s. 57A (inserted by ERA 1999).
54 ERA 1996, ss. 80F–I (inserted by EA 2002, s. 47).
55 ERA 1996, s. 1.
56 ERA 1996, s. 198.

appointments. The right to a redundancy payment is only available to employees who have worked for one year.[57] The same is usually true of the right not to be unfairly dismissed,[58] although there are some reasons for dismissal (pregnancy, for example) which are actionable from the moment the employment starts.[59] The justification given for these qualifying periods is that they give firms the flexibility to hire people on a short-term basis and to try them out without fear of legal action if it turns out that they are unsuitable.

Thus, the law adopts a multi-layered approach instead of the 'rights for all' strategy suggested by many rights theorists and by some new institutional economists. We saw earlier that such an approach might be justifiable if it was intended to ensure that all workers benefited from a minimum set of fundamental rights. However, English law fails to grant workers a coherent body of protection. Workers do get the right to the minimum wage, which can be regarded as an aspect of the fundamental right to dignity at work. But there are some significant omissions. For example, the right not to be discriminated against on the grounds of trade union membership or non-membership is available only to employees. This is a key part of freedom of association: there is little point in saying that individuals are free to join a union if the employer can discriminate against them for doing so. Another non-discrimination right confined to employees is the right not to be discriminated against on the ground of having a fixed-term contract. While this is not quite so fundamental, it is part of a set of initiatives (to be discussed below) aimed at eliminating discrimination against atypical workers. It seems strange that it should be granted only to those who have a contract of employment.

It remains to be seen how the government will use the power in ERA 1999, s. 23 to extend to workers any of the rights currently granted to employees.[60] The power could be used to extend *all* employee rights to workers. In effect, this would abolish the employee/worker distinction, leaving only two categories: worker and self-employed person. This could be justified either on new institutional economics arguments or on a 'rights for all' basis. It would also reduce the need for costly litigation because there would only be one boundary in dispute (worker/self-employed) in place of the two we have at present (worker/self-employed and worker/employee). Alternatively, the government could use its s. 23 power to refine the current three-tier system, for example, by ensuring that workers got some of the fundamental rights identified above. The government might decide to do this if it remained persuaded that it would be too costly to give workers all the current employee rights. However, as we saw in the theoretical discussion, this option is difficult to justify, not least because it gives employers the power to decide whether an individual should be an employee or a worker and thus what rights he or she should get.

57 ERA 1996, s. 155 (as amended).
58 ERA 1996, s. 108(1).
59 ERA 1996, s. 108(2).
60 For discussion, see P. Davies and M. Freedland, 'Labour markets, welfare, and the personal scope of employment law' (2000) 16 *Oxford Review of Economic Policy* 84.

Atypical workers have other problems too

Even if atypical workers can bring themselves within the scope of some or all of mainstream employment law, by showing that they are workers or employees, this may not solve all their problems. This is because employment law is directed at the concerns of typical employees. Atypical workers may face difficulties which simply do not apply to typical employees. The EC's strategy has been to legislate separately for each group of atypical workers.[61] It has therefore been well placed to address the unique concerns of fixed-term workers, teleworkers and so on. Many of the relevant directives have been agreed by the social partners (the European employers' associations and the European Trade Union Confederation) under the social dialogue procedure.[62]

The Fixed-Term Employees (Prevention of Less Favourable Treatment) Regulations 2002 are intended to tackle the specific problems faced by fixed-term employees.[63] First, the Regulations contain a basic protection against discrimination on the grounds of being a fixed-term employee.[64] This means that an individual cannot, for example, be paid less than a permanent worker simply because he or she has a fixed-term contract, unless the employer can give an objective justification for the difference in treatment. Second, the Regulations prevent employers from repeatedly renewing fixed-term contracts over a long period of time.[65] If a person is employed under a succession of fixed-term contracts for a period of more than four years, he or she is deemed by the Regulations to be a permanent employee. However, the employer may escape this result if it can show that there is an objective justification for continuing to employ the person on a fixed-term basis. It remains to be seen how ready the courts will be to accept employers' defences under this provision. However, the main criticism which has been made of the Regulations is that they only apply to employees. As we have seen, more people would have been protected had the term 'worker' been used instead.

A more recent development is the *Framework Agreement on Telework*, concluded by the social partners in 2002. This is the first agreement concluded by the social partners which is to be implemented by employers and unions in the Member States instead of by means of a directive.[66] It has been implemented in the UK by the DTI's *Telework Guidance*, agreed by the CBI, TUC and CEEP UK in 2003. It remains to be seen how much use employers will make of the guidance, particularly where there is no trade union presence in the workplace. The agreement addresses the problems faced by teleworkers, who use information technology in order to do their work from a location other than the employer's premises (usually their

---

61 The EC regards the scope of employment law as a matter for the Member States, so it has played no role in the wider employee/worker debate.
62 Article 139 EC.
63 SI 2002/2034, implementing Directive 99/70/EC. See A. McColgan (2003) 32 *ILJ* 194.
64 SI 2002/2034, regs. 3–4.
65 SI 2002/2034, reg. 8.
66 *Framework Agreement on Telework*, 16 July 2002, para. 12.

home).[67] The agreement is not intended to take effect as legislation, so its drafting is rather informal. But it does lay down a number of important principles. First, it states that telework should be voluntary.[68] If it is not part of the worker's initial job description, the employer should not be able to force a worker to change to telework unless he or she is willing to do so. This is dealt with in the UK guidance through the basic contractual principle that an individual's contract of employment cannot be varied without his or her consent.[69] However, this offers no protection where the employer has left open the possibility of changing to teleworking in the original contract. The agreement also suggests (although the language is less clear) that the worker should be able to give up telework and return to the employer's premises if he or she subsequently chooses to do so. The UK guidance indicates that employers may be able to refuse such requests, for example, where the employer no longer has sufficient office space.[70] Second, both the agreement and the guidance indicate that teleworkers should benefit from the same terms and conditions of employment as comparable workers at the employer's premises.[71] Third, both instruments make specific provision concerning the technology to be used by the teleworker.[72] For example, they indicate that it is usually the employer's responsibility to pay for the teleworker's telephone and internet use.

Other groups of atypical workers have fared less well. 'Traditional' homework has not been given much attention, although the UK government has taken steps to ensure that homeworkers will benefit from the national minimum wage even if they fall outside the definition of 'worker' used in the 1998 Act.[73] Agency workers also receive specific attention in the Act, which provides that they should be paid the minimum wage by whoever pays them, even if there is uncertainty about who counts as their employer in the technical sense.[74] However, attempts to reach an agreement about agency work at the European level have so far been unsuccessful.

The scope of employment law – an issue to remember

The remaining chapters of this book will consider in greater detail the various employment issues we have touched on here: the minimum wage, freedom of association, unfair dismissal and so on. Each chapter will contain a brief reminder of the scope of the rights it is considering: whether they are worker rights or employee rights. As you learn about each new set of rights, you should think back to the arguments made in this chapter and consider whether you agree with the way in which the law has allocated them.

---

67 Above n. 66, para. 2.
68 Above n. 66, para. 3.
69 DTI, *Telework Guidance* (2003), pp. 8–10.
70 DTI, above n. 69, p. 10.
71 Above n. 66, para. 4; DTI, above n. 69, pp. 11–2.
72 Above n. 66, para. 7; DTI, above n. 69, p. 15.
73 NMWA 1998, s. 35.
74 NMWA 1998, s. 34.

Further reading

For a detailed textbook account of this topic, see S. Deakin and G.S. Morris, *Labour Law* (3rd edn., 2001), chapter 3; or H. Collins, K.D. Ewing and A. McColgan, *Labour Law: Text and Materials* (2001), chapter 2. Most of the statistics used in this chapter were drawn from B. Burchell, S. Deakin and S. Honey, *The Employment Status of Individuals in Non-Standard Employment* (DTI URN 99/770) (1999).

J. Atkinson, *Flexibility, Uncertainty and Manpower Management* (1984) is a classic statement of the advantages of atypical work from a business perspective and gives a good insight into the neoclassical arguments. Theorists in this tradition often claim that atypical work is beneficial for the worker too. What benefits might there be? Do they depend on the type of atypical work? Are some types of atypical work never beneficial? Do you agree with the view that legal regulation would stifle job creation? For some ideas, see J. Murray, 'Normalising temporary work' (1999) 28 *ILJ* 269; and S. Fredman, 'Labour law in flux: the changing composition of the workforce' (1997) 26 *ILJ* 337.

C. Kilpatrick, 'Has New Labour reconfigured employment legislation?' (2003) 23 *ILJ* 135, gives an excellent account of new institutionalist arguments. She suggests that the exclusion of atypical workers from protection may be the result of a particular regulatory strategy adopted by successive governments. What is that strategy? Do you think that it is defensible? What does her analysis tell us about the explanatory power of the perspectives adopted in this chapter?

For a stimulating discussion of the development of atypical work from a rights perspective, see Fredman, quoted above. There is a large literature on atypical work in the rights tradition, much of which is mentioned in the footnotes to this chapter, but one of the most recent and thought-provoking contributions is P. Davies and M. Freedland, 'Employees, workers and the autonomy of labour law', in H. Collins, P. Davies and R. Rideout (eds.), *Legal Regulation of the Employment Relation* (2000). Why should atypical workers be protected? How do these writers justify imposing additional costs on employers? What are the implications of the regulation of atypical work for women and members of the ethnic minorities? What are the implications of the regulation of atypical work for trade union membership?

Rights theorists are strongly critical of the role of the courts in interpreting 'employee' and 'worker' in atypical work situations. You may find it helpful to revisit the discussion of the courts in chapter 4, and S. Anderman, 'The interpretation of protective employment statutes and contracts of employment' (2000) 29 *ILJ* 223. If the law was reformed in line with rights arguments, what strategies could the legislature adopt to ensure that the courts gave full effect to the new provisions?

6

Working time

Working time has traditionally been regarded as a matter for collective bargaining or for managerial decision-making. Nowadays, three important aspects of working time are regulated by legislation. First, the Working Time Regulations 1998 (WTR 1998) seek to regulate the working time of all workers, by prescribing limits on the maximum number of hours which can be worked in the week and by requiring employers to give their workers daily and weekly rest breaks and annual holidays. Second, the law forbids discrimination against those who work part-time. Unless the employer can justify treating part-timers differently, it must give them the same benefits as full-timers. Third, the law provides various kinds of leave to enable employees to combine work and family life: maternity leave, paternity leave, parental leave and emergency leave. Parents may also ask for their employer's permission to work part-time or from home or in some other way which will assist them in fulfilling their family responsibilities.

In the international human rights instruments, there is a long-standing tradition of rights to reasonable limits on working hours and to paid holidays. Such rights have been framed as basic minimum standards which are necessary to ensure that all workers are treated fairly by their employers, or sometimes as an aspect of health and safety regulation. Maternity leave is also a well-established right. It reflects the dual concerns that pregnant women might suffer discrimination in the labour market and that certain types of work might pose a health hazard to pregnant women and their babies. More recent instruments have begun to include some version of the right to 'reconcile' work and family life. Some instruments base this right on the needs of working parents of both sexes; others emphasise its role in facilitating women's participation in the labour market. In general, however, the international instruments tend to contain either bare minimum standards or relatively vague aspirations, so theorists have had to elaborate on them in order to develop a detailed critique of English law.

Neoclassical economists focus on the individual's 'labour supply decision': in other words, his or her choice of how many hours to work. This approach tends to be hostile towards legal regulation of working time because it limits individuals' choices. From the new institutional economics perspective, however, controls on working time can be justified in various ways. A common argument is that the relationship between working hours and productivity is not straightforward: shorter working hours may make people more, rather than less, productive. Neoclassical writers are also critical of rights to parental leave, paternity leave and so on, because they are seen as costly for employers. But pro-labour economists argue that such rights may have compensating advantages. In particular, they make it easier for employers to recruit and retain workers, thus giving them access to a wider pool of talent.

Economics perspectives

The working week

Let us begin with a basic neoclassical account of working time.[1] This treats the number of hours worked as a choice made by each employee. Assume that the wage rate is £1 per hour and (implausibly) that the individual could work for up to 24 hours a day. This gives the individual a choice between 24 hours of leisure time and no income, or no hours of leisure time and £24 of income, or (more likely) some position in between, such as 12 hours of leisure and £12 of income. The individual's choice will be governed by a range of personal factors. For example, a mother with young children might place a high value on leisure time because it can be spent with her family, whereas their father might be willing to work extra hours in order to bring in additional income.

If the wage rate increases, the worker's response will depend upon which of two effects is dominant: the income effect or the substitution effect.[2] The income effect in the context of a wage rate increase means that the individual's income goes up even though he or she is working the same number of hours. He or she might decide to spend this extra money on more leisure time: in other words, to reduce the number of hours worked. The substitution effect in the context of a wage rate increase means that the price of leisure (the money foregone by deciding not to work) goes up. It therefore makes sense for the worker to increase his or her working hours. Which of these effects dominates depends, again, on the individual's preferences. So in our example above, an increase in wages might prompt the mother to enter the labour market, because in a few hours she can earn money to purchase additional goods for her family, and it might prompt the father to reduce his hours in order to spend more time with the children. A wage decrease has the opposite effect. The individual's income will fall if he or she continues to work the same hours, so if the income effect is dominant, he or she will increase his or her hours. But the price of leisure will decrease, so if the substitution effect is dominant, the individual will not bother to work so many hours.

What happens if the law steps in to regulate the number of hours people can work? Let us imagine that the law states that no-one may work for more than

---

1 See, generally, P.R.G. Layard and A.A. Walters, *Microeconomic Theory* (1978), chapter 11.
2 See L. Robbins, 'On the elasticity of demand for income in terms of effort' (1930) *Economica* 123.

48 hours per week. This would leave some workers feeling underemployed: their preference would be to increase their income by working for more than 48 hours. Such sentiments are particularly likely to arise among low-paid workers, who may not be able to earn enough to live on if the law restricts their hours. This demonstrates that there is an important relationship between working time and the minimum wage, to be considered in chapter 8. One option for the underemployed worker is to seek a second job to increase his or her hours and income. This defeats the law's aim of ensuring that no-one works for more than 48 hours. But it is difficult to prevent because the law – which regulates individual employers – cannot tackle the cumulative effect of several separate employment relationships.

Imagine now that the only kind of job available is one with a 48-hour working week. This will leave some workers feeling over-employed. They would rather work fewer hours and have more leisure time. Instead, they are left with the difficult choice of working full-time or not working at all. If they take a full-time job, some theorists suggest that they will take more days off (such as sickness absences) because they are unhappy with the hours they are expected to work.[3] The state could intervene to help these workers by encouraging employers to provide more opportunities for part-time working. A neoclassical economist would, of course, advocate keeping the legal rights of part-time workers to a minimum, so that employers would be attracted to part-time work by its cheapness.

The new institutional economists approach the regulation of working time in a very different way.[4] They argue that controls on working time may benefit employers. At first sight, it might seem as if there is a linear relationship between hours worked and productivity: the more hours a worker works, the more productive he or she will be. But on reflection this is clearly not true. If it takes a person one hour to dig a hole of a certain depth, it is unlikely that he or she will be able to dig ten times that depth in ten hours. Even where the measure of productivity is less clear-cut, the quality of the individual's work may suffer. A shop worker may be less polite and helpful to the customers; a doctor may administer the wrong dose of medication. A legal maximum limit on the working week would help employers to get the best out of their workers.

The obvious neoclassical response to this is to point out that no rational employer would require its workers to work long hours if this would be damaging to the firm. And a legal maximum limit would not help firms to improve safety and productivity because it would not fit their specific needs.[5] It might be unsafe for certain workers to work as many as 48 hours in a week, whereas others could work productively for a

---

3 See, for example, S.G. Allen, 'An empirical model of work attendance' (1981) 63 *Review of Economics and Statistics* 77.

4 See, generally, S. Deakin and F. Wilkinson, 'Rights vs efficiency: the economic case for transnational labour standards' (1994) 23 *ILJ* 289.

5 A point made by C. Barnard, 'EC "Social" Policy', in P. Craig and G. de Búrca (eds.), *The Evolution of EU Law* (1999), p. 491, though she advocates regulation in a different form rather than no regulation at all.

much larger number of hours. However, this argument assumes that employers have perfect information about safe working hours, and that they are willing to focus on considerations such as productivity and safety rather than cost. An employer might ask someone to work additional hours without realising that he or she has already reached the limit of his or her productivity. Or the employer might decide to use existing workers to do extra hours instead of incurring the expenses of recruiting and training additional staff. A legal maximum limit on the working week helps to educate employers about safe working hours, and prevents them from making decisions based solely on short-term financial concerns.

New institutional economists also argue that there are benefits for employers in the provision of part-time jobs. The reasons for this are partly macroeconomic. If the UK economy is to be as productive as possible, it must use its labour resources to the full.[6] But not all workers are able to – or want to – work full-time. Those wishing to study for new qualifications or to care for children would often prefer a part-time job. From a macroeconomic viewpoint, it is better to have these people in the labour market on a part-time basis than not at all. And at the microeconomic level, firms will benefit from having access to a wider pool of talent from which to recruit their employees. However, these benefits will only arise if the part-time jobs on offer are sufficiently attractive to persuade more people to enter the labour market. Economists express this idea using the concept of the 'reservation wage'. For someone who is not currently participating in the labour market, the reservation wage is the lowest wage rate at which he or she would be willing to take a job. If part-time jobs are low-paid and have few benefits, they will fall below the reservation wage of many potential workers. But if the law steps in to ensure that part-time workers have the same pay and benefits as their full-time colleagues, and that they are entitled to the minimum wage and other legal rights, the jobs are more likely to be at or above many people's reservation wage. As usual, the rational employer facing recruitment difficulties would take these steps of its own accord, without legal intervention, but concerns about costs and being undercut by competitors might prevent this.

Leave

Neoclassical theorists argue that if the law requires employers to provide various kinds of leave for parents, they will be burdened with substantial costs. One potential cost is that of providing pay and benefits to an employee who is on leave. Of course, the law may specify that some kinds of leave should be unpaid or paid at a lower rate than the employee's usual wage. But where the leave is paid at the normal rate, the employer is receiving no work in return for its outlay. Another type of cost – which arises even if the leave is unpaid – is the cost of providing cover for the employee.

---

6 These arguments feature in many of the government's policy documents. See, for example, HM Treasury/DTI, *Full and Fulfilling Employment: Creating the Labour Market of the Future* (2002).

This may be quite substantial. A suitable person must be recruited and trained, and there may be some loss of productivity while he or she is learning the job.

One way in which the employer might deal with these costs would be to pass them on to employees. The employer could calculate the overall cost of providing family-friendly working policies and deduct this from employees' wages. However, family-friendly policies present a major problem in this regard. They do not benefit all workers. While parents and those who expect to become parents may be willing to pay for the benefits, employees who do not fall into either of these categories would probably prefer to receive a higher salary instead.[7] Moreover, they may be too expensive to be offset by a pay cut. Where the employer cannot offset the costs of family-friendly policies, some redundancies may result. And the employer may be tempted to discriminate against those who are likely to use the policies when it is recruiting new workers.

New institutional economists present a very different picture of parental leave policies, arguing that they can benefit employers as well as employees. One major advantage identified in the literature is that these policies help employers to recruit and retain workers.[8] For example, a woman may be more willing to return to work after maternity leave if she is able to work flexible hours and to have time off if her child is ill. The retention of workers is particularly important for firms which have to provide a substantial amount of training before a new worker can become productive. The employer decides whether or not to provide training by comparing the costs of the training with the benefits of having a skilled individual in the workforce. But these benefits may only outweigh the costs if the worker stays with the employer for a certain number of years after receiving the training.

The real challenge facing the new institutionalists is to demonstrate that it is right for the law to require all firms to provide the various forms of family leave, even if they have low recruitment and training costs and can cope with a high turnover of workers. A number of arguments can be made.[9] One is that a reduced turnover of workers may improve productivity even if training costs are low. This is because new workers always take some time to become as productive as experienced workers. Another is that workers who feel supported by their employer in their attempts to juggle work and family life will respond by being more loyal to the firm. This loyalty may make the workers more productive. Finally, workers who are happy with the way in which their work and home life are balanced will be more focused when they are at work. For example, a worker whose childcare arrangements have fallen through and who is trying to find an alternative will be distracted from his or her work. A worker who is given a day's emergency leave to resolve the problem will

---

7 R. Drago *et al.*, 'The willingness-to-pay for work/family policies: a study of teachers' (2001) 55 *Industrial and Labor Relations Review* 22, casts doubt on this expectation. The authors found that workers who did not expect to benefit from family-friendly policies were willing to pay something towards them.

8 See, for example, DTI, *Work and Parents: Competitiveness and Choice* (2000).

9 DTI, above n. 8.

miss a day's work but will at least be able to concentrate when he or she returns. The new institutionalists might also strengthen their basic argument about recruitment and retention by combining it with human rights arguments, to which we will now turn.

Rights perspectives

International instruments have long been concerned with three of the issues we are considering in this chapter: limits on weekly working hours, paid annual holidays, and maternity leave. Rights to reconcile work with family life are beginning to appear in more recent instruments.

Hours and holidays

Not surprisingly, hours and holidays are the exclusive preserve of economic and social rights instruments. Article 7 of the ICESCR is as follows:

> The States Parties to the present Covenant recognise the right of everyone to the enjoyment of just and favourable conditions of work which ensure, in particular . . .
> (d) Rest, leisure and reasonable limitation of working hours and periodic holidays with pay, as well as remuneration for public holidays.

Article 24 of the UN Declaration is in similar terms. These rights can be seen as part of a minimum set of terms and conditions of employment from which all workers should benefit, including a fair wage and a safe working environment. They were intended to address some of the most abusive forms of work, in which low-paid workers were expected to work extremely long hours in hazardous conditions. The concern is to ensure that workers are treated fairly and with dignity.

The detail of these rights is fleshed out most fully in ILO instruments. Long working hours have been a concern of the ILO from its inception: the first Convention to address working time is Convention No. 1 of 1919.[10] The basic ILO standards are that the working day should be limited to eight hours, the working week should be limited to 48 hours, and that there should be a continuous 24-hour rest period in every seven days. Various exceptions are provided in the interests of business flexibility. Once a worker has completed a year's continuous service, he or she should be entitled to three weeks' paid holiday.[11] All these standards represent minimum levels of protection, so there is nothing to stop a state from introducing more favourable provisions. The UK has not ratified any of the ILO Conventions concerning working time. This probably reflects the UK's tradition of collective *laissez-faire*: until recently, working hours were seen as a matter for unions and

---

10 Hours of Work (Industry) Convention (No. 1, 1919). See also Weekly Rest (Industry) Convention (No. 14, 1921); Hours of Work (Commerce and Offices) Convention (No. 30, 1930); Weekly Rest (Commerce and Offices) Convention (No. 106, 1957).
11 Holidays with Pay (Revised) Convention (No. 132, 1970).

employers to decide through collective bargaining.[12] Legislation was only passed where workers were felt to be particularly vulnerable to exploitation.[13]

The ILO has also adopted a Convention on part-time work.[14] The ILO acknowledges that part-time work is an important source of job opportunities, but argues that part-timers need protection of various kinds.[15] The Convention has not been ratified by the UK. It sets out three main principles. First, part-timers should be guaranteed the same legal rights as full-time workers in various areas, including trade union membership and activities, discrimination, maternity protection, and unfair dismissal.[16] The concern here is that legislation may discriminate against part-timers even though the problems they may face in these areas are no different to those faced by full-timers. Second, part-timers should be paid the same hourly rate as full-timers.[17] This addresses the problem of discrimination by firms against their part-time employees. Third, 'where appropriate, measures shall be taken to ensure that transfer from full-time to part-time work or vice versa is voluntary in accordance with national law and practice'.[18] This encourages governments to grant individuals a right to choose the hours they work, but its wording is rather vague.

Leave

The ICESCR provides a basic right to maternity leave in Article 10(2):

> Special protection should be accorded to mothers during a reasonable period before and after childbirth. During such period working mothers should be accorded paid leave or leave with adequate social security benefits.

The ESC 1961, which has been ratified by the UK, specifies that maternity leave should be for a minimum duration of 12 weeks.[19] The revised ESC 1996[20] and the ILO Maternity Protection Convention[21] specify a minimum of 14 weeks. The right to maternity leave itself implies a right to return to work, but CEDAW expressly states that the woman should be able to return without loss of seniority.[22] Some instruments, including the ILO Convention[23] and the ESC 1996,[24] also provide that a woman who returns to work while she is still breastfeeding should be given time off for this purpose. Several instruments state that pregnancy or the taking of maternity

---

12 See chapter 1.
13 Examples include the Employment of Women, Young Persons and Children Act 1920 and the Coal Mines Regulation Act 1908.
14 Part-Time Work Convention (No. 175, 1994).
15 Above n. 14, Preamble.
16 Above n. 14, Articles 4 and 7.
17 Above n. 14, Article 5.
18 Above n. 14, Article 10.
19 Article 8.
20 Article 8.
21 Maternity Protection Convention (No. 183, 2000).
22 Article 11(2)(b).
23 Above n. 21, Article 10.
24 Article 8.

leave should not be permitted as grounds of dismissal.[25] Finally, it is common to find a requirement that pregnant women or women who are breastfeeding should not be required to engage in hazardous work or night work.[26]

Modern human rights instruments have begun to look beyond the basic provision of maternity leave and to consider the longer-term problems of balancing work and family life faced by working parents of both sexes. Formulations of the right to reconciliation vary considerably. Perhaps the most detailed right is that contained in the ESC 1996:

> With a view to ensuring the exercise of the right to equality of opportunity and treatment for men and women workers with family responsibilities and between such workers and other workers, the Parties undertake:
>
> 1. to take appropriate measures:
>   (a) to enable workers with family responsibilities to enter and remain in employment, as well as to re-enter employment after an absence due to those responsibilities, including measures in the field of vocational guidance and training;
>   (b) to take account of their needs in terms of conditions of employment and social security;
>   (c) to develop or promote services, public or private, in particular child daycare services and other childcare arrangements;
> 2. to provide a possibility for either parent to obtain, during a period after maternity leave, parental leave to take care of a child, the duration and conditions of which should be determined by national legislation, collective agreements or practice;
> 3. to ensure that family responsibilities shall not, as such, constitute a valid reason for termination of employment.[27]

Some of the less detailed rights place a particular emphasis on the provision of childcare facilities. This is true of CEDAW and of the Convention on the Rights of the Child.[28] The latter gives the children of working parents a right to childcare services. Others, such as the EU Charter, focus on the provision of parental leave.[29]

The international instruments also differ in the underlying basis they give to the right. The ESC right focuses on discrimination against working parents.[30] The concern is that their childcare responsibilities might make it more difficult for them to fulfil the demands made by employers, and that they might therefore need protection against unfavourable treatment. CEDAW, not surprisingly, is concerned with the elimination of discrimination against women, but so is the ILO Convention on Workers with Family Responsibilities.[31] This justification reflects the fact that

---

25 ESC 1961, Article 8; ESC 1996, Article 8; CEDAW, Article 11(2)(a).
26 ESC 1961, Article 8; ESC 1996, Article 8; ILO, above n. 21, Article 3; CEDAW, Article 11(2)(d).
27 Article 27.
28 CEDAW, Article 11; CRC, Article 18(3).
29 Article 33.
30 Article 27, quoted above.
31 CEDAW, Article 11; ILO Workers with Family Responsibilities Convention (No. 156, 1981), Preamble.

although many mothers now have paid employment and although social attitudes have changed, women still take the primary responsibility for childcare in most households. The reasons for women's role are complex. One is that some stereotypes remain: a man who chooses to take time out from his job to care for his children may still meet with surprise and even derision. Another is labour market discrimination: since women have to interrupt their careers to give birth, and since they earn less than men on average,[32] it may be rational for them to prioritise childcare over labour market work. Yet another is the substantial proportion of lone parent families, the vast majority of which are headed by women. These women have no choice but to take a substantial role in childcare. Taking all these factors together, many writers have concluded that since the burden of childcare falls most heavily on women, the right to reconcile work and family life should be seen as an aspect of women's right not to be discriminated against.[33]

The sex discrimination basis for the right to reconciliation has one major benefit: it links this novel right into well-established and powerful anti-discrimination norms. It becomes harder to argue against a right such as parental leave once it is made clear that discrimination against women may continue if the right is denied. However, there are two important disadvantages which will be outlined here: the temptation to stereotype women, and the tendency to focus solely on childcare.[34] These difficulties are not insurmountable but they do require careful attention when the right to reconciliation is being implemented in practice.

The stereotyping problem occurs where additional protections for working parents are available only to women or are designed in such a way as to make it likely that only women will use them. Although such protections would solve women's immediate problems of balancing work and family life, they would do nothing to promote equal parenting or to change assumptions for the future. Instead, they would serve to promote the idea that the main responsibility for childcare lies with women. Interestingly, the drafters of CEDAW were alert to this concern. Article 5(a) requires states to work towards the elimination of stereotypical assumptions about men's and women's roles. It is coupled with Article 5(b), which requires states:

> To ensure that family education includes a proper understanding of maternity as a social function and the recognition of the common responsibility of men and women in the upbringing and development of their children, it being understood that the interest of the children is the primordial consideration in all cases.

This is an important statement of two principles: first, that pregnancy and maternity should be distinguished from the task of raising children, and second, that men and women both have responsibility for the latter. These two principles can be summed up in the phrase 'equal parenting'. From a rights perspective, any new

---

32 See chapter 8.
33 See, for example, C. McGlynn, 'Reclaiming a feminist vision: the reconciliation of paid work and family life in European Union law and policy' (2001) *Columbia Journal of European Law* 241.
34 McGlynn, above n. 33.

development in parental leave rights must be tested for its ability to promote equal parenting.

A second problem with using sex discrimination as the underlying justification for the right to reconciliation is that it may lead to a focus on the raising of children as the only 'version' of family life. In practice, many workers also play a major role in caring for their elderly relatives. Some commentators would argue that this burden also falls more heavily on women, so rights to time off work to care for family members other than children could still be based on a sex discrimination rationale. In our discussion of the law, we will need to look at whether any of the rights it grants extend beyond childcare.

The law on working time

The law on working time is quite complex, and can only be explained in outline here. The discussion will be divided into two sections. The first will consider working time rules which apply to all workers regardless of their family status, and the second will consider rules which are specifically designed to deal with the problems faced by workers with family responsibilities.

Rules applicable to all

This section will consider the WTR 1998, which seek to regulate the working week, and the Part-time Workers Regulations 2000, which address some of the issues faced by part-timers. It will be argued that while both sets of regulations seem to reflect rights or new institutional economics perspectives, they contain a number of provisions which respond to neoclassical concerns about the cost of rights. These provisions may serve to undermine their apparent aims.

The WTR 1998[35] implement the EC's Working Time Directive, which was enacted as a health and safety measure designed to protect workers not only against the dangers associated with exhaustion but also the dangers of repetitive and monotonous work.[36] It remains to be seen whether the Regulations will make any impact on the UK's 'long-hours culture'. In 1999, for example, male full-time workers did an average of 45.2 hours per week.[37] This can be contrasted with an EU average of 41.2 hours per week. Women full-time workers tend to work fewer hours than men, but their hours are still long by European standards. In the UK, the average for 1999 was 40.7, whereas the EU average was 39.0.

---

35 SI 1998/1833, as amended by SI 1999/3372; SI 2001/3256; SI 2002/3128. See, generally, C. Barnard (1999) 28 *ILJ* 61 and (2000) 29 *ILJ* 167.

36 Directive 93/104/EC on the organisation of working time, enacted under the then Article 118a EC (which now forms part of Article 137 EC). The UK government brought an unsuccessful challenge of the Directive's treaty basis: Case 84/94 *UK v EU Council* [1996] ECR I-5755. For a detailed analysis of the Directive, see B. Bercusson, *European Labour Law* (1996), chapter 21.

37 Source: EUROSTAT *Labour Force Survey* (1999) (http://europa.eu.int/comm/eurostat).

The Regulations apply to employees and workers, so their scope is broad.[38] They require the employer to give each worker four weeks' leave from work each year.[39] This leave may be used for any purpose and must be paid at the worker's usual wage.[40] The working week is governed by two major rights. According to reg. 4, the maximum number of hours worked in a week (including overtime) should not exceed 48, averaged over a 17-week period. And under reg. 11, the worker is entitled to a continuous rest period of 24 hours in seven days or 48 hours in 14 days, at the choice of the employer. The working day is also regulated in two main ways. Under reg. 10, the worker is entitled to a rest period of 11 consecutive hours in each 24-hour period. And under reg. 12, the worker is entitled to a rest break of at least 20 minutes, to be spent away from his or her workstation, if his or her working day is longer than six hours. Some of these rights interact in important ways. In particular, although the maximum working week of 48 hours is only an *average* requirement, the employer's ability to demand some very long working weeks is limited by the obligation to provide daily and weekly rest breaks.

At first sight, the legislation appears to reflect either the rights theorists' concern with protecting the dignity of workers, or the new institutional economists' concern with promoting productivity. However, the rights are far from absolute. The drafters of the Directive were concerned to balance the goal of protecting workers against employers' need for flexibility.[41] The most significant example of this is that the individual worker can waive his or her right to the 48-hour working week if he or she signs a written agreement to that effect. This is not permitted under ILO standards.[42] Nor is it formally permitted under Article 6 of the Working Time Directive, but derogation from the absolute standard laid down in that Article is permitted under Article 18. In late 2003, the EC is due to review whether or not to continue to allow this derogation. Rights theorists have condemned the derogation, fearing that workers will be put under pressure by employers to waive the maximum limit,[43] despite the fact that it is unlawful for the employer to discriminate against a worker in these circumstances.[44] Even if no pressure is applied, workers may sign a waiver form at the commencement of their employment without realising what it is or that they need not sign it. From a new institutional economics perspective, the possibility of waiver means that employers can in effect ignore the new legislation. This will prevent them from learning any lessons about how to maximise their

---

38 WTR 1998, reg. 2.
39 WTR 1998, reg. 13.
40 WTR 1998, reg. 16.
41 Directive 93/104/EC, Preamble, states that: 'it appears desirable to provide for flexibility in the application of certain provisions of this Directive.'
42 Above n. 10.
43 F. Neathey and J. Arrowsmith, *Implementation of the Working Time Regulations* (DTI URN 01/682) (2001), found some evidence of this: p. 29.
44 ERA 1996, s. 45A, gives workers a right not to be subjected to any detriment by their employer, and s. 101A protects employees against dismissal, on grounds of asserting their rights under the WTR 1998.

workers' productivity. But the waiver makes sense from a neoclassical viewpoint: it upholds individuals' right to choose how many hours they work.

Of course, both rights theorists and new institutionalists would support some elements of flexibility in the Regulations. For example, the rights to rest periods and rest breaks do not apply in 'special cases', such as where there is an unforeseeable emergency.[45] The Regulations would clearly have absurd results if they did not permit employers to ask their workers to stay late if an accident had occurred. Moreover, some of the flexible provisions only allow the employer to negotiate with trade union representatives or with the elected representatives of the workforce, rather than with workers as individuals. For example, the averaging period for the 48-hour working week can be extended from 17 weeks to any period up to 52 weeks, where this is for 'objective or technical reasons or reasons concerning the organisation of work', by collective or workforce agreement.[46] From a new institutional perspective, this is a valuable compromise. It offers a greater chance that the law will be beneficial to firms because it allows them to adapt it to their needs. And workers are less likely to be intimidated if they are able to negotiate as a group. From a rights perspective, the implications of this provision and others like it depend on who has the greatest bargaining power: the employer or the representatives.[47]

The other topic to be discussed in this section is the legal regulation of part-time work. The UK has a substantial part-time workforce. There is no standard definition of part-time working – legislation defines a part-time worker as a person who does fewer hours than full-time workers in the same establishment[48] – but for statistical purposes we will take it to be anyone who works 30 or fewer hours per week. On this basis, 26.4% of all persons in employment are part-timers.[49] Part-time working is more prevalent among women than men: around 11.2% of male workers are part-timers whereas the figure is 44.2% for women. Women make up around 77% of the part-time workforce. For many years, the law adopted a neoclassical approach towards part-time workers. The law did not require employers to treat them in the same way as full-time workers, and indeed some differential treatment of part-timers was enshrined in legislation. The argument was that part-time work was an important source of new jobs. Employers would not create such jobs unless they were cheap. Nowadays, more emphasis is placed on a rights approach: part-timers' dignity is infringed where they are treated differently.

The fact that the part-time workforce is predominantly female has played a significant role in the development of legal protection for part-timers. In the past,

45 WTR 1998, reg. 21.
46 WTR 1998, reg. 23.
47 For early empirical evidence, see Neathey and Arrowsmith, above n. 43, chapter 5.
48 Part-time Workers (Prevention of Less Favourable Treatment) Regulations 2000 (SI 2000/1551), reg. 2.
49 Source: National Statistics *Labour Force Survey* (March–May 2003) (http://www.statistics.gov.uk).

legislation discriminated against part-timers by making it more difficult for them to qualify for certain legal rights, such as the right not to be unfairly dismissed.[50] Those who worked for fewer than eight hours per week could not claim at all, and those who worked for fewer than 16 hours per week could only claim after they had worked for the employer for five years, whereas the requirement for full-timers was two years' continuous service. These exclusions were challenged using sex discrimination law. In *ex p. EOC*, it was held that the requirements to work for more than eight hours per week and to work for five years for the same employer before a claim could be brought were harder for women than men to comply with because a majority of part-timers were women.[51] This amounted to indirect discrimination on grounds of sex and was unlawful.

As part of the EU's strategy of regulating various forms of 'atypical work', the social partners have agreed a Directive on part-time work[52] which was transposed into English law by the Part-time Workers (Prevention of Less Favourable Treatment) Regulations 2000 (PTWR 2000).[53] In contrast to the sex discrimination solution, the Regulations protect men who work part-time as well as women. The main provision is reg. 5, which states that an employer may not treat a part-timer less favourably than a comparable full-timer. Importantly, however, the employer's obligation to treat part-timers in the same way as comparable full-timers is not absolute. The employer may continue to treat part-timers differently where it can offer objective justification for its actions.[54]

The main criticism of the Regulations from a rights perspective relates to the way in which a 'comparable full-timer' is defined.[55] To be comparable, the full-timer must be engaged in broadly similar work and must work under the same type of contract.[56] This means that a part-time employee can only compare him- or herself with a full-time employee, and that a part-time worker can only compare him- or herself with a full-time worker.[57] Thus, no comparison will be possible in the (highly plausible) situation in which all the full-timers are employees and all the part-timers have workers' contracts. According to the government's own figures, only one-sixth of all part-time workers have a comparator within the meaning of the Regulations.[58] As a result, the Regulations fall short of international standards. The PTW Directive does refer to the nature of the comparator's contract as a relevant consideration, so

---

50 Employment Protection (Consolidation) Act 1978, Sch. 13.
51 *R v Secretary of State for Employment, ex p. EOC* [1995] 1 AC 1.
52 Directive 97/81/EC, extended to the UK by Directive 98/23/EC. See M. Jeffrey, 'Not really going to work? Of the Directive on Part-Time Work, "Atypical Work" and attempts to regulate it' (1998) 27 *ILJ* 193.
53 SI 2000/1551, as amended by SI 2002/2035.
54 PTWR 2000, reg. 5(2).
55 A. McColgan, 'Missing the point? The PTWR 2000' (2000) 29 *ILJ* 260.
56 PTWR 2000, reg. 2.
57 There is an exception which allows individuals who have changed from full-time to part-time work to compare their new terms and conditions with their old ones, regardless of contract type: PTWR 2000, regs. 3 and 4.
58 DTI, *PTWR Regulatory Impact Assessment*, available at http://www.dti.gov.uk/er/ptriasum.htm.

on a narrow reading the government's transposition may be justified.[59] However, as McColgan explains, the Directive provides that where this strict comparison cannot be made, 'comparison shall be made ... in accordance with national law, collective agreements or practice'.[60] In the SDA 1975 and RRA 1976, a hypothetical person may be used as a comparator.[61] So it could be argued that the government should have provided this as an option because it would have been 'in accordance with national law'. The ILO standard requires that the comparator be employed in similar work and in the same type of employment relationship, but it is nevertheless quite generous in that it allows the worker to compare across firms if necessary. The comparator:

> is employed in the same establishment or, when there is no comparable full-time worker in that establishment, in the same enterprise or, when there is no comparable full-time worker in that enterprise, in the same branch of activity

as the part-time worker.[62] Thus, although the law purports to adopt a rights approach, its bold stance is undermined by the technical hurdles it places in the way of claimants. Again, it seems that concerns about the cost to firms of granting generous protection may have had some influence.

Rules applicable to workers with family responsibilities

So far, we have focused on the ways in which the law addresses the needs of full-time and part-time workers in general. We will now turn to a group of measures which are designed specifically to address the problems faced by workers with family responsibilities. Balancing work and family life is a serious issue for many workers. For example, in 2002, of the women whose youngest child was under five, 36% worked part-time and 17% worked full-time.[63] Of the women whose youngest child was between five and ten, 44% were working part-time and 26% full-time.

Several of the international instruments discussed above oblige the state to take measures to ensure that workers have access to childcare facilities. However, there is a considerable shortfall of places in the UK. In 2001, there were 5,709,403 children under the age of eight,[64] and a mere 1,176,000 childcare places for this age group.[65] Inevitably, the shortage of places serves to raise the price which can be charged for them, so that they are affordable only to high- or middle-income families. Access to childcare is a particular problem for lone parents who are unable to share their responsibilities with a spouse or partner and are therefore more dependent on state- or market-provided services. However, the measures which might be taken to

---

59 Directive 97/81/EC, Annex, Clause 3.
60 McColgan, above n. 55.
61 See chapter 7.
62 ILO, above n. 14, Article 1.
63 Source: National Statistics *Social Trends* (2003) (http://www.statistics.gov.uk).
64 Source: National Statistics *Census 2001* (http://www.statistics.gov.uk).
65 Above n. 63.

improve the availability of childcare are largely beyond the scope of this book. They include things like giving employers tax incentives to set up workplace crèches and providing more opportunities for people to train and qualify as childminders. We will focus instead on the obligations the law places on employers to help workers balance their jobs with family life.

The law provides four types of leave. The first is maternity leave.[66] All employees who are expecting a baby, regardless of their length of service, are entitled to ordinary maternity leave of 26 weeks.[67] Those who have completed 26 weeks' service with the employer before the fourteenth week prior to the expected date of childbirth are entitled to additional maternity leave of a further 26 weeks.[68] Additional maternity leave is unpaid. Ordinary maternity leave is paid, but at a special rate. In outline, a woman who has worked for the employer for 26 weeks ending with the fifteenth week before the expected date of childbirth, and whose earnings have reached a specified minimum amount, qualifies for Statutory Maternity Pay (SMP).[69] For the first six weeks, SMP is 90% of the woman's normal weekly earnings. For the remaining 20 weeks, SMP is 90% of the woman's normal weekly earnings or £100, whichever is *lower*.[70] Employers are reimbursed by the government for the SMP payments they make.[71] Women who do not qualify for SMP may be able to claim social security benefits instead. The employee is entitled to return from ordinary maternity leave to the same job on the same terms and conditions as if she had not been away.[72] The same entitlement applies in the case of additional maternity leave unless it is not reasonably practicable for the employer to permit this. In such situations the employer must offer suitable alternative work.[73]

The law also provides a much more limited right to paternity leave.[74] This is available to employees who have worked for 26 weeks ending with the fifteenth week before the expected date of childbirth.[75] They must either be the biological father of the child or the spouse or partner of the mother, and must expect to have responsibility for the child's upbringing.[76] The leave may be for one week or two

---

66 The provisions on maternity leave are contained in ERA 1996, ss. 71–5, but they have been substantially amended, most recently by the EA 2002. Details are fleshed out in the Maternity and Parental Leave etc. Regulations 1999 (SI 1999/3312) (MPLR 1999), as amended by SI 2001/4010 and SI 2002/2789. For their basis in EC law see the Pregnant Workers Directive (Directive 92/85/EEC).

67 ERA 1996, s. 71.

68 ERA 1996, s. 73; MPLR 1999, reg. 5.

69 Social Security Contributions and Benefits Act 1992, s. 164 (SSCBA 1992) (as amended). Details are set out in the Statutory Maternity Pay (General) Regulations 1986 (SI 1986/1960) which have been significantly amended by SI 2002/2690.

70 SSCBA 1992, s. 166.

71 SSCBA 1992, s. 167.

72 MPLR 1999, reg. 18(1). Where there is a redundancy situation, reg. 10 applies.

73 MPLR 1999, reg. 18(2).

74 ERA 1996, ss. 80A–E, inserted by EA 2002. Detail is set out in the Paternity and Adoption Leave Regulations 2002 (SI 2002/2788) (PALR 2002).

75 PALR 2002, reg. 4.

76 PALR 2002, reg. 4.

consecutive weeks (at the employee's choice)[77] and must in general be taken within 56 days of the birth of the child.[78] Most employees are entitled to Statutory Paternity Pay (SPP) which is 90% of the employee's weekly earnings or £100, whichever is the lower.[79] Since the leave period is relatively short, the employee is entitled to return to the same job at the end of it.[80]

The right to parental leave is available to parents who wish to have time off work to look after their child.[81] To qualify, the parent must be an employee who has worked for the same employer for one year.[82] The entitlement is to 13 weeks' leave per child.[83] It must be taken before the child is five years old.[84] There is no obligation on the employer to pay the employee while he or she is on parental leave. The employee is entitled to return to his or her old job if he or she has taken leave of up to four weeks. If he or she has taken a longer period of leave, he or she is entitled to return to the same job unless this is not reasonably practicable, in which case a suitable alternative must be offered.[85]

The final statutory right to leave is the right to emergency leave contained in ERA 1996, s. 57A.[86] This right is available only to employees but there is no requirement to have worked for the employer for any period of time before using the right. It can be invoked when an emergency occurs concerning one of the employee's dependants: a spouse, child or parent, or another person living in the same household such as a partner or another relative.[87] The emergencies covered include: when a dependant is ill or injured, when a dependant dies, when it is necessary to make arrangements for the care of a dependant, or when established care arrangements break down.[88] The entitlement is to take a 'reasonable' amount of time off to deal with the emergency.[89] The government's guidance, which is not legally binding, gives as an example the case of an employee whose child has chickenpox.[90] The guidance suggests that two weeks' leave to care for the child until he or she is better would not be reasonable, whereas two days' leave to take the child to the doctor and to make arrangements for his or her care for the remainder of the illness would be reasonable. If the employer and employee cannot agree on the appropriate duration of the leave, the employee can complain to the Employment Tribunal and seek compensation.[91] There is no

---

77 ERA 1996, s. 80A(3); PALR 2002, reg. 5.
78 ERA 1996, s. 80A(4).
79 SSCBA 1992, ss. 171ZA–J; Statutory Paternity Pay and Statutory Adoption Pay (General) Regulations 2002 (SI 2002/2822).
80 PALR 2002, regs. 13–14.
81 ERA 1996, ss. 76–80 (inserted by ERA 1999, s. 7, Sch. 4), implementing the Parental Leave Directive (Directive 96/34/EC) agreed by the social partners. For detail see MPLR 1999 (as amended).
82 MPLR 1999, reg. 13.
83 MPLR 1999, reg. 14.
84 MPLR 1999, reg. 15.
85 MPLR 1999, regs. 18 and 18A. Where there is a redundancy situation, reg. 10 applies.
86 Inserted by ERA 1999, s. 8, Sch. 4, implementing the Parental Leave Directive (Directive 96/34/EC).
87 ERA 1996, s. 57A(3)–(5).
88 ERA 1996, s. 57A(1).
89 ERA 1996, s. 57A(1).
90 DTI, *Time Off for Dependants* (URN 99/1186) (1999), p. 7.
91 ERA 1996, s. 57B.

legal obligation on the employer to pay the employee during a period of emergency leave.

A first point to note about these various rights is that they are available only to employees, and sometimes only to employees who have satisfied a qualifying period. As we saw in chapter 5, this is difficult to justify from a rights perspective. Atypical workers are not left wholly unprotected: they may be able to claim under the SDA 1975. The courts assume that women have a greater role in childcare than men, so if the employer ignores a woman's childcare responsibilities it may be discriminating against her. Moreover, the *Dekker* decision makes clear that any discrimination on grounds of pregnancy counts as direct sex discrimination.[92] However, this creates a considerable degree of uncertainty for workers, who may have to resort to litigation to determine their rights. From a neoclassical perspective, the fact that these rights are not granted to workers makes a major contribution to the cheapness of atypical work. Theorists in this tradition argue that employers will create more jobs as a result.

A second point to note is that much of this leave is unpaid, or paid at a rate which is much lower than most workers' usual earnings.[93] Neoclassical theorists would argue that this is essential: employers cannot be expected to pay workers while they are absent. Moreover, employers will in any event face the expense of hiring and training substitute workers, particularly for longer periods of leave. A new institutional critique would take a very different stance. The new institutionalists are concerned to get more workers into the labour market and to retain them even when they start a family. This goal will only be achieved if the leave provisions make a practical difference to workers' lives. Many workers may not be able to manage without their pay for 13 weeks while they take parental leave. Many women may not be able to avail themselves of their right to additional maternity leave because it is unpaid. This does not necessarily mean that employers should be made to pay: subsidies could be provided by the government. The real question is whether the rights are sufficiently useful to persuade people to combine paid work with family life.

A third point relates to the concern expressed in our rights discussion that parental leave provisions might have the unfortunate side-effect of stereotyping women and perpetuating the view that childcare is their responsibility alone. Theorists in this tradition find much to criticise in the law as it currently stands. The fact that parental leave is unpaid makes it unlikely that men will use it. One reason for this is that due to the gender pay gap, women earn less on average than men. If anyone is to give up their wage, it is rational for the woman to do so where she is less well paid. These predictions are reinforced by the empirical evidence from other European countries.[94] Where parental leave is paid, the take-up among men is significantly higher than where it is unpaid. The introduction of a right to unpaid

---

92 Case C-177/88 *Dekker v VJV-Centrum* [1991] IRLR 27.
93 See, generally, A. McColgan, 'Family-friendly frolics: the MPLR 1999' (2000) 29 *ILJ* 125.
94 S. Fredman, *Women and the Law* (1997), pp. 219–20.

parental leave will do nothing to promote the cause of equal parenting. Moreover, the rights as they currently stand also reinforce the view that the only type of family responsibility is parental responsibility. With the notable exception of the right to emergency leave, which can be used for parents or other relatives living in the same household, the law does nothing to help those who care for people other than children.

The rights we have considered so far give employees the possibility of taking specific periods of time off work in order to perform their family responsibilities. However, these rights do not help with the daily struggle to make sure that someone is free to collect the children from school each day or to care for them during the holidays. Many parents deal with this by working part-time or working flexible hours. But a major difficulty is that employers often insist that certain jobs can only be done on a standard full-time basis. This means that a person who wishes to work flexibly or part-time may have to resign and seek a new job. Research shows that many women who work part-time are overqualified for their jobs.[95] This suggests that those moving to part-time work may have to move to lower-paid and less challenging work.

The law has tackled this in two main ways. First, some cases have held that an employer's insistence that a job can only be done full-time may be unlawful under the SDA 1975.[96] The courts acknowledge that women have a greater responsibility for childcare. This means that when an employer imposes a requirement of full-time working, the proportion of women who can comply is considerably smaller than the proportion of men who can comply. This amounts to indirect discrimination,[97] although the employer does have the opportunity of defending itself by showing that there are good business reasons for the requirement to work full-time. The SDA 1975 may also help male workers, but only where the employer allows women with childcare responsibilities to work part-time. If the employer denies this right to male workers in a similar position, the employer is committing an act of direct sex discrimination.[98]

Second, the government has recently introduced a right to request flexible working which is available to both men and women independently of the SDA 1975.[99] The right is afforded to employees (not workers) who have worked for at least 26 weeks for their employer.[100] They must be the parent of a child under six and they must be seeking to work flexibly in order to care for that child.[101] The employee

---

95 S. Horrell, J. Rubery and B. Burchell, 'Unequal jobs or unequal pay?' (1989) 20 *Industrial Relations Journal* 176.

96 For example, *Home Office v Holmes* [1984] IRLR 299. The SDA 1975 is explained in more detail in chapter 7.

97 SDA 1975, s. 1(1)(b).

98 SDA 1975, s. 1(1)(a).

99 ERA 1996, ss. 80F–I, inserted by EA 2002, s. 47.

100 ERA 1996, s. 80F(1); Flexible Working (Eligibility, Complaints and Remedies) Regulations 2002 (SI 2002/3236) (FWER 2002), reg. 3.

101 ERA 1996, s. 80F; FWER 2002, reg. 3.

may ask the employer for permission to do one of three things: to work a different number of hours, to work at different times, or to work from home.[102] For example, the employee could ask to work part-time or to work only during school hours. Detailed provision is made for the employer to hold a meeting with the employee to discuss the request and to provide written reasons for its decision.[103] Under ERA 1996, s. 80G(1)(b), the employer may only refuse the employee's request if one of a set of listed reasons applies. They include 'additional costs', 'inability to re-organise work among existing staff', 'inability to recruit additional staff', 'detrimental impact on performance' and so on.

The right to request flexible working has been highly controversial. From a neoclassical perspective, it interferes with the employer's ability to organise the workplace as it sees fit. For rights theorists, it is inadequate: the employee is only allowed to make a request and the employer who wants to refuse can easily identify a legitimate reason for doing so. More fundamentally, rights theorists argue that the right to reconcile work and family life should be given a bolder interpretation in English law. This would involve not only providing rights for working parents, but also reviewing traditional patterns of working time more generally. If it were made compulsory, the 48-hour week could play a role in helping working parents by forcing working fathers to reduce their hours, thus giving them more time to spend with their families. And part-time work could be viewed in a wholly different light. If part-time work is seen as a vital technique for parents seeking to reconcile work and family life, the right not to be discriminated against on the grounds of working part-time does not go very far towards meeting their needs. First, it can be argued that everyone should have the right to choose part-time working (perhaps with exceptions where the employer could show a business justification for full-time working) so that they can reconcile work and family life.[104] The right to request flexible working points in this direction but its impact is limited by the fact that the employer can easily refuse a request. Second, it could be argued that part-time workers should benefit from some protection with regard to the duration and timing of their work.[105] If the purpose of part-time work for many is to reconcile work and family life, it is very important that the work is regular and reliable. A worker who needs to organise childcare is unlikely to be able to come in to work at very short notice. Some employers have designed contracts which ensure that part-timers are given notice before their hours are increased, or which limit working hours to school terms, in order to enable workers to manage their childcare arrangements.[106] For some writers, the right to reconciliation is a radical force with implications for all

---

102 ERA 1996, s. 80F(1)(a).
103 ERA 1996, s. 80G; Flexible Working (Procedural Requirements) Regulations 2002 (SI 2002/3207).
104 The government considered this option before introducing the right to request flexible working but decided that it was too strict.
105 See M. Jeffery, 'Not really going to work? Of the directive on part-time work, atypical work and attempts to regulate it' (1998) 27 *ILJ* 193.
106 M. Cully *et al.*, *Britain at Work* (1999), p. 75, found that 19% of workplaces studied offered term-time only contracts.

aspects of working time, not just parental leave provisions. It is not difficult to imagine the neoclassical response.

Further reading

For detailed textbook accounts of this topic, see S. Deakin and G.S. Morris, *Labour Law* (3rd edn., 2001), chapters 4.6 and 6.6; or H. Collins, K.D. Ewing and A. McColgan, *Labour Law: Text and Materials* (2001), chapter 4.

The most substantial body of literature concerns family-friendly rights. To get a flavour of the new institutional economics arguments, one of the most useful sources is the DTI's Green Paper, *Work and Parents: Competitiveness and Choice*, published in 2000. It is sometimes argued that rights for working parents are counterproductive. Employers become hostile to working parents because they might invoke costly rights, and co-workers become resentful because they have to cover parents' absences from work. Do you think these are real risks? If so, can the law be used to change people's attitudes? Would the Green Paper persuade people who were hostile or resentful? For a detailed analysis of the empirical evidence about the costs to employers of family-friendly policies, see S. Holtermann, 'The costs and benefits to British employers of measures to promote equality of opportunity', in J. Humphries and J. Rubery (eds.), *The Economics of Equal Opportunities* (1995).

For a good introduction to the rights perspective, see S. Fredman, *Women and the Law* (1997), chapter 5; and J. Conaghan, 'Women, work and family: a British revolution?', in J. Conaghan *et al.* (eds.), *Labour Law in an Era of Globalization* (2002). C. McGlynn, 'Reclaiming a feminist vision: the reconciliation of paid work and family life in European Union law and policy' (2001) *Columbia Journal of European Law* 241, offers an excellent theoretical discussion of the right to reconciliation and a critique of the EC's approach. When reading these articles, you need to think about the core problem of how to implement the right to reconciliation without perpetuating stereotypes about the role of women in childcare. Which aspects of the current law might perpetuate stereotypes? How should they be reformed? What are the limits of labour law in promoting equal parenting? What other government policies might be relevant? For a broader discussion of the issues, see J. Williams, *Unbending Gender: Why Work and Family Conflict and What To Do About It* (2000).

There is very little theoretical literature on the rights and economics aspects of working time more generally. For a detailed critique of the legislation, see C. Barnard (1999) 28 *ILJ* 61 and (2000) 29 *ILJ* 167. To learn more about the Directive and its regulatory technique, see either C. Barnard, 'EC "Social" Policy', in P. Craig and G. de Búrca (eds.), *The Evolution of EU Law* (1999); or B. Bercusson, *European Labour Law* (1996), chapter 21.

The role of negotiations with trade union representatives or worker representatives in modifying the obligations set out in the WTR 1998 has attracted particular interest. Labour lawyers who are particularly concerned with collective rights have welcomed this development as an opportunity for trade unions to re-establish themselves in the workplace. It has also been supported as an example of 'smart' regulation in the new institutional tradition: see H. Collins, 'Is there a third way in labour law?', in J. Conaghan *et al.*, *Labour Law in an Era of Globalization* (2002). What are the benefits of alienable rights for firms? What are the benefits of such rights for workers? What are the risks for workers associated with alienable rights? And what costs do firms face when negotiating with worker representatives about these rights?

Working time rights are often cited as an example of the 'utopian' nature of economic and social rights. Do you agree? Are they more powerful if they are based on the right to safe and healthy working conditions? Is the Working Time Directive genuinely based on health and safety rights? Could working time rights be more effectively justified using the right not to be discriminated against or the right to reconcile work and family life?

7

Discrimination

Discrimination is perhaps one of the most controversial topics in labour law when it is viewed from the rights and economics perspectives. First, there is controversy between the two camps. Rights theorists are almost universally in favour of legislation to combat discrimination, whereas some (though by no means all) economists argue that governmental intervention is unnecessary. Second, there is controversy within each camp. Within the rights camp, for example, there is a fierce debate surrounding the concept of equality. Within the economics camp, there is a debate about the costs and benefits of tackling discrimination and even a debate about whether or not discrimination exists at all.

This chapter will begin by considering economics perspectives on discrimination, since they offer a good introduction to the debate as to whether or not the law should intervene at all in this area. We will then consider the rights perspectives, which will help to explain what form legal intervention should take if it occurs. And we will conclude with a discussion of English law. The law adopts a rights perspective, but we need to ask which rights perspective it is and whether it is at all influenced by economic factors.

Economics perspectives

Our discussion of economic accounts of discrimination will be divided into two sections: those accounts which do not support legal intervention, and those which may be used to do so. In the former category, we find the argument that much alleged 'discrimination' may not be discrimination at all, and the argument that discrimination does exist but will ultimately be cured by the market itself. In the latter category, we find the statistical discrimination and crowding theories.

Arguments against legal intervention

Some theorists argue that what may appear to be discrimination in the labour market can be explained in other ways. This argument is most commonly made in relation to sex discrimination and we will take this as our example. One version of the argument is based on theories about investments in 'human capital'.[1] This is economists' shorthand for education or training which makes a worker more productive. Let us imagine the case of someone deciding whether or not to go to university. He or she must weigh the cost of getting a degree against the salary he or she will be able to secure as a graduate. If the salary is likely to be sufficient to pay off student loans and to make up for three years without earnings, the rational person will do a degree. Now imagine a woman who plans to leave the labour market after a couple of years in order to raise a family. She will only earn the higher salary for a short period of time, so she may calculate that it would not be rational to go to university because the costs of doing so would be higher than the benefits. On this theory, many of the women in the labour market will be less well qualified than men. As a result, they will end up in lower-paid jobs. But this is due to the choices they have made, not to discrimination.

Another version of the theory focuses less on human capital and more on the degree of effort men and women are willing to expend on their jobs.[2] This approach starts with the assumption that although women now participate in the labour market to a very great extent, they still retain primary responsibility for childcare and housework. This means that their energies are divided between labour market work and domestic work. Two results follow. First, women expend less energy when they are at work. Because they are less productive than men, they earn less. Second, women seek jobs which are less energy-intensive. This explains why many women seek part-time work, or avoid jobs which involve commuting or foreign travel. These jobs tend to be lower-paid. Again, therefore, women's disadvantage in the labour market can be explained by their choices and may not be the result of discrimination.

Not surprisingly, the rational choice approach has prompted a furious reaction from critics. One response is to argue that women's choices may be made in the light of the discrimination they expect to encounter in the labour market[3] (a possibility acknowledged by Becker in his account of the effort theory[4]). For example, a woman may be aware that because of employers' prejudices, she is unlikely to be promoted beyond a certain level in the firm. It would not be rational for her to seek additional qualifications when she is unlikely to get a better job which would enable her to recoup her training costs. Another response is to argue that women's so-called 'choices' are in fact constrained by various factors such as social attitudes.[5] A woman's 'choice' of a part-time job located near her home might reflect the fact that her partner, family and friends assume that she will have primary responsibility for her children. She might prefer a different job, but her choice is *constrained* by the need to fulfil social expectations about the role of a mother. Whichever approach is

---

1 See, generally, G. S. Becker, *Human Capital* (3rd edn., 1993).
2 G.S. Becker, 'Human capital, effort, and the sexual division of labor' (1985) 3 *Journal of Labor Economics* S33–S58.
3 S. Fredman, *Women and the Law* (1997), p. 406.
4 Becker, above n. 2.
5 Fredman, above n. 3.

adopted, the underlying argument is the same: discrimination, not women's choices, is the cause of women's disadvantage.

In fact, most economists acknowledge some force in their opponents' claims. The real debate turns on how much of women's disadvantage to attribute to non-discriminatory factors and how much to discriminatory ones. A number of empirical studies have sought to disentangle women's choices from the discrimination they encounter, but given the complexity of the issues involved, these studies are rarely conclusive.[6] For our purposes, the important point is that few would deny the existence of *some* discrimination.

Nevertheless, not all would acknowledge that discrimination is a problem which requires a legal solution. Many economists claim that discrimination will ultimately be eliminated by market forces. Again, the pioneering work on this issue has been done by Becker.[7] He argues that discrimination is a 'taste' or preference for which employers are willing to pay. For example, a homophobic employer might be willing to pay an extra £2 per hour (called a 'discrimination coefficient') in order to obtain a workforce made up entirely of heterosexuals. This might mean paying £10 an hour to heterosexual workers but only hiring a gay or lesbian worker if he or she was willing to accept less than £8 per hour. According to Becker, this situation is not sustainable over the longer term. The employer's products must compete in the market. A non-discriminating competitor could easily take advantage by employing gay and lesbian workers at £8 per hour. The competitor's products would be cheaper and would ultimately drive the discriminating firm out of the market.

The main criticism of Becker's theory is that it is not supported by the empirical evidence. Discrimination against homosexuals and other disadvantaged groups has persisted over time, and although it has become less prevalent in many cases, it has not been eliminated altogether. There are some obvious explanations for this. First, Becker's model assumes that employers know that the workers from the favoured and unfavoured groups are equally productive. In reality, however, employers' prejudices may lead them to think that certain groups are less productive than others.[8] The government's policy that gays and lesbians could not be employed in the armed forces was based, in part, on the argument that their presence would impede operational efficiency.[9] Where employers hold beliefs of this nature, they will not perceive any advantage in employing members of the unfavoured group, even at a lower wage. Second, Becker's model assumes that there is perfect competition in the employer's product market. Any tiny difference in labour costs could make or break a firm's fortunes. However, this may not be the case in practice.[10] Some

---

6 For a critique, see B.R. Bergmann, 'Does the market for women's labor need fixing?' (1989) 3 *Journal of Economic Perspectives* 43.

7 G.S. Becker, *The Economics of Discrimination* (1957).

8 Fredman, above n. 3.

9 See *R v Ministry of Defence, ex p. Smith* [1996] QB 517 (CA).

10 See Bergmann, above n. 6, at 50.

firms may have a monopoly or may sell in markets in which consumers' decisions are not based solely on price.

Arguments which might support legal intervention

Some economists have produced alternative explanations of discrimination in labour markets which may be more supportive of legal intervention. The theory of 'statistical discrimination' suggests that discrimination may benefit employers. This means that it is unlikely to disappear unless the law intervenes. But it also suggests that anti-discrimination laws would impose costs on employers. The 'crowding model' demonstrates that discrimination is inefficient for society as a whole. This theory supports legal intervention more clearly because it identifies a positive economic benefit which would flow from anti-discrimination policies.

When an employer is making a hiring decision, it gathers information about each applicant. But information-gathering is costly, so employers make some decisions based on the average characteristics of the group to which the person belongs. These decisions are accurate in themselves, but they discriminate against anyone in the group who does not share the average characteristics. This is the theory of 'statistical discrimination'.[11] Imagine that the employer is looking for someone to do a job involving heavy lifting. The employer considers that it would be too expensive to conduct a medical check on all applicants. But the employer has evidence that a majority of people over the age of 50 have health problems which make them unsuitable for physical work. As a result, it decides to exclude all applicants who are 50 or over. This discriminates against anyone in that group who is physically fit enough to do the job.

The statistical discrimination theory presents employers as the beneficiaries of discrimination. Their use of statistics sometimes means that they miss out on productive workers who do not fit the characteristics of their group. But this is not a hiring mistake on the part of the employer. The employer is acting rationally because the benefits of identifying that worker are not sufficient to outweigh the costs of more comprehensive investigations at the hiring stage. Employers only make hiring mistakes on this theory when they use out-of-date or inaccurate statistics. The theory could be used to justify legal intervention in the sense that it shows that employers have no incentive to combat discrimination by themselves: why would they seek to eliminate it if they are its beneficiaries? However, it also shows that anti-discrimination laws impose costs on employers. Instead of making stereotypical assumptions about individuals on the basis of their membership of a group, employers would be obliged to seek detailed information about each individual as part of the hiring process. In our example, the employer would be forced to conduct costly medical checks.

11 One of the earliest versions is E.S. Phelps, 'The statistical theory of racism and sexism' (1972) 62 *American Economic Review* 659. For refinements see D.J. Aigner and G.G. Cain, 'Statistical theories of discrimination in labor markets' (1977) 30 *Industrial and Labor Relations Review* 175. See also L.C. Thurow, *Generating Inequality* (1976), chapter 7.

Another theory of discrimination is the 'crowding model'.[12] This theory focuses on the empirical evidence that women and members of the ethnic minorities have often found it difficult to enter certain jobs (often ones which are well paid) and tend to end up 'crowded' into other (usually low-paid) occupations. A simple model will help to explain the theory. Imagine that there is a workforce of 60 men and 60 women, and three jobs: truck driver, car mechanic and childminder. There is an equal demand for workers to do each of the three jobs, so ideally there should be around 40 workers in each job. But employers make the stereotypical assumptions that women are bad drivers and cannot fix cars but are good at caring for children. This means that the 60 men will be employed either as truck drivers or as car mechanics (say 30 of each) and the 60 women will be employed as childminders. Because the men are in short supply, they will receive high wages. And because there are too many women fighting over the childminding jobs, their wages will be low.

What would happen if anti-discrimination laws were passed? Assuming that the laws were effective, women workers would be able to move into the hitherto forbidden occupations of truck driver and car mechanic. Since we assumed that the demand for labour in all three jobs was equal, the market should ultimately achieve the equilibrium position in which there are around 40 workers in each job: 10 women would give up childminding to become mechanics, and 10 women would give up childminding to become truck drivers. At this point, the wages for all three occupations would be equal. Wages for childminders would increase because there would no longer be an oversupply of workers. Wages for car mechanics and truck drivers would decrease because there would no longer be a shortage of workers. Because men would lose out, it seems unlikely that the discriminating employers would bring about this change of their own accord: it would be too unpopular with their workers. Legislation would be required.

But the significant difference between the crowding model and the other theories we have examined is that it does identify an economic benefit from ending occupational segregation. It leads to a more efficient allocation of labour. When the 20 women leave childcare, there is a loss of output in that sector. But there is a gain in output in car mechanics and truck driving because of the extra 10 women in each. Since the pay in these last two occupations is higher than was the women's pay when all the women were childminders, it is apparent that employers place a higher value on their output in these new jobs. In other words, the value to the employer of each extra mechanic or driver is greater than the value of additional childminders. If certain assumptions are made,[13] economists can demonstrate that this additional value to the employer is equal to the additional value to *society as a whole* of having more people working in those jobs. This is common sense: the artificial labour shortages created by discrimination cannot be good for the economy.

---

12 See B.R. Bergmann, *The Economic Emergence of Women* (1986), chapters 5 and 6.
13 The key assumptions are perfect competition in the labour market and perfect competition in the market for the firm's products.

Of course, in the real world, these advantages might take some time to materialise. The simple model we have been using assumes that there are no costs involved for the women in changing careers. But this is obviously not the case in practice. The women would have to acquire the necessary training in order to become mechanics or truck drivers. They might find that this training is unavailable to them because of discrimination. Or they might decide not to incur the costs of training in case they meet with prejudice and are unable to get a new job at the end of it. These concerns seem to be borne out by the empirical evidence, which shows that some careers remain heavily male-dominated despite the long-standing prohibitions on discrimination contained in English law.

The statistical discrimination and crowding models are, of course, interrelated. Crowding may occur for many reasons. Some employers may simply be prejudiced: they may make assumptions about the capabilities of particular groups without any evidence at all to support their views. Others may contribute to crowding because of their use of statistical data. For example, an employer which has to provide costly training to its staff and needs them to stay in work for a considerable period in order to recoup those costs might decide not to employ young women because they are statistically more likely than other groups to take breaks from the labour market in order to have children. This might result in women being crowded into occupations which do not require much training.

The two theories we have considered in this section suggest that there may be economic costs and benefits if anti-discrimination laws are enacted. Employers may face greater hiring costs, but the value of outputs across the economy as a whole may be increased. However, even those who advocate anti-discrimination laws on economic grounds would probably accept the need to look to rights arguments as well. As we have seen, although the crowding model predicts some advantages if discrimination is ended, these advantages may take some time to materialise. In the meantime, employers' concerns about their increased hiring costs may come to seem overwhelmingly important. Rights arguments can help to combat these problems by supporting the enactment of legislation even if the economic benefits are insubstantial or delayed. And rights arguments are useful for another reason. Anti-discrimination legislation comes in many different shapes and sizes. Rights arguments can help us to choose among the various possibilities.

Rights perspectives

All the major international human rights instruments contain a right to equal treatment. The only significant difference between them lies in the groups they seek to protect. Some groups have secured public support relatively recently, so they are protected only by more modern instruments. But equality is not a simple concept, so we will need to draw on the literature and on some of the more detailed instruments in order to determine exactly what the right to equal treatment means.

Who is protected?

Most instruments offer a list of those groups who are deemed to be protected against discrimination. The traditional formulation is:

> race, colour, sex, language, religion, political or other opinion, national or social origin, property, birth or other status.[14]

A more modern and comprehensive list is to be found in the EU Charter, which states in Article 21(1) that:

> Any discrimination based on any ground such as sex, race, colour, ethnic or social origin, genetic features, language, religion or belief, political or any other opinion, membership of a national minority, property, birth, disability, age or sexual orientation shall be prohibited.

The inclusion of 'genetic features' is a useful illustration of how discrimination law needs to develop over time. It is only in relatively recent years that it has become possible for scientists to identify the genes which are responsible for particular medical conditions. This opens up the possibility that an employer might refuse to hire someone on the grounds that he or she was likely to develop an illness in later life.

The advantage of listing the groups to be protected is that it guides states in their efforts to comply with international standards, and judges in their attempts to interpret those standards. The disadvantage is that it can be inflexible, making it difficult to accommodate newly recognised victims of discrimination.[15] Most instruments deal with this by indicating that the list of prohibited grounds is not exhaustive. Article 14 of the ECHR begins its list with the phrase 'such as' (to show that the list is illustrative) and ends it with 'or other status' (to make clear that other grounds can be added). But in order to work out what else could legitimately be added to the list, we need to develop some understanding of what it is that the various recognised grounds of discrimination have in common.

It is clear when one looks at the historical development of discrimination law that political factors have played a key role in determining which characteristics would be included. Affected groups have secured the law's protection after mounting extensive lobbying campaigns.[16] Nevertheless, commentators continue to search for some underlying theoretical basis for discrimination law. A leading contender is the notion of 'immutability'.[17] We should ignore some characteristics because they cannot be changed by the individual concerned. The individual cannot do anything about his or her race, so we should not treat it as a relevant factor when making

14 United Nations Universal Declaration of Human Rights (UDHR), Article 2; ICESCR, Article 2(2); ICCPR, Article 2(1).

15 S. Fredman, *Discrimination Law* (2002), pp. 67–8.

16 For history, see Fredman, above n. 15, chapter 2.

17 For discussion, see S.A. Marcosson, 'Constructive immutability' (2001) 3 *University of Pennsylvania Journal of Constitutional Law* 646.

employment decisions. However, there are two problems with immutability. First, some characteristics we usually ignore can in fact be changed: for example, religion, sex, and political opinion. But a common response to this is to argue that although individuals can change these characteristics of their own volition, it would be wrong to compel them to do so, because the psychological costs would be enormous. This makes the characteristics immutable in practice. Secondly, we do sometimes use immutable characteristics when making employment decisions. Intelligence is the most obvious example. But the advocates of immutability explain this by saying that society could not function properly if this characteristic was ignored, because it is highly relevant to an individual's ability to do certain jobs.

Other theories about the underlying basis of discrimination law also exist. One is the irrelevance theory: that we disregard certain characteristics because they are not relevant to an individual's ability to do the job.[18] But as we shall see below, there are some exceptional cases in which a person's characteristics may be relevant. The irrelevance theory cannot explain these cases. Another approach is to say that we protect certain characteristics because those who have them have been victims of discrimination in the past. But if a new ground of discrimination were to emerge, like genetic features, this approach would require us to wait for people to suffer discrimination instead of taking preventative action.[19] Finally, some would argue that we should look to a more general, flexible criterion such as whether the treatment of a particular group makes members of that group feel as if they are not valued by society.[20] You need to consider which of these various approaches you find most persuasive.

What constitutes discrimination?

Most of the major human rights instruments we have been considering prohibit 'discrimination' without specifying what is meant by this. At first sight, the answer might seem simple: discrimination occurs when two people who are equal in terms of skills and abilities are treated unequally because one of them has a particular characteristic (is female or Asian or gay or disabled, for example). The problem is that there are at least three different interpretations of what a government needs to do in order to ensure that people are treated equally.

The first is often labelled 'equality as consistency' or 'formal equality'. According to CEDAW, Article 1:

> 'discrimination against women' shall mean any distinction, exclusion or restriction made on the basis of sex which has the ... *purpose* of impairing or nullifying the recognition, enjoyment and exercise by women ... of human rights.[21]

18 J.H. Ely, *Democracy and Distrust* (1980), chapter 6.
19 P.T. Kim, 'Genetic discrimination, genetic privacy: rethinking employee protections for a brave new workplace' (2002) 96 *Northwestern University Law Review* 1497 at 1500.
20 Fredman, above n. 15, p. 82.
21 Emphasis added. See also International Convention on the Elimination of All Forms of Racial Discrimination (ICERD), Article 1; Convention 111, Article 1.

This is the simple idea that likes should be treated alike. It helps to overcome blatant forms of discrimination such as an outright refusal to employ the over-50s. But commentators have pointed out the many limitations of this approach.[22] One is that it depends on finding a 'comparator', a similarly qualified person with whom to claim equal treatment. If an employer dismisses a woman because she is pregnant, we might intuitively respond that this should amount to unlawful sex discrimination. On a strict interpretation of equality as consistency, however, it does not: she cannot show that she has been treated less favourably than a similarly situated man because men cannot be similarly situated and there is therefore no comparator.[23] Another problem is that formal equality only requires equal treatment, not fair treatment. Thus, if the law condemns an employer for refusing to allow people with certain genetic conditions to have access to employer-sponsored health insurance, the employer could respond either by permitting them to join or by ceasing to provide insurance for any of its employees. Both responses treat all the employees equally, but the latter is clearly a bad outcome for all concerned.

A further limitation of formal equality leads us neatly to our second conception, equality of opportunity.[24] The relevant ILO Convention[25] provides:

> Each Member for which this Convention is in force undertakes to declare and pursue a national policy designed to promote, by methods appropriate to national conditions and practice, *equality of opportunity* and treatment in respect of employment and occupation, with a view to eliminating any discrimination in respect thereof.[26]

There is no point in saying that a particular job – say, as an architect – is open to people of all races if the educational system disadvantages young people from certain ethnic groups. Formal equality does nothing to help those individuals who have not been able to obtain the qualifications they need in order to apply for the job. Equality of opportunity seeks to solve this problem by creating what is often called a 'level playing field' between all groups in society. Governmental intervention would be designed to help people from disadvantaged groups to apply for jobs and to have a realistic prospect of success. The state would provide, for example, special training for women who wanted to enter traditionally male-dominated careers. Equality of opportunity usually involves policies outside the scope of employment law. Employers themselves are obliged only to comply with formal equality and to make decisions based solely on merit.

The third interpretation is 'equality of results'.[27] This picks up on another limitation of equality of opportunity. Advocates of equality of results point out that the creation of a 'level playing field' (even if the strategy was properly resourced by the

---

22 Fredman, above n. 15, pp. 7–11.
23 A conclusion reached in the early case of *Turley v Allders Department Stores Ltd* [1980] ICR 66.
24 Fredman, above n. 15, pp. 14–15.
25 Convention 111, Discrimination (Employment and Occupation), 1958.
26 Convention 111, Article 2 (emphasis added). See also CEDAW, Article 3; ICERD, Article 2(2).
27 Fredman, above n. 15, pp. 11–4.

government) would still not guarantee that more individuals from disadvantaged groups would secure particular jobs. They propose at least two solutions. The first and less radical option is to attack the criteria used by employers when selecting people for jobs. The concern is that employers might use criteria which comply with formal equality but in practice operate to the disadvantage of members of a particular group. To quote Article 1 of CEDAW again:

'discrimination against women' shall mean any distinction, exclusion or restriction made on the basis of sex which has the *effect* . . . of impairing or nullifying the recognition, enjoyment and exercise by women . . . of human rights[28]

For example, the employer might require the individual to work all day on a Friday. This applies equally to workers from all religious backgrounds but it may be harder for Muslims to comply with because it interferes with their obligation to attend Friday prayers. Under an equality of results approach, these criteria would be banned, because although they are formally neutral, they *result* in discrimination. As we shall see below, however, employers usually have the opportunity to justify their use of these criteria where they reflect a genuine business need.

Some writers would adopt an even stronger focus on the results of employers' practices. They advocate a second option: that employers should be required to engage in 'positive discrimination' or 'affirmative action'.[29] This means deliberately favouring members of under-represented groups during the recruitment process until equality has been achieved:

Adoption by States Parties of temporary special measures aimed at accelerating *de facto* equality between men and women shall not be considered discrimination as defined in this Convention, but shall in no way entail, as a consequence, the maintenance of unequal or separate standards; these measures shall be discontinued when the objectives of equality of opportunity and treatment have been achieved.[30]

Affirmative action is controversial because it involves discriminating against one group in order to advance the interests of another group. However, its advocates point out that this is only unfair if the two groups are equal to start with. If they are unequal, there is nothing unfair about favouring the previously disadvantaged group. Affirmative action policies may take many different forms. One option is to favour the member of the disadvantaged group only where his or her qualifications are equal to those of applicants from the advantaged group. This can be justified by saying that since their qualifications are equal, it is impossible to choose between them as individuals. Selecting a person in pursuit of the social goal of equality is as fair as, if not fairer than, selecting a person at random. A more controversial option is to favour the member of the disadvantaged group

---

28 Emphasis added. See also ICERD, Article 1; ILO Convention 111, Article 1.
29 See, generally, Fredman, above n. 15, chapter 5.
30 CEDAW, Article 4. See also ICERD, Article 1(4); ILO Convention 111, Article 5.

where he or she is *sufficiently* qualified to do the job, even if there are other applicants from the advantaged group who are better qualified. This makes a greater inroad into the principle that jobs should be allocated on merit and is more likely to prompt claims on the part of members of the advantaged group that they are being treated unfairly. But its advocates offer at least two justifications. One is that members of disadvantaged groups find it difficult to obtain qualifications, despite equal opportunities policies, so this approach will help more people than the equal qualifications option. The other is that members of the advantaged group cannot complain of unfairness since they start from a position of privilege in society, even if they themselves have never been responsible for the discriminatory treatment of others.

Can discrimination ever be justified?

We have already seen that some commentators think that discrimination can be justified. 'Positive discrimination' can be viewed as discrimination against members of a previously advantaged group, but it is justified by the need to redress the balance in favour of members of a disadvantaged group. But the question with which we are concerned in this section is a slightly different one. Is it ever possible to justify discrimination against a *disadvantaged* group?

One circumstance in which discrimination may be justified is in the field of equality of results. We saw in our discussion above that employers might sometimes use selection criteria which seemed neutral but in fact resulted in discrimination against members of a particular group. Such criteria are *prima facie* discriminatory. But it is generally accepted that they may be used where they are genuinely related to the job in question. According to Article 1(2) of the ILO Discrimination Convention, 'any distinction, exclusion or preference in respect of a particular job based on the inherent requirements thereof shall not be deemed to be discrimination'. Thus, an employer would be allowed to use the criterion 'ability to lift heavy weights' for the job of construction worker, even though it would discriminate against women and those with physical disabilities, because it reflects an essential feature of that job.

Another situation in which discrimination might be permitted is where a person's characteristic (race, sex and so on) is what *qualifies* him or her to do the job in question.[31] This exception is also permitted by Article 1(2) of the ILO Convention, quoted above. There are some straightforward examples. If a theatre company is looking for someone to play King Lear, it should be allowed to advertise for a male actor. It would be absurd if this amounted to discrimination. More controversially, if a police force is looking for officers to work on an estate inhabited largely by a particular ethnic group, it might argue that it should be allowed to appoint officers from that group because they are more likely to understand the needs of, and to be

---

31 Note that this differs from affirmative action, in which everyone's qualifications are assessed neutrally, and their characteristics are only used as a tie-breaker.

trusted by, the residents. There is clearly some force in this argument, though it does run the risk of perpetuating stereotypes. It denies people from other ethnic groups the opportunity to demonstrate that they could do the job effectively. Arguments about qualifications always require careful scrutiny.

English law

English law does prohibit discrimination, so it is clear that policy-makers have not adopted two of the economics arguments we considered: that discrimination does not exist at all, and that discrimination will eventually be eliminated by market forces. Instead, the law reflects rights arguments and, more recently, a version of the crowding theory: the argument that employers will benefit if they can recruit from a wider pool of talent. We will concentrate on two key questions. To what extent does the law implement a rights approach, in the scope of protection it offers and in its definition of discrimination? And to what extent does the law reflect the economists' point that anti-discrimination policies might be costly for employers to implement, at least over the short term?

Who is protected?

As we saw in chapter 5, we must always ask whether any particular piece of employment legislation protects employees or workers. English anti-discrimination legislation protects workers and uses the broadest possible definition of that concept.[32] Thus, it includes self-employed people where they undertake to perform the work personally, as well as employees and workers narrowly defined. This reflects the fact that fundamental human rights are at stake. The legislation applies to all aspects of the employment relationship: selection procedures, hiring decisions, terms and conditions of employment, opportunities for promotion and training, and detrimental treatment and dismissal.[33]

For many years, English law concentrated largely on protecting workers against race and sex discrimination. Other groups, if they were to be protected at all, had to bring themselves within these categories. Attempts were made to argue that sex discrimination laws protected against discrimination on grounds of sexual orientation,[34] and that religious discrimination could also constitute racial discrimination.[35] These arguments had varying degrees of success. Recently, the EU's competences were extended to cover a wide range of possible grounds of discrimination.[36] This has led to the enactment of a Framework Directive on Discrimination[37] and

---

32 For example, Employment Equality (Sexual Orientation) Regulations 2003 (SI 2003/1661, EE(SO)R 2003), reg. 2(3).
33 For example, EE(SO)R 2003, reg. 6.
34 See, for example, Case C-249/96 *Grant v South West Trains Ltd* [1998] IRLR 206; *Advocate General for Scotland v Macdonald* [2003] IRLR 512 (HL).
35 See, for example, *Mandla v Dowell Lee* [1983] IRLR 209.
36 Article 13 EC, inserted in 1997.
37 Directive 2000/78/EC.

to new implementing legislation in English law, broadening the scope of our law considerably.[38]

Discrimination on all of the following grounds is prohibited in English law:

- Being male or female (SDA 1975, as amended, ss. 1 and 2;[39] Article 141 EC; Directive 76/207/EEC (the Equal Treatment Directive)[40]).
- Being a transsexual (SDA 1975, s. 2A[41]).
- Being married (but not being unmarried) (SDA 1975, s. 3).
- Race (RRA 1976, as amended, s. 1; Directive 2000/43/EC).

Under s. 3(1), discrimination on racial grounds includes discrimination on grounds of 'colour, race, nationality or ethnic or national origins'. The courts consider factors such as a shared history, a cultural tradition, geographical origin, language, literature and religion when deciding whether or not a particular group constitutes a 'race'.[42]

- Disability (DDA 1995, as amended, ss. 4 and 6; Directive 2000/78/EC).

According to s. 1(1), a person has a disability if he or she 'has a physical or mental impairment which has a substantial and long-term adverse effect on his ability to carry out normal day-to-day activities'.[43] To count as long-term, the disability must have lasted or be expected to last for at least 12 months.[44] The definition includes those who would suffer from a disability were it not for medication,[45] and those who have a progressive condition (such as HIV or multiple sclerosis) which currently has minor effects but might lead to a disability in the future.[46]

- Religion or belief (Employment Equality (Religion or Belief) Regulations 2003 (SI 2003/1660, EE(RB)R 2003), reg. 3; Directive 2000/78/EC).

These new regulations protect people from discrimination on the grounds of 'religion, religious belief, or similar philosophical belief'. This is likely to include non-religious philosophies such as humanism, agnosticism and atheism. However,

---

38 See, generally, S. Fredman, 'Equality: a new generation?' (2001) 30 *ILJ* 145.
39 The Equal Pay Act 1970 is also of relevance, but it will be considered in detail in chapter 8. You should also review the discussion of maternity leave and parental rights in chapter 6.
40 Directive 2002/73/EC amends the Equal Treatment Directive but Member States have until 2005 to implement it.
41 Inserted by the Sex Discrimination (Gender Reassignment) Regulations 1999 (SI 1999/1102), after the ECJ's decision in Case 13/94 *P v S* [1996] ECR I-2143.
42 *Mandla v Dowell Lee* [1983] IRLR 209. See also *Dawkins v Department of the Environment* [1993] IRLR 284.
43 For detail, see Secretary of State for Education and Employment, *Guidance on matters to be taken into account in determining questions relating to the definition of disability* (1996).
44 DDA 1995, Sch. 1, para. 2; Sch. 2, para. 5.
45 DDA 1995, Sch. 1, para. 6.
46 DDA 1995, Sch. 1, para. 8.

the use of the term 'similar' was deliberately intended by the government to exclude political beliefs from the scope of protection.[47]

• Sexual orientation (EE(SO)R 2003, reg. 3; Directive 2000/78/EC).

These new Regulations protect people from discrimination on the grounds that they are, or are thought to be, homosexual, heterosexual, or bisexual.

Article 14 of the ECHR also contains an anti-discrimination guarantee. This can be enforced in the English courts by virtue of the HRA 1998, so it is just as much a part of English law as the provisions we have been considering. However, a major caveat is in order before we consider the content of Article 14. The Article only protects against discrimination which occurs when an individual seeks to exercise one of the other Convention rights.[48] Thus, if an employer banned members of a particular political party from wearing their membership badges at work, a claim could be brought.[49] There is a prima facie breach of Article 10 (freedom of expression) and Article 14 (discrimination on grounds of political opinion). But if the employer refuses to give someone a job because she is a woman, it is difficult to show that a Convention right has been breached. As a result, Article 14 cannot be invoked.[50]

Although the potential of Article 14 is limited, its scope is very broad. It covers 'sex, race, colour, language, religion, political or other opinion, national or social origin, association with a national minority, property, birth or other status'. Thus, it adds a number of prohibited grounds to those we have been considering, such as property and political opinion. Perhaps most significantly, the Article 14 right is not a closed list: other grounds of discrimination can be added under the category of 'other status'. This could occur in one of two ways. First, the UK courts could be persuaded to add a new ground on their own initiative. Second, the UK courts are bound to take into account the Strasbourg jurisprudence when interpreting the Article, so they could be persuaded to adopt new grounds which have been added by the ECtHR. The Strasbourg court has included a number of other grounds, including sexual orientation[51] and illegitimacy.[52]

If we measure English law against one of the most up-to-date lists of grounds, that contained in the EU Charter, what is missing?[53] One major omission is age. This will soon be the subject of legislation because it is covered by the

---

47 See, for example, Cabinet Office, *Towards Equality and Diversity: Implementing the Employment and Race Directives* (2001), paras. 13.4–13.6.
48 The Article prohibits discrimination in 'the enjoyment of the rights and freedoms set forth in this Convention'.
49 Subject to the issues about horizontal effect discussed in chapter 4.
50 Protocol 12 to the ECHR contains a right not to be discriminated against which would apply even if no other Convention right had been infringed. However, the UK government has not ratified it, nor does it form a part of English law.
51 For example, *Salgueiro da Silva Mouta v Portugal* [2001] 31 EHRR 47.
52 For example, *Marckx v Belgium* [1979–80] 2 EHRR 330.
53 It is highly likely that the EU Charter will form part of the new EU Constitution. It will then become a part of English law, but it will apply only to the EU institutions and to the government when it is implementing EU law.

EU Framework Directive, which the UK is required to implement by 2006.[54] At present, where age discrimination also has gender implications, it may occasionally be dealt with through the SDA 1975. In *Price v Civil Service Commission*, the EAT looked favourably on a claim that an upper age limit of 28 in a job advertisement discriminated against women because they were more likely to take breaks from the labour market in their 20s to have children.[55] The other main omission is discrimination on the ground of a person's genetic features. A genetic predisposition to a particular disease is not protected under the DDA 1995, because that Act only applies once someone has a substantial impairment as a result of their disability (or a minor impairment in the case of a medical condition which is going to get worse). It might be possible to persuade the courts to construe the EU Framework Directive (which does not define disability) broadly,[56] or to include genetic discrimination within Article 14 of the ECHR. But it seems likely that there will be pressure for specific legislation on genetic discrimination at some point in the future. Otherwise, English law broadly measures up to international standards on the scope of protection.

What constitutes discrimination?

English law incorporates both formal equality (through what is often labelled 'direct discrimination') and a version of equality of results (through the concept of indirect discrimination).[57] But it does not satisfy many rights commentators because it forbids affirmative action altogether and does not require employers to pursue equal opportunities policies.

According to reg. 3(1)(a) of the EE(RB)R 2003, A discriminates against B if 'on grounds of religion or belief, A treats B less favourably than he treats or would treat other persons'. Thus, the court must find that B has been treated less favourably than a comparator (who might be real or hypothetical) and that this has occurred because of religion or belief. In *James v Eastleigh BC*, a 'but-for' test was used: but for the man's sex, would he have received the treatment of which he was complaining?[58] This is the test for direct discrimination.

According to reg. 3(1)(b), indirect discrimination occurs where:

A applies to B a provision, criterion or practice which he applies or would apply equally to persons not of the same religion or belief as B, but—

(i) which puts or would put persons of the same religion or belief as B at a particular disadvantage when compared with other persons,

(ii) which puts B at that disadvantage, and

(iii) which A cannot show to be a proportionate means of achieving a legitimate aim.

---

54 Directive 2000/78/EC.
55 [1978] ICR 27.
56 Directive 2000/78/EC.
57 The DDA 1995 defines these concepts in a different way to the other Acts, but space precludes a full discussion of its approach.
58 [1990] IRLR 288.

The first part of this definition describes the situation in which an employer is using apparently neutral selection procedures. The use of 'criterion or practice' is intended to capture not only formal selection requirements but also more informal behaviour which might be discriminatory. For example, recruiting only from among the friends of existing employees instead of advertising vacancies may well be discriminatory since it often tends to perpetuate the racial and gender composition of the existing workforce. Paragraph (i) seeks evidence that the criterion or practice has a disparate impact between groups. The phrase 'particular disadvantage' is intended to be less technical and statistical than the phrase 'considerably smaller proportion' which was used in earlier legislation. Paragraph (iii) will be considered below, in our discussion of justification.

It was noted above that equal opportunities policies were largely beyond the scope of labour law, focusing as they do on education and training. But some training is provided by employers. As we saw above, training is one of the areas in which employers are obliged not to discriminate. But SDA 1975, s. 48(1) contains an exception which allows the employer to encourage members of the under-represented sex to apply for jobs and to favour them in the provision of training. Similar provisions are contained in other pieces of anti-discrimination legislation. However, these provisions do not satisfy rights theorists. They permit employers to help disadvantaged groups but they do not oblige employers to do so. Thus, they will only be of assistance where the employer has a commitment to equal opportunities.

Rights theorists are even more vocal in their criticisms when we turn to the question of positive discrimination or affirmative action. In general, this is not permitted in English law because most of our anti-discrimination legislation is 'symmetrical': it protects traditionally advantaged groups as well as traditionally disadvantaged groups. Thus, as we have seen, the SDA 1975 applies to men and women, and the EE(SO)R 2003 apply to homosexuals, heterosexuals and bisexuals. This means that a positive discrimination measure which favoured a traditionally disadvantaged group, such as women or homosexuals, would be unlawful because it would discriminate against men or heterosexuals. The most significant exception to this is the DDA 1995, which applies only to people with a disability. This permits affirmative action in the sense that a person who did not have a disability would have no grounds for complaint if, for example, an employer advertised a job for disabled people only. However, there is no obligation on the employer to favour people with disabilities. So far, EU law has not acted as a force for change in the field of affirmative action. The relevant Directives permit Member States to use affirmative action but create no obligations to do so.[59] Moreover, the ECJ has been relatively strict in its insistence that any individual who is likely to suffer as a result of affirmative action programmes should have an opportunity to argue that he or she ought to be offered the job despite being a member of the

---

59 Directive 2000/78/EC, Article 7; Directive 2000/43/EC, Article 5; Article 141(4) EC.

advantaged group.[60] This has limited the number of schemes which have been held to be lawful.

Rights theorists have argued that English law's reliance on direct and indirect discrimination alone has not done enough to improve the position of disadvantaged groups, and that a more radical approach – such as affirmative action – should be employed. One problem, noted in our theoretical discussion, above, is that direct and indirect discrimination may not be powerful enough to overcome employers' (and society's) deep-seated prejudices about the abilities of those who belong to certain groups. Another problem is that direct and indirect discrimination must be enforced by individual litigants in the courts. But many potential complainants lack the resources to litigate and may feel that the odds are stacked against them.[61] Public bodies such as the Equal Opportunities Commission (EOC) and the Commission for Racial Equality (CRE) can assist complainants but they too have limited resources and cannot take on every case. Affirmative action would overcome these problems by imposing a positive duty on employers to assist members of disadvantaged groups.

Curiously, although English law is weak on equal opportunities and outlaws affirmative action, it does show some signs of adopting a novel and quite radical strategy for tackling discrimination which has been welcomed by commentators. Sometimes referred to as 'mainstreaming', it involves imposing positive duties on employers to review their actions and policies in order to ensure that they do not discriminate.[62] It is potentially far-reaching because it does not depend on an individual complaint and it could lead to changes which would help many people in the relevant workplace. So far, mainstreaming has largely been confined to public bodies,[63] though it has been extended to private employers in Northern Ireland, who are under a duty to review their employment of Catholics and Protestants and to take affirmative action if the members of one community are not being treated fairly.[64] It is, of course, essential to monitor employers' compliance with this duty. This role is performed by the Northern Ireland Equality Commission.[65] The effectiveness of mainstreaming is likely to depend on whether this body has enough resources to carry out its task effectively. It remains to be seen whether mainstreaming will be extended to private firms elsewhere in the UK.

60　The leading cases are Case C-409/95 *Marschall v Land Nordrhein Westfalen* [1998] IRLR 39; Case C-158/97 *Badeck* [2000] IRLR 432; Case C-407/98 *Abrahamsson v Fogelqvist* [2000] IRLR 732. For discussion see S. Fredman, 'Affirming affirmative action' (1998) *Cambridge Yearbook of European Legal Studies* 199.

61　Fredman, above n. 15, pp. 163–74.

62　Fredman, above n. 15, pp. 176–94; B.A. Hepple, M. Coussey and T. Choudhury, *Equality: a New Framework* (2000), chapter 3.

63　Under RRA 1976, s. 71 (inserted by the Race Relations (Amendment) Act 2000), public bodies in England, Scotland and Wales are required to work towards the elimination of race discrimination. Section 75 of the Northern Ireland Act 1998 requires public bodies in Northern Ireland to promote equality of opportunity more generally.

64　Fair Employment and Treatment (Northern Ireland) Order 1998, Article 55.

65　Fredman, above n. 15, pp. 182–7, discusses enforcement issues.

Can discrimination ever be justified?

English law permits discrimination in two sets of circumstances. One is where someone's characteristics are a 'genuine occupational qualification' for the job in question. Thus, although it would normally be unlawful to offer a job only to a woman, an exception can be made where the job involves acting a female part in a film. The traditional approach to this exception is to list the circumstances in which it applies, thereby reducing the judges' discretion in interpreting it. Thus, the SDA 1975, s. 7, lists authenticity in dramatic performances, the need for decency and privacy, and the provision of personal welfare services, among others, as situations in which sex might be a genuine occupational qualification. More recent legislation takes a more flexible and discretionary approach. Thus, the EE(SO)R 2003, reg. 7(2), carves out an exception for cases in which the employer can show that it is 'proportionate' to treat sexual orientation as a 'genuine and determining' occupational requirement in a particular case. The addition of the word 'determining' indicates that the person's sexual orientation must be essential to the job, not just a desirable characteristic. And the proportionality test, to be discussed below, is relatively difficult to satisfy. This should ensure that the genuine occupational qualification exception is only used in the most limited circumstances and does not perpetuate stereotyping.

A second respect in which discrimination can be justified is in relation to equality of results. Here, the employer is generally forbidden from using criteria which have a disparate impact on a particular group, even if those criteria seem to be neutral. But the employer is permitted to justify the use of such criteria where it can be shown that they are necessary for the job in question. Thus, in *Clymo v Wandsworth LBC*,[66] the council refused to permit the claimant and her husband (who was also employed by the council) to share her job when she returned from maternity leave. The court accepted the council's argument that the job was a management position involving the supervision of junior staff who needed continuity in the instructions they were given, and was therefore unsuitable for job-sharing. From a rights perspective, the scope of the justification test is crucial. If it is too wide, the right to equal treatment will be fatally undermined.

There are three formulations of the test. Older legislation, such as the SDA 1975, provides that the employer discriminates where he applies an ostensibly neutral criterion which has a discriminatory impact and 'which he cannot show to be justifiable irrespective of the sex of the person to whom it is applied'.[67] The more modern formulation is that the employer discriminates where he applies such a criterion 'which [he] cannot show to be a proportionate means of achieving a legitimate aim'.[68] In practice, however, the two formulations may have similar results. This is because the traditional approach has long been construed in the light of the ECJ's decision in the

---

66 [1989] IRLR 241.
67 SDA 1975, s. 1(1)(b)(ii).
68 For example, EE(RB)R 2003, reg. 3(1)(b)(iii).

Bilka-Kaufhaus case.[69] The Court laid down a proportionality test: discriminatory measures can only be justified where they 'correspond to a real need on the part of the undertaking, are appropriate with a view to achieving the objectives pursued, and are necessary to that end'.[70] It is this test which has now been codified in the new legislation. If applied correctly, the test is relatively strict. It forces the courts to judge the validity of the employer's goals and to assess whether or not the employer could have achieved those goals by some other non-discriminatory means.

A third formulation of the justification test is that found in the DDA 1995. Under s. 3A(3), discriminatory treatment is justified 'if, but only if, the reason for it is both material to the circumstances of the particular case and substantial'. This is clearly much less stringent than the proportionality test, since it only requires the reason to be relevant to the individual's case and to carry some weight.[71] The courts have discouraged the idea that it should be interpreted in the same way as the justification tests present in other anti-discrimination legislation.[72] Rather surprisingly, this aspect of the DDA 1995 has not been amended despite the fact that it appears to put the UK in breach of EC law, since the Framework Directive clearly uses a proportionality test.[73]

The justification test responds to a wide-ranging set of cost arguments being put forward by employers. The basic argument is that changing from a discriminatory practice to a non-discriminatory one will be less convenient and therefore more expensive.[74] This argument is familiar from our discussion of the statistical discrimination theory, in which we saw that employers might use statistical information during recruitment because it is easier and cheaper than finding out about individual candidates in detail. But employers' claims are by no means confined to increases in recruitment costs. In *Clymo*, the council was concerned about the possible costs of a new way of organising a job. Most rights theorists are relatively dismissive of employers' claims about costs. They emphasise the fundamental nature of the right to equal treatment and argue that it should trump financial considerations. They also derive some support from the economists' crowding model, which shows that over the longer term, the ending of discrimination will benefit the economy as a whole. The problem is that the courts do not have the tools to measure these wider economic benefits, but they are acutely aware of each employer's arguments about the short-term, transitional costs it will face. We will examine the justification test in more detail in chapter 8, because it has been of particular importance in shaping

---

69 Case C-170/84 *Bilka-Kaufhaus GmbH v Weber von Hartz* [1986] IRLR 317. For the approach of the English courts, see *Allonby v Accrington and Rossendale College* [2001] IRLR 364 (CA).
70 Case C-170/84 *Bilka-Kaufhaus v Weber von Hartz* [1986] IRLR 317 at 320.
71 *Heinz (HJ) Co Ltd v Kenrick* [2000] IRLR 141. For critique, see J. Davies, 'A cuckoo in the nest? A "range of reasonable responses", justification and the DDA 1995' (2003) 32 *ILJ* 164.
72 *Clark v TDG* [1999] IRLR 318 at 322.
73 Directive 2000/78/EC, Article 2.
74 Where there is no real inconvenience the courts are more sympathetic to claimants. See, for example, *London Underground Ltd v Edwards (No. 2)* [1998] IRLR 364.

the law on equal pay, so you may want to look at that discussion before forming a view on it.

Further reading

For detailed textbook accounts of this topic, see S. Deakin and G.S. Morris, *Labour Law* (3rd edn., 2001), chapter 6; or H. Collins, K.D. Ewing and A. McColgan, *Labour Law: Text and Materials* (2001), chapter 3.

For a readable introductory text, written largely from a rights perspective, see S. Fredman, *Discrimination Law* (2002). B.A. Hepple, M. Coussey and T. Choudhury, *Equality: a New Framework* (2000), is a wide-ranging review of discrimination law with many recommendations for reform. Some have now been implemented in response to the Framework Directive, but many remain relevant. There are lots of questions to think about when considering the rights perspective. What conception of equality should the law adopt? Should it be based on equality at all? (For discussion of this last question, see H. Collins, 'Discrimination, equality and social inclusion' (2003) 66 *MLR* 16.) In what circumstances, if any, can discrimination be justified? What is the proper role of affirmative action, if any? What are the advantages and disadvantages of imposing positive duties to refrain from discriminating? What are the limits of labour law in combating discrimination? What other government policies are relevant?

To learn more about age discrimination, have a look at S. Fredman, 'The age of equality', and B. Hepple, 'Age discrimination in employment: implementing the Framework Directive 2000/78/EC', both in S. Fredman and S. Spencer (eds.), *Age as an Equality Issue* (2003). On genetic discrimination, compare A. Silvers and M. Ashley Stein, 'An equality paradigm for preventing genetic discrimination' (2002) 55 *Vanderbilt Law Review* 1341, with P.T. Kim, 'Genetic discrimination, genetic privacy: rethinking employee protections for a brave new workplace' (2002) 96 *Northwestern University Law Review* 1497. Why should these issues be included in the scope of anti-discrimination law? Do they raise any particular problems not shared by the established grounds of discrimination?

For an excellent introduction to the debate between neoclassical and new institutional economists, see M. Sawyer, 'The operation of labour markets and the economics of equal opportunities', in J. Humphries and J. Rubery (eds.), *The Economics of Equal Opportunities* (1995). In the same volume, I. Bruegel and D. Perrons, 'Where do the costs of unequal treatment for women fall?', give an account of the economic benefits for firms and for the economy as a whole which would flow from the elimination of discrimination. How do these writers arrive at such different conclusions to those of the neoclassical economists? What assumptions do they use? More generally, what are the advantages of justifying anti-discrimination laws on the grounds of their economic benefits? Are there any risks associated with this strategy?

One of the most famous neoclassical critiques of anti-discrimination laws is R. Epstein, *Forbidden Grounds: the Case Against Employment Discrimination Laws* (1992), especially chapters 1–3. His work has a strong ideological basis in the doctrine of freedom of contract. What are the advantages of a market solution to the problem of discrimination? What assumptions does Epstein make in setting out his theory? Why might markets fail to eliminate discrimination? For a shorter piece focusing in particular on the costs of anti-discrimination laws, see R. Posner, 'An economic analysis of sex discrimination laws' (1989) 56 *University of Chicago Law Review* 1311. To what extent should we be concerned about the costs of anti-discrimination policies? Is there a case for saying that the costs should simply be ignored?

8

Wages

In the days of collective *laissez-faire*, a book on labour law would not have contained a chapter on wages.[1] Workers' pay was seen as pre-eminently a matter for collective bargaining between trade unions and employers. Even when the law did intervene, through the creation of Wages Councils to determine wage rates for the lowest paid, this was viewed as a substitute for collective bargaining rather than as a new approach to pay determination.[2] Nowadays, however, the position is very different. English law regulates pay in two ways. Firstly, the National Minimum Wage Act 1998 (NMWA 1998) seeks to ensure that all workers receive a minimum hourly rate for their work. This is intended to improve the working conditions of the lowest paid workers. Secondly, the Equal Pay Act 1970 (EqPA 1970) and the anti-discrimination legislation seek to ensure that workers who make an equal contribution to the firm are paid equally, and that no artificial distinctions are made on the basis of sex, race, religion and so on. The discussion of equal pay in this chapter will concentrate primarily on equality between the wages of women and men, because this has received most attention in the cases and the literature. However, it is important to bear in mind that unequal pay may affect other groups too, particularly the members of certain ethnic minorities.[3]

Neoclassical economists are hostile to legal regulation of wages. They argue that it is the function of markets to set wages, so any interference with the usual interplay of market forces will be inefficient and counterproductive. The minimum wage will artificially inflate the wages of some workers to a level above their market value, leading to redundancies for some workers and an inefficient use of labour in the economy as a whole. Equal pay legislation is unnecessary because the market itself is capable of eliminating inequalities over time. In contrast, the new institutional economists welcome some regulation of wages, arguing that it is important to prevent firms from trying to compete on the basis of low wages in an era of globalisation.

---

1 See chapter 1.
2 O. Kahn-Freund, 'Legal Framework', in A. Flanders and H. Clegg (eds.), *The System of Industrial Relations in Great Britain* (1954), discussed in P. Davies and M. Freedland, *Labour Legislation and Public Policy* (1993), pp. 27–34.
3 According to the CRE, in 1995, full-time ethnic minority employees earned on average 92% of the wages of white employees (CRE, *Employment and Unemployment Factsheet* (1997)).

Instead, firms should compete on the basis of quality and productivity. In turn, this involves harnessing the enthusiasm of the workforce by showing them how much they are valued. On this theory, it is essential to avoid very low wage levels and to ensure that equally productive workers are paid equally, regardless of characteristics such as race or sex.

The other main argument in favour of legal regulation comes from a rights perspective. It can be argued that low pay puts workers' dignity in jeopardy. The very essence of employment is the wage-work bargain: the individual offers to work for the employer in return for a wage. The individual's dignity is violated if he or she is obliged to work for less than he or she needs to live on, or for a lower wage than that earned by an equally productive person of the opposite sex or of another race. On this view, the law's role is to prevent exploitation.

Economics perspectives

We will discuss the minimum wage and equal pay separately, although there is some overlap between the arguments on each topic.

Minimum wages

In order to understand the economics argument against the minimum wage, we need to begin with a simple account of how wages are determined. Employers have a demand for labour, which is determined by a variety of factors, including demand for the products they are selling and the prices of the other resources they are using, such as machinery. In general, employers' demand for labour decreases as the wage rate rises. Workers' labour supply is again determined by a variety of factors, including their preferences for work or leisure and their income from other sources. But in general, workers' supply of labour increases as the wage rate increases. The 'invisible hand' of the market guides employers and workers to the point at which the amount of labour being supplied equals the amount of labour employers want. This is the equilibrium wage. At this price, just enough workers enter the labour market to fulfil employers' demand.

Of course, this model is a simple one and assumes that markets are perfectly competitive.[4] Nevertheless, it helps us to understand the theoretical impact of a minimum wage. If the minimum wage is set at a rate below the equilibrium wage, it will have no impact at all. Employers are already willing to pay a higher rate. But this is unlikely to happen in practice since the purpose of the minimum wage is to improve the conditions of the lowest-paid workers. Thus, the minimum wage will usually be set so that it is higher than the equilibrium wage. Where this is the case, economists

---

4 Where the employer is a monopsonist, the minimum wage might cause employment to increase by countervailing the employer's power to set wages at an artificially low level. However, most economists believe this situation to be rare in practice. See E.G. West and M. McKee, 'Monopsony and "shock" arguments for minimum wages' (1980) 46 *Southern Economic Journal* 883.

predict three main effects.[5] First, since the cost of labour has increased, employers will employ fewer workers. Some people – usually disadvantaged individuals on the fringes of the labour market – will lose their jobs because of the minimum wage.[6] Second, since the wage level has increased, more people will be willing to enter the labour market. This means that more people will now be looking for a job so the number of unemployed people will increase. Third, the minimum wage creates allocative inefficiency. The workers who are made redundant as a result of the minimum wage will either not be able to find jobs at all or will only be able to find lower-paying jobs in sectors not covered by the minimum wage. The value of their output to society in their new job (if any) is lower than the value of their output to society before the minimum wage was introduced. Society as a whole loses out because workers are not being allocated to their most valued uses. Of course, employers might offset some of these effects by making savings in other respects: they might be able to keep their overall wage bill down by cutting fringe benefits. But while this might prevent some redundancies, advocates of the minimum wage would not welcome it because it does not leave workers any better off as a result of the wage increase.

There are two ways in which a new institutional economist might defend the minimum wage: the 'shock' theory and the 'efficiency wage' theory. Both theories focus on the role of wages in improving firms' productivity. This reflects the new institutionalists' macroeconomic concern with globalisation. They argue that UK firms cannot hope to compete with firms in developing countries on the basis of price, and should compete instead by being highly productive and by developing innovative goods and services.

The idea behind the 'shock' theory is that employers might respond to the minimum wage by being 'shocked' into improving other aspects of their business so that the minimum wage does not have a damaging effect.[7] If a worker has to be paid £5 an hour instead of £4 an hour, the rational employer will seek to ensure that the worker becomes more productive so that it is worth paying that much for his or her output. This might involve investing in new machinery or providing training. However, critics point out that a firm which is selling in a competitive market will keep matters such as equipment and training under constant review in order to ensure that it is not outdone by its rivals. Thus, the shock theory would only work

---

5 The literature is substantial. See, for example, J. Stigler, 'The economics of minimum wage legislation' (1946) 36 *American Economic Review* 358; J. Mincer, 'Unemployment effects of minimum wages' (1976) 84 *Journal of Political Economy* S87; P. Linneman, 'The economic impacts of minimum wage laws: a new look at an old question' (1982) 90 *Journal of Political Economy* 443. For critique and counter-arguments, see D. Card and A. B. Krueger, *Myth and Measurement: The New Economics of the Minimum Wage* (1995).

6 H. Hutchison, 'Toward a critical race reformist conception of minimum wage regimes: exploding the power of myth, fantasy and hierarchy' (1997) 34 *Harvard Journal on Legislation* 93, argues that the minimum wage in the US is a form of institutionalised racism because it has an adverse impact on the employment levels of African-American workers.

7 See, generally, A. Rees, *The Economics of Work and Pay* (1973), pp. 80–3.

where a firm was not operating in a fully competitive market. And the effect of the shock might be to make the employer realise that it has too many workers, thereby leading to redundancies.[8]

The other possible way of justifying the minimum wage would be to treat it as an application of the 'efficiency wage' theory.[9] This theory seeks to explain why it might sometimes be to an employer's advantage to pay workers more than the equilibrium wage. The traditional model of wage determination assumes that all workers are equally productive. The efficiency wage theory assumes that workers differ in their degree of productivity and that they can be motivated by higher wages to be more productive. Workers will value their jobs more highly if they are paid an efficiency wage. They will have more to lose if they are dismissed. This should deter them from being lazy or unproductive (often referred to as 'shirking').[10]

Some figures will help to illustrate the benefits to the employer. Under the traditional model, if the employer hires workers at a wage above the equilibrium wage, it will simply be increasing its costs unnecessarily, because equally productive workers could have been hired at the equilibrium wage. The rational employer would not hire a worker to produce four units of output for £6 an hour when it can get the same output at the equilibrium wage of £4 an hour. But now imagine that while the worker paid £4 an hour will produce four units of output, the worker paid £6 an hour will produce eight units of output. By paying an efficiency wage, the employer in fact makes a saving. Instead of paying two workers £4 an hour to get eight units, the employer can get them by paying one worker £6 an hour.

The efficiency wage theory was first used to explain employers' voluntary decisions to pay above the market rate, but it can be adapted in support of the minimum wage. A worker who receives very low pay is, on this theory, unlikely to put much effort into his or her work. An increase in pay prompted by the introduction of a minimum wage will increase the value of the job to the worker and encourage him or her to be more productive in order to keep the job. Of course, the employer might decide to pay an efficiency wage to this group of workers without legislative intervention,[11] but the usual concerns about undercutting by competitors might serve to prevent this.

However, the efficiency wage theory has been developed for a relatively specific set of circumstances: the situation in which the employer cannot monitor or measure its employees' performance. Most of the time, firms can find cheaper ways of preventing shirking. Many workers can be monitored: the output of workers on a production

---

8 West and McKee, above n. 4.
9 R. Solow, 'Another possible source of wage stickiness' (1979) 1 *Journal of Macroeconomics* 79; C. Shapiro and T. Stiglitz, 'Equilibrium unemployment as a worker discipline device' (1984) 74 *American Economic Review* 433.
10 Some writers argue that efficiency wages can be used to combat other problems as well as shirking, such as high employee turnover.
11 See C. Jolls, 'Fairness, minimum wage law, and employee benefits' (2002) 77 *New York University Law Review* 47.

line in a factory can be checked by a supervisor. Or workers' pay can be related to performance. Traditionally, many workers have been paid piece-rates: they are paid for each shirt they sew rather than for each hour they work. Other examples include offering performance-related bonus payments or giving workers the chance to be promoted to a better job if they perform well. Moreover, worker loyalty can be generated by pay and pension schemes which reward those who stay with the firm for longer.[12] For those who take the view that efficiency wages are helpful only on the rare occasions when these strategies do not work, a legally imposed minimum wage is an unduly costly way of improving productivity.

Equal pay

The standard neoclassical argument against equal pay laws is that they are unnecessary. Becker's 'taste for discrimination' model identifies discrimination as a preference for which employers are willing to pay.[13] Preferring an all-male workforce, they are willing to pay men a premium, and will only employ women if they are prepared to work at a lower wage. The difference between the wage offered to men and that offered to women is the 'discrimination coefficient'. However, Becker suggests that this behaviour cannot be sustained over time. Non-discriminating employers will take advantage of the supply of cheap female labour and will drive their discriminating competitors out of the market. Legislative intervention to require employers to pay men and women equally imposes unnecessary costs on employers. As we saw in chapter 7, this theory has been much criticised for the fact that its predictions have not been borne out: women's average earnings remain considerably lower than men's despite long-standing awareness of the issue of unequal pay.

Unequal pay might also be addressed through the 'crowding' analysis we explored in chapter 7.[14] On this view, the problem is not that women are paid less than men even though they are equally productive. Women are paid according to the value of their output to the employer (and to society as a whole). The problem is that due to discrimination, women are segregated into certain occupations instead of being equally represented throughout the economy. This means that there is an oversupply of workers in female-dominated occupations – which pushes their wages down – and an undersupply of workers in male-dominated occupations – which pushes their wages up. This theory can be used to support legal intervention to give women access to hitherto excluded jobs. The correction of crowding has benefits for employers and for society because it leads to a more efficient allocation of labour.

Interestingly, however, it also follows that the crowding model does *not* support legal intervention to raise women's pay. First, equal pay laws would not tackle the root cause of discrimination: occupational segregation. Second, such laws would

12 J.M. Malcomson, 'Work incentives, hierarchy, and internal labour markets' (1984) 92 *Journal of Political Economy* 486.
13 G.S. Becker, *The Economics of Discrimination* (1957).
14 B.R. Bergmann, *The Economic Emergence of Women* (1986), chapters 5 and 6.

rarely be applicable in practice. If women are crowded into particular jobs, they will not be able to identify any men doing the same work who are being paid more than they are. They will not be able to demonstrate the existence of unequal pay. And third, if an equal pay law could be invoked, it would require the employer to pay the women workers above their market value, which would have the same harmful consequences as the minimum wage, discussed above. The crowding model only supports laws which seek to give women access to jobs which have previously been unavailable to them.

However, there are some economic justifications for equal pay legislation. Both the shock theory and the efficiency wage theory which we used to justify minimum wage legislation can also be employed here. A firm which was required by law to increase the pay of its female workers to the same level as that of its male workers might be 'shocked' into adopting new production methods or providing additional training to improve its productivity. Or, on the efficiency wage theory, if the women's pay was improved, they might become more productive because they would value their jobs more highly. Of course, the introduction of equal pay would not necessarily involve paying the women a wage which was above equilibrium in the new, non-segregated labour market. But it would involve paying them more than they had previously earned. It would also combat any resentment they might have felt at the unequal way in which they were being treated, which might have made them less loyal to the firm.

Rights perspectives

The right to a minimum wage appears in a number of economic and social rights instruments, but inevitably – given the different economic conditions in the signatory states – governments are given a substantial degree of discretion to determine the rate and the criteria to be used in setting it. The right to equal pay is dealt with explicitly in economic and social rights instruments, and since it is a part of the right not to be discriminated against it can be read into civil and political rights instruments too. Again, however, the exact scope of the right is unclear.

Minimum wages

Article 7 of the ICESCR provides that there is a right to 'remuneration which provides all workers, as a minimum, with ... a decent living for themselves and their families'.[15] The key phrase here is 'decent living'. This requires the state to determine how much money a person needs in order to have a reasonable existence and to ensure that remuneration is determined accordingly. Article 23(3) of the UDHR is, if anything, more explicit in identifying the relevant standard. It specifies that the remuneration should be sufficient to ensure 'an existence worthy of human

---

15 ESC 1961, Article 4(1) (which was unchanged in 1996) is in similar terms.

dignity'. But the most specific provision is Article 3 of the ILO's Minimum Wage Fixing Convention:

> The elements to be taken into consideration in determining the level of minimum wages shall, so far as possible and appropriate in relation to national practice and conditions, include—
>
> (a) the needs of workers and their families, taking into account the general level of wages in the country, the cost of living, social security benefits, and the relative living standards of other social groups;
> (b) economic factors, including the requirements of economic development, levels of productivity and the desirability of attaining and maintaining a high level of employment.[16]

This identifies in some detail the factors which must be taken into account when determining how much workers need to live on. The cost of living is clearly essential. An effective minimum wage must enable workers to fulfil basic needs such as food and accommodation. But the references to wage levels and other social groups suggest that the minimum wage should be about more than just survival. It should ensure some level of equity between different groups in society, so that the living standards of those on the minimum wage bear some relationship to the living standards of other groups. But the most significant feature of this provision is para. (b), in which attention is drawn to the potential costs of the minimum wage for employers and, indirectly, for workers. A minimum wage may result in redundancies for some workers, or may deter foreign firms from setting up business in the country. These effects are likely to increase the higher the wage is set. This provision cautions states not to set the minimum wage at too high a level and to balance its potential benefits against the potential costs.

States are generally given some discretion as to whether or not the entire responsibility for the minimum wage should fall on employers. Obviously, it is inherent in the idea of a minimum wage that it is paid by employers. But a state might decide to provide a decent standard of living through a combination of a minimum wage paid by employers and social security benefits paid directly by the state. This approach is accepted by the ILO. Article 3 of the Convention (quoted above) indicates that social security benefits are one of the factors to be taken into account when setting the level of the wage. The UDHR also makes clear that remuneration from employers can be 'supplemented, if necessary, by other means of social protection'.[17] This is a significant limitation on the use of human rights arguments to support a minimum wage. Employers can argue that the responsibility for upholding workers' rights need not fall entirely on them.

---

16 Convention 131, Minimum Wage Fixing Convention, 1970, Article 3. This has not been ratified by the UK. The other ILO Convention in this area is Convention 26, Minimum Wage-Fixing Machinery Convention, 1928. This was originally ratified by the UK but denounced in 1985.
17 Article 23(3).

Equal pay

We saw in chapter 7 that the right not to be discriminated against is a fundamental right which features in all the major human rights instruments we are considering. Pay inequality is, of course, a particular type of discrimination, just like discrimination in hiring or promotion prospects, so it is covered by these more general guarantees. But because of the prevalence of unequal pay, many economic and social rights instruments include a specific right to equal remuneration. We will consider these rights here in order to see whether they offer us any more detailed guidance as to what workers are entitled to in this sphere.

The vast majority of instruments focus on pay inequality between men and women. This is true of the ESC, the EU Charter and, inevitably, CEDAW.[18] The ICESCR obliges signatories to implement the principle of equal pay for men and women 'in particular', which implies that states should also give consideration to the issue of whether any other groups deserve particular attention in this respect.[19] Article 5 of ICERD refers to equal pay, thus identifying it as an area in which discrimination might take place on the grounds of race. But the most general right is Article 23(2) of the UDHR, which provides that 'everyone, without any discrimination, has the right to equal pay for equal work'.

The instruments tend to adopt one of two formulations in order to define workers' entitlement. One is 'equal pay for equal work', and the other (which is more common) is 'equal pay for work of equal value'. The former carries the risk that it might be given a narrow interpretation. 'Equal work' implies that the work done by the woman and the person with whom she seeks equality must be the same. Thus, a female catering worker would have to compare herself with a male catering worker doing exactly the same job. This creates particular difficulties where women are 'crowded' into particular occupations. If their job is female-dominated, there may be no men doing the same job for them to compare themselves with. This will prevent them from bringing a claim. The concept of 'work of equal value' is much more radical. It implies that jobs can be allocated a value even if they are ostensibly different. Thus, the job of a female catering worker might involve the same degree of responsibility, effort, skill and so on as the job of a male mineworker, even though the two jobs are quite different. On this approach, a woman might be able to claim equal pay with a man doing a different job, provided that their jobs are of equal value. This makes it easier for women in female-dominated occupations to bring a claim, since they can compare themselves with men doing other jobs. The ILO's Equal Remuneration Convention requires states to take measures, where necessary, 'to promote objective appraisal of jobs on the basis of the work to be performed'.[20] This is intended to assist in the application of the equal value principle.

---

18 ESC 1961, Article 4(3) (not accepted by the UK); ESC 1996, Article 4(3) (not ratified by the UK); EU Charter, Article 23; CEDAW, Article 11(d).

19 Article 7(a)(i).

20 Convention 100, Equal Remuneration Convention, 1951, Article 3. The Convention was ratified by the UK in 1971.

Importantly, the ILO Convention gives employers a defence to an equal pay claim:

> Differential rates between workers which correspond, without regard to sex, to differences, as determined by such objective appraisal, in the work to be performed shall not be considered as being contrary to the principle of equal remuneration for men and women workers for work of equal value.[21]

This means that where the work performed by men and women is not the same, the employer may reflect this in their pay. Thus, if the jobs of catering worker and mineworker were rated equally in an appraisal, but the mineworkers had to spend some nights on call in case of an emergency at the mine, the mineworkers could be paid extra. This is a relatively straightforward defence, but it is of interest because it is narrowly defined. The only excuse it allows is a difference 'in the work to be performed'. As we shall see, English law permits employers to rely on a wider range of factors in defence.

English law

The rights perspective is evident in several aspects of English law on the minimum wage and on equal pay. Considerable efforts have been made to ensure that the rights are available to as many people as possible regardless of their technical employment status. In relation to the minimum wage, the rights and economics perspectives come into sharp conflict when we consider the way in which the rate is determined and the level at which it has been set. In relation to equal pay, controversy surrounds the availability of the 'material factor' defence, which allows employers to argue that unequal pay can be justified where it is the result of market forces.

The National Minimum Wage

The National Minimum Wage Act 1998 (NMWA 1998) created, for the first time in the UK, a minimum wage which applies across all parts of the country and almost all sectors of the economy.[22] The government supported the measure using both rights and economics arguments.[23] In terms of rights, the government argued that a minimum wage was necessary in order to combat the poverty faced by the lowest-paid workers, and to tackle unequal pay, since a high proportion of the beneficiaries would be women and workers from ethnic minority groups.[24] In terms of economics, the government argued that the minimum wage would contribute to

---

21 Convention 100, above n. 20, Article 3(3).
22 For analysis, see B. Simpson, 'A milestone in the legal regulation of pay: the National Minimum Wage Act 1998' (1999) 28 *ILJ* 1; 'Implementing the national minimum wage: the 1999 Regulations' (1999) 28 *ILJ* 171.
23 See the statement by Margaret Beckett to the House of Commons on 18 June 1998 in response to the Low Pay Commission's first report, available at http://www.dti.gov.uk/er/lowpay/response.htm.
24 See S. Fredman, *Women and the Law* (1997), pp. 263–71, for the relationship between the minimum wage and equal pay.

the macroeconomic goal of a high-wage, high-productivity economy. Critics argued that the minimum wage would contribute to unemployment and would discourage firms from investing in Britain.

Entitlement and enforcement

The rights approach to the minimum wage is most apparent in the legislative provisions on entitlement to be paid the minimum wage and on the mechanisms for enforcing that entitlement. Considerable efforts have been made to ensure that the minimum wage is available to the vast majority of working people, and to ensure that it is effectively enforced.

The minimum wage must be paid to all 'workers'.[25] This term is defined in s. 54(3) of the NMWA 1998 to exclude those who are genuinely self-employed. The Act also makes specific provision for certain groups who would not otherwise fall within this definition. These groups include agency workers who do not have a workers' contract with either the agency or the user,[26] and homeworkers who do not necessarily undertake to perform the work personally.[27] Moreover, in s. 41, the Secretary of State is given a power to extend the Act to other groups who do not count as workers. This gives the Secretary of State the opportunity to close loopholes in the coverage of the Act.[28] The breadth of coverage indicates that the minimum wage is being seen as a fundamental right which should be secured to as many workers as possible.

As we have seen in previous chapters, the enforcement of employment rights is generally a matter for the affected individual. He or she must bring a case before the Employment Tribunal. This is also one mechanism for the enforcement of the minimum wage.[29] However, those workers who are likely to benefit from the minimum wage are among the most disadvantaged people in society. It was not considered reasonable to expect these individuals to bear the entire burden of enforcing this basic entitlement. Two main mechanisms have been employed to assist them.[30] First, the government sought to ensure that employers would comply with the minimum wage voluntarily, without the need for enforcement. Thus, the introduction of the minimum wage was surrounded by considerable publicity, and changes to the minimum wage rate are widely advertised.[31] The choice of a single hourly rate for all regions and sectors was intended to make the law easy to understand. However, commentators argue that this strategy has not been entirely successful.[32] For

---

25 B. Simpson, 'A milestone in the legal regulation of pay: the National Minimum Wage Act 1998' (1999) 28 *ILJ* 1 at 4–5.

26 NMWA 1998, s. 34.

27 NMWA 1998, s. 35.

28 The discussion in chapter 5 will give you some idea of the kinds of loopholes which might emerge.

29 NMWA 1998, ss. 17, 18, 28.

30 See, generally, P. Skidmore, 'Thinking about enforcement: the minimum wage in practice', in H. Collins *et al.*, *Legal Regulation of the Employment Relation* (2000).

31 NMWA 1998, s. 50.

32 B. Simpson, 'Implementing the national minimum wage: the 1999 Regulations' (1999) 28 *ILJ* 171 at 180–1.

example, the government abandoned a plan to oblige employers to give workers a statement with their pay explaining how they were being paid the minimum wage. Employers argued that this would be too costly to administer, but it would clearly have helped workers to understand – and to challenge – their employers' calculations.

The government's second strategy for ensuring that the minimum wage would be enforced was to grant enforcement powers to a public body, the Inland Revenue.[33] Revenue officials can identify employers who may be in breach of the NMWA 1998 either by looking at tax records or by acting on information from disadvantaged workers, and can investigate those employers using an array of statutory powers to gather evidence.[34] Where a breach is identified, the Inland Revenue can issue an 'enforcement notice' requiring the offending employer to start paying the minimum wage and to pay workers any money they are owed due to the employer's prior failure to comply with the Act.[35] If the employer does not comply, the Revenue can sue on behalf of the workers for the money they are owed, and can require the employer to pay a penalty to the Secretary of State.[36] There have been some initial difficulties with these provisions. In particular, it was held in *Inland Revenue Commissioners v Bebb Travel* that an enforcement notice could not relate to workers who were no longer employed by the offending employer, thus limiting the Revenue's ability to obtain the money owed to those workers.[37] The National Minimum Wage (Enforcement Notices) Act 2003 was passed to remedy this problem.

The rate

The most controversial aspect of the minimum wage is, of course, the rate at which it is set. Despite the rights arguments and new institutional economics arguments adopted by the government in its advocacy of a minimum wage, the rate as finally set reflects to a considerable extent the concerns of those economists who are hostile to the policy. The relatively weak positions taken by international human rights instruments mean that it is difficult to construct a powerful human rights critique of the minimum wage rate.

The adult minimum wage is set at £4.50 per hour which works out at £216 per week on the basis of the maximum 48-hour week set by the WTR 1998.[38] From a human rights perspective, the test must be whether this sum is sufficient to ensure a 'decent' standard of living for the worker and his or her family. Not surprisingly, this is very difficult to determine. The government sets the 'poverty line' at 60% of the median income of the population as a whole (£311 per week in 2001–2),[39]

---

33 See Simpson, above n. 25, at 25–8.
34 NMWA 1998, ss. 13–5.
35 NMWA 1998, s. 19.
36 NMWA 1998, ss. 20–1.
37 [2003] 3 All ER 546.
38 From 1 October 2003.
39 *Households Below Average Income* survey, available at http://www.statistics.gov.uk.

which means that those who earn £187 per week or less are officially living in poverty. Of course, in working out these figures it is important to take into account the number of people making up the household which must live on this income. The official figures are calculated for couples. This means that £216 per week is enough to take either a single person or a childless couple above the poverty line. However, the picture changes when we take account of the needs of households with children. Government figures enable us to calculate the 'real' value of £216 per week to different sizes of household.[40] Thus, if we imagine a couple with two children, aged six and nine, the 'real' value of £216 per week is £150, taking that family below the poverty line.

Nevertheless, it is difficult to say that the minimum wage is not enough to fulfil the criteria set by international human rights instruments. First, our picture of household income was deliberately simplified. For example, we assumed that the household only had one income. A household with two minimum wage earners would be much less likely to fall below the poverty line. Second, we did not take into account the social security benefits to which low income families are entitled. A system of tax credits has recently been introduced to help those in work who have low incomes, and benefits such as income support may be available to some working families.[41] As we saw above, international standards permit the government to fulfil the obligation to provide a minimum wage in part by supplementing workers' wages with social security benefits. Third, the ILO standard requires states to take into account the economic consequences of fixing the minimum wage at too high a level. When the minimum wage was first introduced, the government made very clear that it was seeking to set the wage at a level which would not create unemployment. Many commentators felt that the government had given too much credit to employers' claims that they might have to make workers redundant. Nevertheless, a sensible human rights argument must allow for the relevance of these concerns.

The delicate balance between workers' rights and economic concerns is highlighted particularly clearly by the government's decision to introduce a separate 'development rate' of £3.80 per hour (£182.40 for a 48-hour week). This applies primarily to workers aged 18–21 but can also apply to older workers where they are receiving training during the first six months of a new job.[42] Workers under the age of 18 are not entitled to the minimum wage at all. The government made two main claims in favour of these decisions. First, it was argued that those under the age of 21 should be encouraged to stay in education for as long as possible by making work unattractive to them. This can be linked to new institutional economics arguments about creating a highly skilled and therefore highly productive workforce. Second, it was argued that employers should be encouraged to hire younger workers in order to ensure that those who did enter the labour market did not experience

---

40 Using the equivalence scale variants from above n. 39, Appendix 2.
41 See, generally, N. Wikeley, A.I. Ogus and E.M. Barendt, *The Law of Social Security* (5th edn., 2002).
42 NMWA 1998, s. 3; National Minimum Wage Regulations 1999 (SI 1999/584, NMWR 1999) (as amended).

unemployment. This reflects neoclassical concerns with the costs of the minimum wage.

The government's choices can be challenged from both rights and new institutional economics perspectives. The right to a decent living for the worker and his or her family applies universally in the human rights instruments, regardless of age. A couple which has one income at the development rate for a 48-hour week would be below the poverty line. The position would be exacerbated for a couple with children. Moreover, the development rate can be criticised as a breach of the dignity considerations which underlie the minimum wage.[43] It allows employers to pay equally productive younger workers less than their older colleagues for doing exactly the same job. It also creates potential for abuse: employers could hire only younger workers and dismiss them as soon as they became entitled to the adult rate. These possibilities are worrying if our goal is to pursue a high-productivity economy in which workers' loyalty is secured through the payment of a decent wage.

A final feature of the NMWA 1998 which has been much criticised by commentators is that there is no obligation on the government to review the rate. One option would have been to index-link the rate, so that it would have risen (or fallen) automatically in line with inflation. Another, less radical, option would have been to place the Secretary of State under a statutory duty to review the minimum wage on a regular basis and to give a reasoned decision as to whether or not it was set at the right level. However, the government did not pursue either of these options and retains complete discretion over the rate. It seems possible to criticise this from virtually any of the perspectives we have been examining. In a situation of high inflation, the minimum wage might cease to provide a decent living or to act as an incentive to workers to be productive. In a situation of low inflation, the minimum wage might become a burden on business and a cause of unemployment. Of course, it is to be hoped that the government would use its discretion to alter the rate in these circumstances, but the absence of any legal safeguards to ensure that this takes place must be seen as a flaw in the Act.

Equal pay

English law appears to adopt the rights perspective on equal pay. It makes an equal pay claim available not only to women but to other groups as well, and adopts a broad definition of those workers who can bring such a claim. However, commentators have argued that the law does not fully implement this approach. It places too many technical hurdles in the way of those seeking equal pay, and it gives too much credit to neoclassical economic arguments about the cost of implementing equal pay.[44] They point out that limited progress has been made in tackling pay inequalities.

---

43 It has been condemned by the ESC Committee as a breach of ESC 1961, Article 7(5) (the right of young persons to a fair wage). See K.D. Ewing, 'The Council of Europe's Social Charter of 18 October 1961: Britain and the 15th cycle of supervision' (2001) 30 *ILJ* 409.
44 See, generally, Fredman, above n. 24, chapter 6.

In 2002, women working full-time earned 81% of the average full-time earnings of men.[45] This percentage has remained largely unchanged since the mid-1990s. Our discussion will focus in particular on the Equal Pay Act 1970 (EqPA 1970), which must be read in the light of the Equal Pay Directive.[46] A woman may also base a claim directly on Article 141 EC.

Eligibility and enforcement

According to EqPA 1970, s. 1(6)(a), the Act applies to workers broadly defined, so it includes employees, workers and those self-employed people who undertake to perform work personally. Sex discrimination is the only field in which a separate statute governs pay issues. The other anti-discrimination legislation protects individuals against unequal pay alongside other forms of discrimination, such as unfairness in hiring or promotion. Thus, although many international human rights instruments concentrate on the problem of unequal pay faced by women, English law protects people against pay discrimination on grounds of race, sexual orientation, religious belief and so on. As we saw in chapter 7, the broad worker definition is used in these contexts too. The main mechanism for enforcing equal pay is individual litigation, though some claimants may be able to get help from statutory bodies such as the EOC and CRE.[47]

To bring a claim under EqPA 1970, a woman must show that she is doing 'like work' or 'work of equal value' to that of a man 'in the same employment' (her 'comparator').[48] The concept of 'like work' covers the situation in which the woman is doing the same or broadly similar work to her comparator.[49] The concept of 'work of equal value' applies where their jobs are different but can be rated as equivalent in terms of effort, skill, responsibility and so on.[50] A major difficulty faced by women seeking to bring a claim lies in identifying a man 'in the same employment' with whom they can compare their pay. The man must be a real person. The woman cannot argue that she has been treated less favourably than a hypothetical man *would have been* treated.[51] And the man must be employed by the same employer or an associated employer and must work at the same establishment.[52] The woman can only compare her treatment with that of a man at one of the employer's other establishments if 'common terms and conditions of employment' are observed at both.[53] Thus, it is difficult for a woman to compare herself with a man at another

---

45 Source: EOC, *Women and Men in Britain: Pay and Income* (2003).
46 Directive 75/117/EEC. The Directive is, of course, directly effective against public sector employers.
47 At the time of writing, the government has announced plans to create a single Commission for Equality and Human Rights which would take over this role.
48 EqPA 1970, s. 1(1) and (2).
49 EqPA 1970, s. 1(4).
50 EqPA 1970, s. 1(2)(c).
51 This type of comparison is permitted under the other discrimination legislation, even for pay issues. See below.
52 EqPA 1970, s. 1(6).
53 See *Leverton v Clwyd CC* [1989] IRLR 28; *British Coal Corporation v Smith* [1996] IRLR 404.

branch of the same firm, and wholly impossible for her to compare herself with men at other firms.

Of course, it is the very essence of a claim based on formal equality that the woman is seeking to compare her treatment with that of someone else: she is seeking equality *with* her male comparator. But the need for a comparator is highly problematic when we consider the degree of occupational segregation in the labour market. Many women have few options for comparison. Imagine a woman working as a carer in a nursing home. All the other carers are women. Her employer owns another home at which some of the carers are men, but she cannot use them as comparators because they have different terms and conditions. Thus, even if she suspects that her pay is low and that if there were any male carers in her workplace, they would be paid more highly, she cannot prove that she is being treated unequally.

Rights theorists tend to favour more radical equal pay laws which would allow women a broader range of comparisons. One of the least controversial options would be to permit comparisons to be made with hypothetical male workers. This is permitted under the SDA 1975 and the other anti-discrimination legislation, so it is only women seeking to bring an equal pay claim who are precluded from adopting this strategy. A more controversial option would be to allow women to compare themselves with men working for other firms.[54] This has been permitted where the same collective agreement applies to both groups of workers.[55] However, this exception is of limited value since collective agreements between a union and more than one employer are unusual nowadays outside the public sector. To allow comparisons in the absence of a common collective agreement is more problematic. A difference between the pay of women working for one firm and men working for another might be attributable to a wide range of factors other than discrimination, such as the different market conditions faced by the two firms. Thus, even if the legislation made such a claim possible, it might be very difficult to persuade a court of its validity.

A very different solution is suggested by the crowding model. From this perspective, equal pay laws – however radical – are doomed to failure because they do not tackle the root cause of women's disadvantage. Because of discrimination, women are 'crowded' into certain sectors of the economy. The oversupply of women in these sectors drives down their pay. Equal pay laws do not help because men tend not to work in 'women's' jobs, so women rarely have an obvious comparator. Instead of trying to strengthen the equal pay laws, we should focus on anti-discrimination legislation and other policy measures which would improve women's access to hitherto excluded jobs. Pay inequalities would disappear as women workers became more evenly distributed throughout the labour market.

---

54 See Fredman, above n. 24, pp. 247–50.
55 *South Ayrshire Council v Morton* [2002] IRLR 256 (Inner House). The ECJ in Case C-320/00 *Lawrence v Regent Office Care Ltd* [2002] IRLR 822 suggested that cross-firm comparisons could be permitted where the employees were in the same establishment or service, but the claim in the case failed on the facts.

Employers' defences

Perhaps the most direct conflict between the rights and economics perspectives comes when we consider the defence an employer may raise when faced with a *prima facie* claim of unequal pay. The ILO position is that the employer should only be able to pay a woman less than a man where this reflects a genuine difference in the work they do.[56] Otherwise, unequal pay is a breach of fundamental rights and cannot be defended. But for many economists, there is the overriding concern that the cost of implementing equal pay will be unsustainable for firms, leading to redundancies for the very women the legislation was seeking to help.

Under EqPA 1970, s. 1(3), the employer can escape the obligation to pay the man and the woman equally where it can prove that the difference in their pay is 'genuinely due to a material factor which is not the difference of sex'.[57] This clearly includes a difference in the work they are doing. However, judicial interpretations have revealed that it is much broader. In the case of *Rainey v Greater Glasgow Health Board*, for example, the employer wished to expand the prosthetics service at a particular NHS hospital.[58] To do so, it needed to recruit new staff from the private sector. They had much higher salaries than those who were already working for the NHS. The vast majority of the private sector workers were men; the vast majority of the NHS workers were women. The hospital offered higher salaries to the new recruits. This gave rise to a *prima facie* case of unequal pay, because the female NHS workers remained on their old lower salaries, but the hospital successfully invoked the 'material factor' defence. The fact that the men would not have joined the NHS if they had not been offered more money was a 'material factor' justifying the difference in pay.

For rights theorists, this decision makes a mockery of the equal pay legislation, in at least two respects. First, the fact that the right to equal pay can be defeated by business considerations indicates that it is not being regarded as a fundamental right at all. A genuine right is one which 'trumps' other factors instead of giving way to them. Second, the courts are slow to identify possible instances of discrimination. In *Rainey*, the court assumed that it was an accident that most of the private sector workers were men. But as Fredman points out, women may have been unable to obtain lucrative private sector jobs because of discrimination.[59] If so, the *Rainey* decision allowed the NHS to perpetuate this discrimination.

For those economists who are concerned with the costs of equal pay legislation, the 'material factor' defence is an important acknowledgement of the risks of redundancies and business failures associated with a strict insistence on equal pay. In the *Rainey* case, the NHS would not have been able to expand its prosthetics service to

---

56 Convention 100, above n. 20, Article 3(3).

57 The test must be interpreted in the light of the objective justification requirement laid down by the ECJ in Case C-170/84 *Bilka-Kaufhaus GmbH v Weber von Hartz* [1986] IRLR 317.

58 [1987] IRLR 26. In Case C-127/92 *Enderby v Frenchay HA* [1993] IRLR 591, the ECJ indicated that the additional pay offered to attract someone to a job should be proportionate.

59 Above n. 24, pp. 256–7.

the same extent if it had had to increase the pay of its female staff.[60] This would have harmed the users of the service and prevented the creation of new job opportunities in the economy. From this perspective, employers are seen as the 'victims' of market forces: the fact that the invisible hand of the market leads the employer towards a pay structure which is discriminatory should not be regarded as the employer's fault. The burden of reshaping the market should not fall on particular employers against whom claims are brought.

The material factor defence highlights a more fundamental feminist critique of the equal pay legislation. The legislation insists that equality must be achieved within the confines of the existing labour market. But many feminists argue that the market undervalues the jobs which have traditionally been done by women.[61] Jobs such as nursing and childcare are seen as unskilled work which women are inherently able to do because of the caring role they play within the family. The market systematically ignores the degree of responsibility associated with these jobs and the skills they require. This claim is difficult for economists to understand. Economists value jobs by looking at the wages people are prepared to work for and the wages employers are prepared to pay. If employers offer childcare workers low pay but they are prepared to accept it, that is the value of their job. It is not possible to put some other 'objective' value on the job which is higher than its market value. Taken to extremes, the debate about the rights and economics perspectives on equal pay becomes a debate about the very foundations of a market economy.

Further reading

For detailed textbook accounts of this topic, see S. Deakin and G.S. Morris, *Labour Law* (3rd edn., 2001), chapters 4.5 and 6.5; or H. Collins, K.D. Ewing and A. McColgan, *Labour Law: Text and Materials* (2001), chapters 3, 4.5 and 4.6.

There is very little theoretical discussion of the minimum wage from a rights perspective, but for a detailed analysis of the NMWA 1998's provisions, see B. Simpson, 'A milestone in the legal regulation of pay: the National Minimum Wage Act 1998' (1999) 28 *ILJ* 1; 'Implementing the national minimum wage: the 1999 Regulations' (1999) 28 *ILJ* 171. Perhaps the most accessible introduction to neoclassical arguments is J. Stigler, 'The economics of minimum wage legislation' (1946) 36 *American Economic Review* 358. The new institutional economics arguments are summarised in the Low Pay Commission's *First Report* (1998), chapter 1 (http://www.lowpay.gov.uk/er/lowpay/). Does it matter whether the minimum wage is justified on a rights or a new institutional economics basis? Is it preferable to justify the minimum wage using a social justice perspective? What factors should be taken into account when defining a 'decent' wage? What is the appropriate

---

60 *Rainey v Greater Glasgow Health Board* [1987] IRLR 26.
61 Fredman, above n. 24, pp. 241–4.

role of cost considerations? Is the minimum wage currently set at an acceptable level? Should younger workers receive the same protection as adults?

S. Fredman, *Women and the Law* (1997), chapter 6, introduces the topic of equal pay from a rights perspective. Is it helpful to think about pay discrimination separately from other kinds of discrimination? To what extent should it be possible for an employer to justify unequal pay? What would the implications be for employers if the 'market forces' defence was not allowed? Should the enforcement strategy applied to the minimum wage be used in relation to equal pay? Or should employers be placed under a positive duty to promote equal pay (see chapter 7)? Or does the problem lie in the way in which pay is determined? On the last question, see A. McColgan, 'Regulating pay discrimination', in H. Collins *et al.*, *Legal Regulation of the Employment Relation* (2000). Finally, do equal pay laws tackle the right set of issues, or is occupational segregation or 'crowding' the real problem? Many of the suggestions for further reading in chapter 7 also discuss the issue of equal pay, so you may find it helpful to review them when considering these questions.

9

Dismissal

Most people place a high value on their jobs. Even if they do not enjoy their work, they need the income their jobs bring in. If they do enjoy their work, their jobs are a source of personal fulfilment and social contacts. And most employers value their workers. Their labour helps to make the firm productive and profitable. But this does not necessarily mean that the employer will want to keep the same individuals in their jobs for life. A downturn in the business might lead to a reduction in the firm's demand for labour. Or an individual worker might stop being productive, through illness or even laziness. Sometimes, individuals leave their jobs of their own volition, when they retire or move on to a better opportunity at another firm. It is when the employer wants to terminate a worker's employment against that worker's wishes that the interests of the firm and the interests of the worker come into sharp conflict.

Neoclassical economists would resolve this conflict in favour of the employer. The law should not seek to control the circumstances in which an employee is dismissed because to do so would impose additional costs on the employer and make it more difficult to run a productive business. Legal intervention would ultimately harm other workers and the economy as a whole. In contrast, new institutionalists would argue that some legal control over dismissal could benefit employers. These writers suggest that employers have an interest in providing a degree of job security, because it will make their workers more loyal and, as a result, more productive. The difficulty is that employers may sometimes forget this long-term goal and dismiss people to save money in the short term. The law can play an important role in preventing employers from giving in to this temptation.

Few international human rights instruments even consider the issue of dismissal. Nevertheless, many commentators have tried to identify an underlying human rights basis for laws on this topic. The most radical approach involves arguing that a job is a form of property. This would suggest that employees could not be deprived of their jobs without their consent and would therefore limit employers' freedom considerably. Other writers have invoked principles such as dignity and autonomy in order to advocate a lesser degree of job security which does allow the employer to dismiss employees provided that there is a good reason for doing so and provided that fair procedures are followed.

Economics perspectives

Arguments against regulation

One of the most strident critics of controls on the employer's power to dismiss is Epstein. In a well-known article, he challenged the trend in many states of the US to abandon 'employment at will' (in which the employer may dismiss employees at any time and for any reason) and to replace it with legal regulation of dismissals.[1]

According to Epstein, the employment at will doctrine has three main attractions for employers: it motivates employees, it is flexible, and it is cheap to administer. We will consider each in turn. Epstein's first point about motivation is fairly obvious. If employees know that they can easily be dismissed for a poor performance, they will work harder. If the law grants them job security, they will be more tempted to shirk. The second major advantage from the employer's perspective is flexibility. The employer needs to respond to changes in its product markets. For example, the market price might fall because of the entry of a new competitor with lower production costs. In this situation, the employer would need to reduce its expenditure by selling machinery and dismissing workers. Any constraint on dismissals would reduce the employer's ability to remain competitive. The third advantage is that the employment at will doctrine is cheap to administer because no-one can challenge the employer's decisions. An unfair dismissal law would allow aggrieved employees to sue. The employer might incur substantial costs in defending litigation even if the claimant did not have a good case.

An obvious criticism of employment at will is that while it benefits employers, it does not benefit employees at all. They are vulnerable to dismissal at any time and for any reason, good or bad. But Epstein argues that employees do have job security under employment at will because market forces prevent employers from behaving arbitrarily. According to Epstein, the employer would face two main disadvantages if it dismissed a productive employee for a bad reason. First, the employer would lose the benefit of that person's skills and would have to incur the costs of hiring and training a replacement. Second, the employer's reputation would suffer. Members of the current workforce who saw that the employer had dismissed someone arbitrarily might decide to look for a new job elsewhere with a better employer. Alternatively, they might decide to reduce their level of effort: there is no point in working hard if it is no guarantee of job security. Outside the workplace, people looking for work might find out about the employer's behaviour and decide not to apply for vacancies. This would reduce the employer's chances of being able to choose among the best candidates when recruiting. These problems should be enough to deter employers from dismissing employees without a good reason. On this view, job security laws are unnecessary.

Neoclassical economists also claim that job security laws may be positively harmful to employees, because they lead to cuts in wages and a reduction in the demand

---

1 R.A. Epstein, 'In defense of the contract at will' (1984) 51 *University of Chicago Law Review* 947.

for labour. This argument is developed by Harrison in particular.[2] As we saw above, job security laws increase employers' costs, because of the higher risk that dismissed employees might bring a claim. These costs are likely to be passed on to employees through cuts in their wages. Thus, whether a job security law benefits employees depends on whether they value job security more highly than the pay they will lose. Moreover, job security laws may make it more difficult for the unemployed to find work. Under employment at will, if there is a rise in demand in the employer's product market, it would hire additional workers and dismiss them if demand dropped again. Under a job security law, the employer may decide to delay hiring the additional workers until it is sure that the rise in demand is likely to be of long duration. This is because the law puts obstacles in the way of dismissing workers who are no longer needed. Thus, job security laws are potentially counterproductive for employees.

Arguments in favour of regulation

Those economists who argue in favour of legal regulation generally do so by attacking one or more of Epstein's underlying assumptions. We will consider arguments which challenge his suggestion that the rational employer would never dismiss a productive employee, his arguments about harm to the employer's reputation, and his claim that employment at will is a good way to motivate employees.

Some writers have argued that – contrary to Epstein's claims – there are at least two situations in which it would be rational for the employer to dismiss a productive employee. Both involve 'opportunism' on the part of the employer: ignoring long-term goals, such as maintaining a good reputation, in order to make a saving in the short term. First, when an employee is accused of misconduct, Epstein would argue that the employer should investigate the allegations in order to decide whether or not the employee is productive and thus whether or not he or she ought to be retained. But an investigation imposes immediate and obvious costs on the employer, whereas the benefits of keeping the productive employee will manifest themselves over the longer term. So the employer might respond to short-term imperatives and dismiss the employee without investigation.[3]

A second situation in which the employer might dismiss a productive worker arises where the employer has adopted what economists sometimes refer to as 'deferred benefit' payment schemes. A simple example is a bonus to be paid to the salesperson when an order is delivered to a new customer. The salesperson works to obtain the order but does not receive the bonus until the deal has been finalised. A more complex example is the payment of workers on a salary scale which increases with age. Workers at the top of the scale may be paid more than they are worth to the employer in productivity terms. But the purpose of the scheme is to motivate

2 J.L. Harrison, 'The "new" terminable at will employment contract: an interest and cost incidence analysis' (1984) 69 *Iowa Law Review* 327.
3 H. Collins, *Justice in Dismissal* (1992), pp. 110–1.

those at the bottom of the scale to remain loyal to the company and to work hard in the hope of retaining their jobs and rising to the top of the scale. In both these situations, the employer can make a short-term cost saving by dismissing a worker before he or she becomes entitled to the bonus or to the higher salaries at the top of the scale.[4] Again, the employer has an incentive to behave opportunistically by dismissing a productive worker.

Epstein's response to these arguments would be to point to the damage such behaviour would do to the employer's reputation. If job applicants find out that the employer dismisses people without investigating the circumstances they will look for a job with a fairer employer. If workers know that they are likely to be dismissed before they receive a bonus, they will realise that the promised payments are a trick and they will not be motivated by them. The second step in the counter-argument must therefore be to challenge Epstein's claims about reputation. Although Epstein's theory works when all parties have perfect information, this underlying assumption does not hold true in practice.[5] Prospective employees may not be able to find out very much information about a firm's hiring and firing practices. Even those who currently work for the firm may not know about the employer's behaviour. The employer may be able to disguise opportunistic dismissals as redundancies, for example, so that workers do not realise the true motivation behind them. Thus, it can be shown that opportunism is a real threat and that it is unlikely to be corrected by market forces. This might justify legal intervention to control the employer's power to dismiss.

Another way to challenge Epstein's arguments is to reconsider his claim about the motivation of employees. Epstein suggests that employment at will is a good motivator: employees will work hard in order to avoid being dismissed. But Fox argues exactly the opposite.[6] If employees feel insecure, they will do the minimum required of them and seize opportunities to shirk. He claims that employees respond best in a high-trust environment. If they feel that the employer trusts them to do a good job, they will repay that trust by working hard and doing their best for the firm. The employer can create a high-trust environment by giving employees discretion instead of continuously checking up on them, and by avoiding a situation in which they feel that they are constantly under threat of dismissal. From this perspective, it is arguable that some legal control over the power of dismissal could benefit employers by improving workers' loyalty and productivity.

Rights perspectives

The literature on unfair dismissal is littered with rights terminology. As we shall see, it is sometimes argued that individuals have a right to job security or even to the 'ownership' of their jobs. Even those theorists who make the more moderate claim that

---

4 Note, 'Employer opportunism and the need for a just cause standard' (1989) 103 *Harvard Law Review* 510.
5 Above n. 4.
6 A. Fox, *Beyond Contract: Work, Power and Trust Relations* (1974), especially chapter 1.

individuals should be treated fairly when their dismissal is being considered often base this on a right to be treated with dignity and respect. Nevertheless, the right not to be unfairly dismissed does not feature heavily in the international instruments, and the ILO has only relatively recently made it the subject of a detailed Convention.

Perhaps the most basic right an employee can have is a right to notice: to be warned in advance that he or she is going to be dismissed. Although this does not offer any control over the employer's reason for dismissal, it does at least enable the employee to start looking for another job. Article 4(4) of the ESC requires states to recognise the right of all workers to a 'reasonable' period of notice before their employment is terminated.[7] A similar right is afforded by Article 11 of the ILO Termination of Employment Convention, although it contains two significant exceptions.[8] First, the employee may be given compensation instead of notice. This is more flexible for employers since it gives them the opportunity to make immediate changes to the workforce. Moreover, it may not disadvantage the employee, since he or she may be able to live on the compensation until he or she has found a new job. Second, the employee need not be given notice at all if he or she is guilty of serious misconduct (stealing from the employer, for example). This exception is relatively uncontroversial because the employer cannot be expected to continue employing someone it no longer trusts.

The right to notice does not protect the employee against arbitrary decision-making by the employer. To do this, the law must control the employer's reason for dismissal. Only one international instrument, the ESC 1996, provides a detailed right of this kind. Article 24 provides:

> With a view to ensuring the effective exercise of the right of workers to protection in cases of termination of employment, the Parties undertake to recognise:
>
> (a) the right of all workers not to have their employment terminated without valid reasons for such termination connected with their capacity or conduct or based on the operational requirements of the undertaking, establishment or service;
> (b) the right of workers whose employment is terminated without a valid reason to adequate compensation or other appropriate relief.
>
> To this end the Parties undertake to ensure that a worker who considers that his employment has been terminated without a valid reason shall have the right to appeal to an impartial body.[9]

This gives workers a right to stay in their jobs unless the employer can identify a valid reason for dismissing them. It also enables workers to enforce this right by challenging employers' dismissal decisions before an independent body and

---

7 This features in the ESC 1961 as well as the ESC 1996 and has been accepted by the UK.

8 Convention 158, Termination of Employment, 1982. The UK has not ratified this Convention. For detailed discussion, see B. Napier, 'Dismissals – the new ILO standards' (1983) 12 *ILJ* 17.

9 This provision does not appear in the ESC 1961 and has not therefore been ratified by the UK. The EU Charter, Article 30, also grants a right to protection against unfair dismissal 'in accordance with Community law and national laws and practices'.

receiving a remedy if they are successful. We will examine each of these elements in turn.

The list of legitimate reasons for dismissal is drawn directly from the ILO Convention.[10] The first two reasons, capacity and conduct, relate to the characteristics of the employee to be dismissed. 'Capacity' applies where the employee is no longer able to do the job, for example, because of illness. Article 6 of the ILO Convention provides that 'temporary absence from work because of illness or injury shall not constitute a valid reason for termination'. This means that the employer can only dismiss on grounds of incapacity where it lasts or is likely to last a long time. 'Conduct' applies where the employee has disobeyed the employer's rules. Article 7 provides that where a worker's employment is to be terminated on grounds of 'conduct or performance', the worker should usually be given an opportunity to defend him- or herself. This is analogous to the fundamental right to a fair trial. The third reason for dismissal permitted by the ESC and the ILO Convention is the 'operational requirements' of the firm. This covers cases in which the firm is experiencing a downturn in business, and can no longer afford to retain all its staff. It allows the employer to dismiss individuals on economic grounds even though there is nothing wrong with their work.

The ILO Convention also highlights certain reasons which *cannot* be relied upon by the employer when dismissing an employee.[11] Some of these forbidden reasons feature in other international human rights instruments, even ones which do not deal with unfair dismissal *per se*. Examples include dismissing an employee because she is pregnant or taking maternity leave,[12] dismissing an employee on discriminatory grounds, such as race or religion,[13] and dismissing an employee because he or she has sought office as a trade union or workforce representative. These cases highlight an important point about dismissal. It is that protection against dismissal may be necessary to ensure that other rights are upheld. There is no point in providing women with a right to maternity leave if the employer can dismiss them as soon as they take the leave. Thus, as well as being important in itself, the right not to be unfairly dismissed is an important component in the protection of workers' rights in general.

The second component in the ESC right, quoted above, is that the worker should be able to challenge his or her dismissal before an impartial body. The ILO Convention allows states to choose whether this should be a 'court, labour tribunal, arbitration committee or arbitrator'.[14] If the dismissal is found to be unlawful, the ESC states that the worker should be given 'compensation or other appropriate relief'. The ILO Convention also accepts the possibility of compensation as a

---

10 Convention 158, above n. 8, Article 4.
11 Convention 158, above n. 8, Article 5.
12 CEDAW, Article 11(2)(a); ESC 1961 and 1996, Article 8(2) (not accepted by the UK); EU Charter, Article 33(2).
13 ESC 1996, Article 20 (sex discrimination).
14 Convention 158, above n. 8, Article 8(1).

remedy but seeks to make it secondary to the remedy of reinstatement. However, the provision is drafted relatively weakly and does not impose any particular obligation on the state to make reinstatement available:

> If the bodies referred to in Article 8 of this Convention find that termination is unjustified and if they are not empowered or do not find it practicable, in accordance with national law and practice, to declare the termination invalid and/or order or propose reinstatement of the worker, they shall be empowered to order payment of adequate compensation or such other relief as may be deemed appropriate.[15]

The Convention does not offer further guidance on how the 'adequacy' of compensation is to be determined.

The ESC right is simply described as a right for 'workers', but the ILO Convention offers more specific guidance as to the limitations states may place on who is protected.[16] It permits states to exclude three main groups: workers on fixed-term contracts (provided that employers are not permitted to use these contracts as a means of evading unfair dismissal laws), workers serving a reasonable period of probation, and casual workers. The state may, after consultation with the social partners, exclude other groups where certain conditions are met, for example, where they work for a small business.

Despite – or perhaps because of – the lack of emphasis on the right not to be unfairly dismissed in the human rights instruments, there is a considerable literature on the topic which does seek to attribute a powerful human rights basis to unfair dismissal laws. The most radical approach is to argue that workers have 'ownership' of their jobs in the same way as they own any other piece of property.[17] It is usually suggested that workers acquire this ownership over time just as a squatter can eventually acquire prescriptive rights over land. Of course, workers' contribution to the firm is rewarded with the payment of wages. But advocates of job property argue that this is not enough to compensate workers for their efforts. Workers may have learnt skills which are only useful in that particular firm. They may also have spent time finding out how the firm works and getting to know other members of staff. These investments will only be rewarded if they are allowed to keep their jobs for a reasonable period of time.

But what does it mean to say that a worker 'owns' his or her job? The fact that I own my car means that I can sell it to whoever I choose. But a worker cannot 'sell' his or her job to another person when he or she does not want it any more. Even those who advocate the job property approach would not make this claim. It would force the employer to form an employment relationship with a person chosen by the former employee, a person who might not even be qualified to do the job. The fact that I own my car also means that no-one is entitled to take it away from me

---

15 Convention 158, above n. 8, Article 10.
16 Convention 158, above n. 8, Article 2.
17 See, for example, D.H.J. Hermann and Y.S. Sor, 'Property rights in one's job: the case for limiting employment-at-will' (1982) 24 *Arizona Law Review* 763.

without my consent. This is both the virtue and the downfall of the job property theory.[18] If employees own their jobs, the employer cannot take them away without the employees' consent. This gives employees a very high level of protection against dismissal. But a moment's reflection reveals that it goes too far. It would not allow the employer to dismiss an employee who was incapable of doing the job or even an employee who was flatly refusing to do any work at all. This would clearly benefit the employee, but it would cause harm to the employer, and consequently to the firm's other employees and to the economy as a whole. Some theorists have acknowledged that a realistic conception of job property would have to allow employers to dismiss on the three grounds listed in Article 24 of the ESC.[19] But these theorists have made such a big concession that it no longer seems appropriate to describe them as advocates of 'job property'.

Since the property approach is problematic, theorists have looked for some other way of linking the right not to be unfairly dismissed to more general human rights. The challenge is to find a basis which gives the employee some job security but (unlike the property approach) also allows the employer to dismiss the employee where there is a good reason for doing so. In an important analysis of the English law of unfair dismissal, Collins has identified dignity and autonomy as the two key principles which underlie the right to job security.[20] We will examine each in turn.

The employee's right to be treated with dignity requires that the employer's decision to dismiss should have a rational basis. A dismissal which has no rational basis infringes the employee's dignity by showing that he or she is at the mercy of the employer's whims. This approach rules out dismissals for bad reasons, such as a dismissal on the ground of an employee's sexual orientation or a dismissal because the employee has sought to enforce his or her entitlement to the minimum wage. It also rules out dismissals for potentially good reasons where the employer has not investigated the circumstances properly. If an employee is accused of persistent lateness, for example, the employee's dignity is respected only where the employer investigates the accusations and gives the employee a chance to defend him- or herself. But it does not rule out all dismissals. If the employer has a good reason for dismissing the employee – he or she has been caught stealing, for example – the employee's dignity is not affronted because there is no irrational behaviour on the part of the employer.

The second principle advocated by Collins is respect for the employee's autonomy. This helps to acknowledge the fact that work is an important way in which people bring meaning to their lives. The employer is under an obligation to respect this aspiration insofar as it is compatible with running an efficient business. For example, Collins argues that the rules which govern the workplace should be published. This allows employees to guide their behaviour accordingly. He also argues

---

18 Collins, above n. 3, pp. 9–12.
19 Hermann and Sor, above n. 17, at 767.
20 Collins, above n. 3, pp. 15–21.

that the employer should not in general seek to interfere with what employees do outside their working time. Both requirements show respect for employees as autonomous individuals who need to be able to plan their lives. The employer can set limits in the interests of the business but these limits must be appropriate. Again, therefore, the employer is obliged to behave in certain ways but is not forbidden from dismissing an employee altogether. An employee who disregarded work rules which were well-publicised and fair could be dismissed without any violation of his or her autonomy.

The principles of dignity and autonomy help to strike a balance between employees' and employers' interests and offer a middle way between the employment at will and job property approaches. However, the principles are not self-executing: they require interpretation to decide what they mean in particular situations. For example, it is not clear whether the vindication of an employee's dignity requires that he or she should get his or her job back after an unfair dismissal, or whether a substantial award of compensation would be a sufficient remedy. These controversies will become apparent in our discussion of English law.

English law

English law offers two types of claim when a person's employment is terminated: wrongful dismissal and unfair dismissal. In a *wrongful* dismissal claim, the employee alleges that the employer is in breach of the terms of the contract of employment. For example, if the contract states that the employee is entitled to four weeks' notice before dismissal, and the employer fails to comply, a wrongful dismissal claim would be available. In an *unfair* dismissal claim, the employee alleges that the employer has failed to comply with the statutory requirements concerning dismissal set out in the ERA 1996 and EA 2002. These govern the employer's reason for dismissal and the procedure it adopts before deciding who to dismiss. The two claims have advantages and disadvantages depending on the employee's circumstances, so we will compare and contrast them under four headings: eligibility to claim, control over the employer's reason for dismissal, control over the employer's dismissal procedure, and remedies.

From a rights perspective, the law presents a mixed picture. It rejects the two extreme positions: employment at will and job property. But in trying to strike a balance between the interests of employers and employees, the legislators have given considerable weight to the argument that dismissal laws impose costs on employers. The EA 2002 in particular has been driven by the government's desire to reduce the number of unfair dismissal claims, which at the moment make up around one-third of all applications to tribunals.[21] Thus, the issue for rights theorists adopting the dignity and autonomy perspective, and for economists concerned with preventing

---

21 ACAS, *Annual Report 2002–3* (2003), p. 41.

opportunism and promoting productivity, is whether the law offers employees *enough* job security in order to fulfil the values they are advocating.

Eligibility to claim

The law of dismissal largely protects employees, rather than workers. This stems from the fact that much of the legislation dates from the 1960s and 1970s, long before the needs of the wider category of workers had been recognised.

Wrongful dismissal claims are based on the employer's breach of the express or implied terms of the contract. A claim based on the express terms of the contract is a straightforward one whether the individual is an employee or a worker. However, the employee is better protected because ERA 1996, s. 86, sets out the minimum period of notice the employee must be given, depending on how long he or she has worked for the employer. No such minimum standards apply in a worker's contract. Where the contract is silent on the question of notice, the employee can again rely on the statutory minimum notice periods. But if a worker's contract did not contain a notice clause, it would be up to the courts to decide how much notice the worker was entitled to.[22] It seems unlikely that the courts would find that casual workers were entitled to long notice periods, given the inherent instability of their jobs.

The law of unfair dismissal applies only to employees. According to ERA 1996, s. 94(1), 'an employee has the right not to be unfairly dismissed by his employer'. Moreover, in most cases the employee must have worked continuously for one year for the employer before a claim can be brought.[23] The use of a qualifying period is permitted by the ILO Convention.[24] The usual justification is that it allows the employer a period of time in which to decide whether or not the employee is suitable. Critics point out that the law of unfair dismissal would not stop the employer dismissing an unsuitable employee, so that the law could apply from the beginning of the employment. But the counter-argument is that an employer might still have to incur the costs of defending a claim, and that job creation in the economy would be stifled as a result. The only exceptions to the one-year rule are those cases in which the employer's reason for dismissal is prohibited under any circumstances, for example, where the employee is dismissed because she is pregnant.[25] These exceptions fit neatly into the dignity rationale suggested by Collins. The employee's dignity is violated when he or she is dismissed for a prohibited reason, regardless of length of service.

For many commentators, the absence of any protection against unfair dismissal is one of the most serious gaps in the law relating to workers. Unlike employees, they are constantly at the mercy of the whims of their employer. But the suggestion that the law should be extended to them is highly controversial. As we saw above,

---

22 For discussion of the courts' likely approach to such cases, see S. Deakin and G.S. Morris, *Labour Law* (3rd edn., 2001), pp. 393–4.
23 ERA 1996, s. 108.
24 Convention 158, above n. 8, Article 2.
25 ERA 1996, s. 99; MPLR 1999, reg. 20.

even the ILO Convention allows states to exclude various kinds of atypical workers. You may find it helpful to review chapter 5 once you have considered the law of unfair dismissal in more detail.

Controls over the employer's reason for dismissal

The law of wrongful dismissal focuses largely on the procedure adopted by the employer when dismissing the employee, and in particular on the notice he or she is given. It is only the law of unfair dismissal which attempts to control the employer's reason for dismissal. The employer's reason may be automatically fair, automatically unfair, or potentially fair. It is automatically fair to dismiss an employee who is taking unofficial industrial action, a concept which will be discussed further in chapter 12.[26] For now, we will concentrate on the other two categories.

Automatically unfair reasons are those which can never be relied upon by the employer, whatever the circumstances. They include dismissals on discriminatory grounds,[27] for pregnancy or taking maternity leave,[28] for taking other forms of parental leave,[29] for participating in trade union activities[30] or acting as a workers' representative,[31] and for asserting statutory rights such as the right to be paid the minimum wage or to work no more than 48 hours per week.[32] They reflect the argument made by Collins that certain grounds for dismissal violate the employee's dignity and should not be permitted. They also reflect the role of unfair dismissal law in protecting other fundamental rights, such as the right to the minimum wage. There is little point in providing employees with these rights if the employer is allowed to dismiss them whenever they bring a claim. English law is largely in compliance with Article 5 of the ILO Convention in this area.

Potentially fair reasons for dismissal are those which the employer can rely on provided that it has acted 'reasonably' in dismissing the employee for that reason. The law offers four options: conduct, capability, redundancy, and 'some other substantial reason' which would justify the dismissal of the relevant employee.[33] Space precludes a full discussion of all four reasons, so we will concentrate instead on tribunals' general approach. The first stage in the process is the identification of the employer's reason for dismissal.[34] This is a simple factual inquiry: what motivated the employer to dismiss the employee? Then, the tribunal must ask whether the employer acted reasonably in treating this as a justification for dismissal.[35] This second stage is governed by a test laid down in *Iceland Frozen Foods Ltd v Jones*, which

26 TULRCA 1992, s. 237.
27 For example, SDA 1975, s. 6(2)(b). Equivalent provisions are contained in the other anti-discrimination legislation.
28 ERA 1996, s. 99; MPLR 1999, reg. 20.
29 ERA 1996, s. 99; MPLR 1999, reg. 20.
30 TULRCA 1992, s. 152.
31 ERA 1996, s. 103.
32 ERA 1996, ss. 101A and 104A respectively.
33 ERA 1996, s. 98. These standards reflect Article 4 of the ILO Convention (above n. 8) quite closely.
34 ERA 1996, s. 98(1).
35 ERA 1996, s. 98(4).

requires the tribunal to ask whether the dismissal was 'within the band of reasonable responses' open to the employer.[36] This suggests that the employer has a large area of discretion when deciding how to respond to the situation and that the tribunal should only interfere when the employer's reaction is extreme. The approach is analogous to the test of *Wednesbury* unreasonableness in administrative law.[37] It has led many commentators to suggest that tribunals are not performing their intended role under the Act.[38] Instead of setting standards for employers which indicate how employees' dignity and autonomy should be respected, tribunals are simply reflecting normal behaviour on the part of employers. Thus, if it is 'normal' for employers to dismiss employees for behaviour which takes place outside working hours and does not impinge on their work, for example, this will be a fair dismissal even though it is arguably an infringement of those employees' autonomy.

For many commentators, then, the only control exercised over the employer's reasoning is when a prohibited ground such as sex discrimination is the motivation behind the dismissal. On the one hand, this approach can be seen as offering inadequate protection to employees' rights, and an insufficient deterrent to employers who are tempted to make opportunistic dismissals. On the other hand, it can be argued that the employer is best placed to assess the needs of its own business, and that interference from the tribunal would come too close to the unsustainable job property approach.

Controls over the employer's procedures

If the law offers limited control over the employer's reason for dismissal, attention inevitably shifts to the employer's procedures. The law of wrongful dismissal controls the employer's procedures in two main ways. First, it requires the employer to give the employee notice before he or she is dismissed. ERA 1996, s. 86, specifies that those who have worked for between one month and two years should have a week's notice. The entitlement increases gradually up to 12 weeks for those who have worked for 12 years or more. The contract may expressly provide for a notice period but it must be at least as long as the employee's statutory entitlement.[39] The employee may waive his or her right to notice or accept a payment in lieu,[40] but the employer can only dispense with notice where the employee has committed a repudiatory breach of the contract, often known as 'gross misconduct'.[41] For example, a shop worker caught in the act of stealing from the till could be dismissed without notice. These various provisions are in line with ILO standards. A second respect in which the law

---

36 [1983] ICR 17, recently reaffirmed in *Post Office v Foley, HSBC (formerly Midland Bank plc) v Madden* [2000] IRLR 827.
37 *Associated Provincial Picture Houses v Wednesbury Corporation* [1948] 1 KB 223. See P.L. Davies and M.R. Freedland, 'The impact of public law on labour law, 1972–1997' (1997) 26 *ILJ* 311.
38 For example, Collins, above n. 3, pp. 37–40; A. Freer, 'The range of reasonable responses test: from guidelines to statute?' (1998) 27 *ILJ* 335.
39 ERA 1996, s. 86(3).
40 ERA 1996, s. 86(3).
41 ERA 1996, s. 86(6).

of wrongful dismissal controls the employer's procedures is where the contract itself specifies that the employee can only be dismissed after a certain procedure has been followed. Many public sector employees have detailed contractual entitlements of this kind which the courts will uphold.[42]

The law of unfair dismissal provides much better procedural protection because it requires all employers to follow a fair procedure regardless of whether or not any such procedure has been voluntarily included in the contract of employment. This protection comes in two layers. The EA 2002 sets out minimum procedures which attract penalties for employers and employees who do not follow them. But long before this was introduced, the employment tribunals had developed a substantial jurisprudence about procedures. A dismissal might also be found to be unfair if the employer does not comply with these more stringent procedures. We will consider each layer in turn.

The EA 2002 inserts a statutory disciplinary procedure and a statutory grievance procedure into every contract of employment and requires both employer and employee to comply with those procedures.[43] The procedures are set out in Sch. 2 to the Act and are relatively simple. Under the disciplinary procedure, the employer must inform the employee of the case against him or her, arrange a meeting to discuss the issue, and provide the employee with a possibility of appeal against the initial decision. Under the grievance procedure, the employee must inform the employer of his or her complaint in writing, and the employer must arrange a meeting to discuss the issue and provide a possibility of appeal if the employee is unsatisfied with the outcome of the initial meeting. Harsh penalties apply if the requirements are not met. If the employer fails to use the disciplinary procedure, the dismissal will be automatically unfair.[44] If the employee fails to send a written statement of his or her grievance to the employer, he or she will be barred from bringing an unfair dismissal claim to a tribunal.[45] If either party fails to complete the procedure, this may be reflected in the damages award, to be discussed below. The government's aim in introducing these provisions was to reduce the number of claims which reached a tribunal hearing – by encouraging the parties to resolve their problems themselves through the procedures – and consequently to reduce the costs faced by employers in defending unfair dismissal claims.[46] However, critics have argued that employers, and employees in particular, may not be aware of the penalties they face if they ignore the procedures.[47] This means that the penalties will not be an effective deterrent.

---

42 See the discussion of remedies, below.
43 EA 2002, s. 30(1).
44 ERA 1996, s. 98A.
45 EA 2002, s. 32.
46 For discussion of the government's rationale, see B. Hepple and G.S. Morris, 'The Employment Act 2002 and the crisis of individual employment rights' (2002) 31 *ILJ* 245. A similar concern is evidenced by the introduction of an arbitration procedure for unfair dismissal claims under the Employment Rights (Dispute Resolution) Act 1998, noted by R. Lewis (1998) 27 *ILJ* 214.
47 Hepple and Morris, above n. 46.

From the employer's perspective, the minimum procedures are also confusing because compliance with them does not guarantee that a dismissal will be found to be fair. This is because they do not reflect the Advisory, Conciliation and Arbitration Service (ACAS) Code of Practice which has hitherto guided tribunals,[48] nor do they reflect the jurisprudence of the tribunals themselves. Hepple and Morris give a number of examples of where the minimum procedures fall short.[49] One of the most striking is that there is no express obligation on the employer to investigate the circumstances surrounding the reason for dismissal. Thus, the employer could follow the minimum procedure but a tribunal could still find that it had behaved unreasonably. However, the employer can avail itself of a defence in these circumstances. If the employer can show that it would have dismissed the employee anyway, the dismissal is not deemed to be unfair simply because the employer failed to follow a procedure other than the minimum one.[50] The government argues that this provision will encourage employers to adopt better procedures than the minimum, because they can do so without fear of liability if those procedures are not always followed. However, this allows the employer to publish a procedure and then ignore it in some cases: a clear violation of employees' dignity.

The EA 2002 has brought about an interesting shift in the nature of unfair dismissal law. Traditionally, the law has been regarded as strong in its procedural requirements even if its scrutiny of the employer's reason for dismissal was weak. The insertion of disciplinary and grievance procedures into every contract of employment looks like a further advance in the protection of employees' dignity. However, for many rights advocates it is undermined by the minimal nature of those procedures and by the government's underlying motivation to cut costs for employers.

Remedies

The remedy offered by the law to an employee who has been wrongfully or unfairly dismissed is an important indicator of the value placed by the law on the employee's rights. For example, if a substantial award of compensation is given when an employee's dignity has been violated, it can be regarded as clear condemnation by society of the employer's behaviour. Substantial remedies are also important from the new institutional economics perspective: if employers are to realise the benefits of providing job security to their employees, they need to be deterred from opportunistic dismissals. However, most commentators agree that the remedies are relatively weak: Epstein's concerns about costs have prevailed again.

The remedies for wrongful dismissal are those available in the law of contract. If an employee has been wrongfully dismissed without notice, he or she can claim the wages which would have been paid during the notice period. However, the

---

48 ACAS Code of Practice 1, *Disciplinary and Grievance Procedures* (2000).
49 Above n. 46.
50 ERA 1996, s. 98A(2).

usual contract rules apply, so the employee must mitigate his or her loss by seeking another job. The damages will be reduced if he or she finds another job or if the court considers that he or she has not made enough of an effort to do so. The sums available on this approach are relatively small for most claimants.

One way to increase the damages available at common law might be to argue that an unfair dismissal amounted to a breach of 'mutual trust and confidence'.[51] A term requiring both parties to behave in ways which preserve the relationship of mutual trust and confidence between them is implied into every contract of employment by the courts. Among other things, this term forbids arbitrary behaviour on the part of the employer. However, in *Johnson v Unisys Ltd*, the House of Lords held that the term did not apply to dismissals, on the grounds that this would subvert Parliament's intentions in creating the doctrine of unfair dismissal and its associated remedies.[52] Hope has been revived somewhat by the recent decision in *King v University of St Andrews*, in which the claimant was allowed to recover damages for a breach of mutual trust and confidence during the disciplinary procedure which led to his dismissal.[53] The court limited the effect of the *Johnson* decision by holding that it only began to apply once the employer had made the decision to dismiss. However, it remains to be seen whether this approach will be upheld by the higher courts.

As we have seen, some employees are lucky enough to have contractual terms which require the employer to follow a procedure before dismissing them. These employees have access to a more advantageous set of remedies at common law. First, they may be able to claim additional damages if the employer does not go through the contractual disciplinary procedure. Logically, the damages should consist of the wages the employee would have received while the disciplinary procedure took place, and some compensation for the loss of the chance that the employee might not have been dismissed. However, whilst the courts have accepted the former element they have not so far seen fit to include the latter.[54] Second, the employee may be able to seek an injunction to force the employer to conduct the disciplinary procedure. The employee must act quickly to show that he or she has not accepted the employer's repudiatory breach of contract so that the contract remains in existence.[55] Then, the court will grant an injunction if there is still a relationship of mutual trust and confidence between the parties so that it is not unfair to the employer to be required to keep the employee on. This sounds like an impossible hurdle but in practice the courts have been quite willing to find that mutual trust and confidence are present.[56] By forcing the employer to go through the disciplinary procedure, the employee not only gets his or her wages during that period but also gets a chance to show that he or she has not done anything to deserve dismissal. This offers a strong protection

---

51 See, generally, D. Brodie, 'Beyond exchange: the new contract of employment' (1998) 27 *ILJ* 79.
52 [2003] 1 AC 518. See H. Collins (2001) 30 *ILJ* 305.
53 [2002] IRLR 252 (Outer House). See D. Brodie (2002) 31 *ILJ* 294.
54 *Gunton v Richmond LBC* [1980] ICR 755; *Boyo v Lambeth LBC* [1995] IRLR 50.
55 See *Gunton v Richmond-upon-Thames LBC* [1980] ICR 755.
56 *Irani v Southampton and West Hampshire AHA* [1985] IRLR 203; *Jones v Gwent CC* [1992] IRLR 521.

for the employee's dignity-based right to have the issue of dismissal carefully considered by the employer. Now that all contracts of employment contain procedural requirements under the EA 2002, the common law remedies of additional damages or an injunction could be used much more widely as a means of enforcing the statutory procedures. However, if the courts keep to the policy expressed in *Johnson*, of ensuring that the common law does not interfere with the unfair dismissal regime, it seems unlikely that such claims will succeed.[57]

Two remedies are available to the employee who brings a successful unfair dismissal claim: re-employment and damages.[58] In principle, re-employment offers a high level of protection to employees because it allows the court to *override* the employer's decision to dismiss. Job property theorists view it as an important instance of their approach: the employee has been unfairly deprived of his or her property and should be given that property back. However, re-employment is the remedy in a tiny fraction of cases so it does not operate as a strong remedy in practice.[59] Some critics argue that this is one of the legislation's failings. Tribunals are too ready to find that it is not 'practicable' for the employer to take the employee back,[60] and even when they do order re-employment, the employer who breaches the order is only required to pay a small amount of additional compensation which is insufficient to act as a deterrent.[61] Others argue that the remedy is unrealistic and should be abandoned. Returning to the workplace after an acrimonious dismissal is an unattractive option for many people, and this is borne out by the fact that few claimants request re-employment.[62] On this view, it is more realistic to compensate employees and deter employers using substantial awards of damages.

An award of damages for unfair dismissal is made up of two elements: the basic award and the compensatory award.[63] The basic award is calculated using a formula which reflects the claimant's age, length of service with the employer and usual weekly wage,[64] up to a limit of £270 per week.[65] The maximum available under this heading is £8100. This means that employees who earn more than £270 per week cannot be fully compensated. The second element is the compensatory award.[66] This is a sum that the tribunal considers 'just and equitable', normally up

---

57 Hepple and Morris, above n. 46, at 253–5.
58 The statute provides for the employee to be reinstated in his or her old job (ERA 1996, s. 114) or re-engaged by the employer in comparable employment (ERA 1996, s. 115). 'Re-employment' does not appear in the statute but is a useful umbrella term.
59 In 2002–3, re-employment was awarded in a mere 16 out of a total of 4158 successful tribunal applications. Source: Employment Tribunals Service, *Annual Report and Accounts 2002–3* (2003).
60 ERA 1996, s. 116(1)(b).
61 ERA 1996, s. 117.
62 ERA 1996, s. 116(1)(a).
63 The figures used to calculate these awards must be revised once a year by the Secretary of State in line with the retail price index: ERA 1999, s. 34. The amounts applicable from 1 February 2004 are set out in the Employment Rights (Increase of Limits) Order 2003 (SI 2003/3038).
64 ERA 1996, ss. 119–22.
65 ERA 1996, s. 227.
66 ERA 1996, ss. 123–4.

to a maximum limit of £55,000. The purpose of this award is to compensate the employee, not to punish the employer, so the tribunal usually looks quite closely at the employee's losses. Again, awards under this heading tend to be relatively low. In 2002–3, the average compensation for unfair dismissal was £6776.[67] These modest awards help to keep employers' costs down. But they can be criticised for failing to vindicate employees' rights and for failing to encourage employers to maintain a policy of job security. They also help to explain why some employees, like the claimant in *Johnson*, have felt the need to pursue their claims at common law as well.

Where the employee has failed to complete a grievance or disciplinary procedure under the EA 2002, his or her unfair dismissal damages must be reduced by 10% and may be reduced by up to 50%, unless the tribunal finds that there are exceptional circumstances for not applying these rules.[68] This is intended to promote the use of the statutory procedures and to encourage the parties to resolve their differences without recourse to a tribunal. However, the rule could operate harshly where employees are unaware of it. Hepple and Morris suggest that, at the very least, employers should have been obliged to inform employees of the importance of following the procedures.[69]

In some circumstances tribunals may be able to make higher awards of damages to reflect the seriousness of the employer's actions. The maximum limit on the compensatory award does not apply in cases of discrimination on grounds of sex, race and so on. Where the employer has dismissed the employee on trade union grounds[70] or for acting as a workforce representative,[71] a minimum basic award of £3600 must be awarded regardless of the individual's length of service. And where the employer has failed to complete a disciplinary or grievance procedure under the EA 2002, the employee's damages must be increased by 10% and may be increased by up to 50% unless exceptional circumstances apply.[72] These various provisions fit well with the dignity rationale suggested by Collins. Because they apply either when a forbidden reason for dismissal is used or when basic procedural fairness is ignored, the employee's dignity is violated and particularly strong condemnation is required. However, this interpretation of the EA 2002 is somewhat undermined by the fact that equivalent provisions apply against employees, even though the employer's dignity is not violated by an employee's failure to complete a procedure.

A final point to note is that the statute provides compensation for those who are made redundant even where the redundancy is fair.[73] This compensation is calculated in exactly the same way as the basic award in unfair dismissal, described

---

67 Source: Employment Tribunals Service, above n. 59.
68 EA 2002, s. 31(2) and (4).
69 Above n. 46.
70 TULRCA 1992, s. 156.
71 ERA 1996, s. 120.
72 EA 2002, s. 31(3) and (4).
73 ERA 1996, s. 135.

above.[74] It is commonly regarded as a way of acknowledging to employees that a dismissal for redundancy, though justified, is not their fault. However, it can be questioned whether the payments are sufficient to do this, given the relatively low level at which they are set.[75] Moreover, the payments may not be enough to deter employers from behaving opportunistically and ignoring the longer-term goal of job security. In contrast, Collins is critical of the very existence of redundancy payments, arguing that it is in the interests of the economy as a whole that employers should not be deterred from reorganising their businesses.[76]

Further reading

For detailed textbook accounts of this topic, see S. Deakin and G.S. Morris, *Labour Law* (3rd edn., 2001), chapter 5; or H. Collins, K.D. Ewing and A. McColgan, *Labour Law: Text and Materials* (2001), chapter 5.

H. Collins, *Justice in Dismissal* (1992), is a thought-provoking study of dismissal laws which draws on both rights and economics arguments. For a critique, see G. Pitt, 'Justice in Dismissal: a reply to Hugh Collins' (1993) 22 *ILJ* 251. What methodology does Collins adopt? Are there problems with it? How does he classify dismissals? What flaws does Pitt identify in his classification? Are the economics arguments he uses primarily neoclassical or new institutional? Do you agree with the balance he strikes between the rights to dignity and autonomy, and cost considerations? Do you find these rights persuasive as the basis for dismissal law, or would you prefer to see it justified in some other way?

B. Hepple and G.S. Morris, 'The Employment Act 2002 and the crisis of individual employment rights' (2002) 31 *ILJ* 245, is an excellent critical analysis of the recent changes brought about by the EA 2002 from a rights perspective. Is the government's worry about the litigation costs associated with unfair dismissal laws a real one? If so, can it be addressed without limiting workers' rights? For discussion of recent procedural reforms, see R. Lewis, 'Recent legislation: The Employment Rights (Dispute Resolution) Act 1998' (1998) 27 *ILJ* 214; J. Earnshaw and S. Hardy, 'Assessing an arbitral route for unfair dismissal' (2001) 30 *ILJ* 289. Might consultation with workers as a group have a role to play here? For some ideas, see the discussion of collective consultation on redundancies in chapter 10.

Should unfair dismissal and redundancy protection be extended to workers as well as employees? Review the arguments presented in chapter 5 on this issue. For an attempt to argue that the qualifying period amounted to discrimination on grounds of sex, see *R v Secretary of State for Employment, ex p. Seymour-Smith (No. 2)* [2000] 1 All ER 857.

---

74 ERA 1996, s. 162.
75 For critique, see R. Fryer, 'The myths of the Redundancy Payments Act' (1973) 2 *ILJ* 1.
76 Above n. 3, chapter 5.

The most accessible account of the neoclassical perspective is R.A. Epstein, 'In defense of the contract at will' (1984) 51 *University of Chicago Law Review* 947. What assumptions does Epstein make in formulating his argument? What do you think motivates people to work hard? Does it depend on the job? Are Epstein's critics right to identify real risks of employer opportunism? Do those risks fully justify English unfair dismissal law or do we need to use other arguments too?

10

Collective representation

This chapter is the first of three chapters dealing with the collective dimension of labour law: in other words, its approach to *groups* of workers. Trade unions are, of course, the classic example of workers grouping together in order to bargain with the employer about terms and conditions of employment. As we saw in chapter 1, the labour law of the 1950s was designed to support collective bargaining. Today, the law continues to play this role to some extent. However, collective bargaining is no longer the sole mechanism through which workers may present their views to the employer. Duties derived from EC law to consult with employees also form an important part of labour law. Consultation may involve trade unions but it need not do so. This chapter will address the two main controversies which arise in this area: whether workers should have a say in the running of the workplace at all, and if so, what form their participation should take.[1]

Human rights instruments generally support some form of worker participation. Civil and political rights instruments usually contain a right to form and join trade unions 'for the protection of [the individual's] interests'. Commentators have argued that this phrase could be used to support a right to engage in collective bargaining, but interpretations (for example, by the ECtHR) have not always confirmed this view. Economic and social rights instruments usually contain an express right to collective bargaining. Consultation is a recent innovation and makes an appearance only in the most modern economic and social rights instruments, such as the EU Charter and the revised ESC 1996.

The economics literature on the role of collective bargaining is substantial and often quite polarised. At the one extreme, there are those who feel that unions are damaging to the national economy and to the interests of individual workers. They argue that unions secure 'rents' for their members: in other words, higher pay than the market would justify. This reduces firms' profits, limits the number of workers they can afford to employ, and increases inequality between unionised and non-unionised workers. At the other extreme, there are those who argue that

---

1 Some countries require companies to have worker representatives as board members. For reasons of space, this will not be discussed in this chapter. For detail, see M. Biagi, 'Forms of employee representational participation', in R. Blanpain and C. Engels (eds.), *Comparative Labour Law and Industrial Relations in Industrialized Market Economies* (7th edn., 2001), pp. 519–22.

unions have a positive effect. Unions improve communication between employers and workers. They increase firms' productivity by supplying information to management about how working practices might be improved, and by reducing the turnover of employees (thus lowering firms' hiring and training costs). Duties to consult employees have not been so fully studied by economists. Some versions of consultation may be closely related to collective bargaining – where a trade union is involved and similar issues are covered – and may therefore have the same balance of advantages and disadvantages. But, as we shall see, the effect of consultation is more difficult to predict the further away we move from collective bargaining.

Rights perspectives

Collective bargaining

Civil and political rights instruments tend not to address the question of collective bargaining. Article 11 of the ECHR is typical: 'Everyone has the right to freedom of peaceful assembly and to freedom of association with others, including the right to form and join trade unions for the protection of his interests.'[2] The phrase 'for the protection of his interests' has been invested with considerable significance by some commentators.[3] They have argued that if the trade union is to protect its members, it must have certain rights, such as the right to engage in collective bargaining and the right to strike. Such rights should therefore be seen as implicit in the right to freedom of association. In the *National Union of Belgian Police* case, the ECtHR appeared to support this view, holding that 'what the Convention requires is that under national law trade unions should be enabled . . . to strive for the protection of their members' interests'.[4] But later cases have not required national governments to protect a right to collective bargaining. In the *Swedish Engine Drivers' Union* case, it was held that a trade union had no right to enter into a collective agreement with the employer,[5] and in *Wilson v UK*, it was held that there was no obligation on the state to maintain a statutory procedure for the recognition of trade unions.[6]

The absence of a right to collective bargaining in civil and political rights instruments reflects their focus on rights for *individuals*. The right to freedom of association can be interpreted as a purely individual right to join associations. The only obligation this right imposes on others (such as employers) is to refrain from discriminating against people because of the associations they have joined. However, some would argue that this approach ignores the reasons which lead individuals to join organisations. In the case of trade unions, individuals often join because they want to use their collective strength in order to bargain with the employer for better

---

2 See also Article 22 of the ICCPR.
3 For discussion, see T. Novitz, *International and European Protection of the Right to Strike* (2003), pp. 225–40; K.D. Ewing, 'The Human Rights Act and labour law' (1998) 27 *ILJ* 275 at 279–80.
4 *National Union of Belgian Police v Belgium* [1979–80] 1 EHRR 578 at 591.
5 *Swedish Engine Drivers' Union v Sweden* [1979–80] 1 EHRR 617.
6 [2002] 35 EHRR 20.

terms and conditions. If the individual's right to join the union is to be rendered truly effective, the union itself must have the rights it needs in order to further its members' interests.

Economic and social rights instruments are more open to the possibility of rights which attach to groups, as well as individuals, which is why they are more likely to contain a right to collective bargaining. Let us look at some examples. Article 28 of the EU Charter states that:

> Workers and their employers, or their respective organisations, have, in accordance with Community law and national laws and practices, the right to negotiate and conclude collective agreements at the appropriate levels and, in cases of conflicts of interest, to take collective action to defend their interests, including strike action.

The ESC (in both the 1961 and 1996 versions) protects a right to bargain, but through more indirect means. Article 6 states that:

> With a view to ensuring the effective exercise of the right to bargain collectively, the Parties undertake:
> . . . 2. to promote, where necessary and appropriate, machinery for voluntary negotiations between employers or employers' organisations and workers' organisations, with a view to the regulation of terms and conditions of employment by means of collective agreements.

In the ILO, collective bargaining is governed by two Conventions. The first, Convention 98 on the Right to Organise and Collective Bargaining (1949), provides in Article 4 that:

> Measures appropriate to national conditions shall be taken, where necessary, to encourage and promote the full development and utilisation of machinery for voluntary negotiation between employers or employers' organisations or workers' organisations, with a view to the regulation of terms and conditions of employment by means of collective agreements.

The UK has ratified this Convention.[7] Further detail is provided in Convention 154, the Collective Bargaining Convention of 1981. Article 5 requires states to promote collective bargaining, and specifies in some detail the aims to be pursued. These aims include ensuring that collective bargaining is possible for all employers and groups of workers, extending the scope of collective bargaining to cover terms and conditions of employment and relations between employers and workers and their respective organisations, encouraging the parties to agree procedural rules for collective bargaining, and ensuring that collective bargaining is not hindered where no procedural rules have been agreed. This provides the most detailed international statement of the state's responsibilities in relation to collective bargaining, but it has not received widespread support. It has been ratified by a mere 34 countries, not including the UK.

---

7 The ESC 1961, discussed above, draws heavily on this Article.

All these rights clearly oblige the state to refrain from preventing or interfering in collective bargaining voluntarily undertaken by employers and unions. The obligation to 'promote machinery' for collective bargaining is, however, rather more difficult to interpret. The use of phrases such as 'appropriate to national conditions' and 'in accordance with ... national laws and practices' indicates that states have a substantial discretion in the way that they implement this obligation. The ILO Freedom of Association Committee has held that the state may not make bargaining compulsory, because this would infringe the fundamental requirement that bargaining should be voluntary.[8] Nor does the duty to promote collective bargaining permit the state to force employers and unions to use conciliation or arbitration when they cannot resolve their disputes. The state may provide such machinery, but recourse to it should be a matter of choice for the employer and union.[9] Finally, the state may help the parties to gain access to information which would assist them in bargaining.[10]

Consultation

Consultation is a relative newcomer and therefore features only in the most recent instruments. The EU Charter contains a basic right to consultation:

> Workers or their representatives must, at the appropriate levels, be guaranteed information and consultation in good time in the cases and under the conditions provided for by Community law and national laws and practices.[11]

As we shall see, there is already a substantial body of EU law on consultation. This right reflects this body of law, and offers little guidance as to how it might be developed in the future. The revised ESC 1996 is the other instrument which contains consultation rights. The UK is not bound by these rights because it has only ratified the ESC 1961, which did not address the issue of consultation. A general right to information and consultation is set out in Article 21:

> With a view to ensuring the effective exercise of the right of workers to be informed and consulted within the undertaking, the Parties undertake to adopt or encourage measures enabling workers or their representatives, in accordance with national legislation and practice:
>
> (a) to be informed regularly or at the appropriate time and in a comprehensible way about the economic and financial situation of the undertaking employing them, on the understanding that the disclosure of certain information which could be prejudicial to the undertaking may be refused or subject to confidentiality; and

---

8 ILO, *Digest of Decisions and Principles of the Freedom of Association Committee* (1996), paras. 844–46.

9 ILO, above n. 8, para. 858.

10 ILO, above n. 8, para. 859.

11 Article 27.

(b) to be consulted in good time on proposed decisions which could substantially affect the interests of workers, particularly on those decisions which could have an important impact on the employment situation in the undertaking.

This right requires workers or their representatives to be provided with information about the state of the business on a regular basis, and to be consulted on specific issues affecting them, such as redundancies. Although it refers to national legislation and practice, it gives a clearer idea than does the EU Charter of the obligations it imposes. It is supplemented by Article 28, which requires states to support workers' representatives by protecting them against detrimental treatment, including dismissal, and by providing them with facilities to carry out their task.[12] The ESC 1996 also contains some more specific consultation rights. For example, Article 29 requires states to oblige employers to consult workers' representatives in the event of collective redundancies. It states that consultation should cover 'ways and means of avoiding collective redundancies or limiting their occurrence and mitigating their consequences'.

One of the major contrasts between consultation and collective bargaining is reflected in the way in which these rights are framed. Collective bargaining requires the active participation of the relevant workers, who must form or join a trade union and seek recognition from the employer. As a result, the state's obligation is confined to providing mechanisms for the workers to use, rather than forcing the workers to use them. Information and consultation does not require the same level of participation. The workers need not join an organisation. They only need to elect representatives. Even if they do not want to do this, the employer can still provide them with information and ask them for their views as individuals. As a result, these rights are more strongly framed. States are required to 'adopt' measures or to 'guarantee' the relevant rights to workers.

This leads to a more profound question about the status of the right to be consulted. Some rights theorists are sceptical about its value to workers. They argue that collective bargaining offers a more effective form of participation because the presence of a trade union helps to equalise the bargaining power of workers and management. Consultation puts workers in a much weaker position. Therefore, consultation should only be promoted as a 'second-best' option when collective bargaining is not available. The two types of participation should not be given equal status by the law. Against this, it might be argued that the right to be consulted in an employment setting is linked to more general rights which *are* regarded as fundamental, such as the administrative law right to be given a hearing by a public authority and even the fundamental human right to a fair trial. On this basis, the right to consultation is an important right to a fair hearing at work.

---

12 Similar obligations are contained in ILO Convention 135, the Workers' Representatives Convention, 1971, which applies both to union representatives and to elected non-union representatives of the workforce. This reference to non-union representatives is unusual given the ILO's traditional focus on collective bargaining as the main mode of worker representation.

Economics perspectives

Trade unions have been a topic of considerable interest to economists. Neoclassical theorists argue that unions lead to unwarranted increases in wages which have harmful consequences for firms, other workers and the economy as a whole. New institutionalists argue that trade unionism can benefit firms by reducing labour turnover and improving productivity. Consultation has not been studied so fully but it is possible to speculate about its likely economic consequences.

Economic arguments against worker participation

An individual worker is unlikely to have much ability to bargain with the employer unless he or she has unique skills. The employer can easily hire a replacement if the worker demands improved terms and conditions. If workers join a trade union, however, the position changes. The larger the proportion of workers who are members of the union, the harder it is for the employer to hire replacements if they demand improved terms and conditions. Moreover, the union may be able to threaten strike action – which would disrupt the employer's business – if its demands are ignored. This enables unions to extract concessions from the employer. This may seem harmless: perhaps the employer is exploiting the non-unionised workers, using its superior economic muscle to pay them less than the market rate for their jobs. But economists do not analyse the situation in this way. If the employer was paying the non-unionised workers less than the market rate for the job, they would simply leave and find jobs elsewhere. So any concessions achieved by the union are 'rents': gains over and above the market rate for the job.[13] These rents are regarded as inefficient. They lead to a misallocation of labour. Because unionised firms will not be able to employ as many workers at the higher wage, some workers in that sector will lose their jobs. In turn, this reduces the output of the unionised sector: fewer workers mean that fewer goods are produced.

By comparing the wages paid to similarly qualified workers in unionised and non-unionised workplaces, economists are able to estimate the extent to which unions are able to secure rents in practice. There are some methodological difficulties with their calculations.[14] In particular, wages in the non-union sector are likely to be influenced by wages in the unionised sector. They may be pushed up by employers who want to protect themselves against union-organising drives. Or they may be pushed down, by the flood of workers into the non-unionised sector who have been made redundant because of wage rises in the unionised sector. A figure representing the difference between wages in the two sectors may therefore be a slight underestimate or overestimate of the union wage effect. Nevertheless, some idea can be given of the union wage effect for particular countries at particular points in time. In their classic study of trade unions, Freeman and Medoff found

13 See F.A. Hayek, *The Constitution of Liberty* (1960), chapter 18; R.A. Posner, *Economic Analysis of Law* (5th edn., 1998), pp. 349–56.
14 D.J.B. Mitchell, *Unions, Wages, and Inflation* (1980), chapter 3.

that in the 1970s, unionised workers in the US were paid 20–30% more than non-unionised workers.[15] More recent figures suggest that the effect for the US in 2000 was around 15%.[16] However, the US is not typical, and tends to show a greater effect than other countries, including the UK. We will examine data for the UK in our discussion of the legal provisions on collective bargaining, below.

Of course, the 'union wage effect' does not always manifest itself in practice. One reason for this is that unions do not pursue high wages at the expense of all other considerations. They are concerned with preserving their members' jobs as well as with securing better pay. So unions will not push for very high wages which would lead to substantial job losses. This is particularly likely to occur when the economy is in recession. If the firm's sales are declining, it may need to make some workers redundant in order to cut its costs and remain profitable. In these circumstances, the union may refrain from asking for a pay rise which would only make matters worse.

When the economy is enjoying a period of growth, the union wage effect is much more of a worry for neoclassical economists. If unions cannot be kept in check by fears about redundancies, some other way must be found to minimise the harm they can do to the economy. Many theorists argue that the law on trade unions can play an important role. It should be used to reduce the power of trade unions and to limit their bargaining power as against employers. For example, some legal systems allow the 'closed shop', in which all workers in a particular workplace can be forced to become members of the union. This makes the union very strong: the employer can hardly ignore the demands of all its workers. So a law which bans the 'closed shop' may help to reduce unions' ability to extract rents from employers. Similarly, unions' bargaining power is strengthened when they are able to make credible threats of strike action. Employers will be keen to avoid the disruption this may cause, so they will be more likely to accept the union's demands. Again, the law can intervene by placing obstacles in the way of strike action. Chapters 11 and 12 will explore these issues more fully.

The impact of consultation has not been analysed so extensively by economists. To begin with, we need to decide how similar consultation is to collective bargaining. If it is very similar, it is likely to have the same impact as collective bargaining: it will enable workers to extract benefits from the employer over and above those they would have achieved in the market. One important difference between the two processes is that consultation leaves the final decision firmly in the hands of the employer. In consultation, the employer asks workers for their opinion and then makes a decision which may or may not reflect their views. In collective bargaining, the aim is to reach an agreement with the union representatives – a 'collective agreement' – which will be respected by both sides. This suggests that consultation is less likely to affect market outcomes because employers can more easily ignore the

15 R.B. Freeman and J.L. Medoff, *What Do Unions Do?* (1984), chapter 3.
16 See B.T. Hirsch and D.A. Macpherson, *Union Membership and Earnings Data Book* (2001).

opinions expressed during consultation. Another important difference between the two processes is that consultation, unlike collective bargaining, does not depend on the presence of a trade union to represent the workers. In collective bargaining, the threat of strike action helps to equalise the bargaining power between the workers and the employer. A similar threat could be used to enforce the demands of representatives in a consultation process. However, this is unlikely unless the workplace is unionised. This is because English law actively discourages non-union industrial action.[17] As a result, the bargaining power of representatives in a consultation exercise may depend heavily on whether or not they have the support of a union. Again, this means that consultation may be a relatively harmless process in which the employer is unlikely to be forced to make concessions to the workers.

Nevertheless, it seems unlikely that neoclassical economists would welcome, or even tolerate, extensive legal obligations on employers to consult with workers. Simply putting consultation procedures in place – supplying information to representatives, holding meetings and so on – costs money. They would see no justification for the imposition of these costs on employers.

Economic arguments in favour of worker participation

Two slightly different claims are commonly used to support the view that worker participation may be beneficial to firms. First, worker participation is said to improve a firm's ability to retain its employees. Second, worker participation may increase productivity by enabling the employer to harness workers' ideas for improving production processes. It might be expected that if these arguments were correct, employers would adopt worker participation mechanisms voluntarily without the need for legal intervention. However, it is commonly argued that legislation is needed to protect 'good' firms from undercutting.

Firms with a high turnover of labour face increased costs because they have to hire replacements and train them to the required standard. Hiring costs include placing job advertisements and using managers' time to conduct interviews. Training costs may be considerable if the job requires firm-specific skills. Some theorists have argued that trade unions can reduce firms' labour turnover. Freeman and Medoff found that unionised firms had lower quit rates than non-unionised firms.[18] They estimated that this reduced firms' labour costs by 1–2%. One explanation for this finding might be the union wage effect, where it exists. For obvious reasons, workers who receive above-average pay are likely to value their jobs more highly. But Freeman and Medoff argued that unions reduced turnover rates even when the unionised and non-unionised firms they compared were paying the same wages. They attributed this to the union 'voice' effect. Workers in unionised firms chose to deal with their grievances by complaining ('voicing'), rather than simply looking for another job

---

17 See chapter 12.
18 Above n. 15, chapter 6.

('exiting').[19] This was because unions encouraged management to put in place grievance and arbitration procedures through which workers' concerns could be resolved. Consultation might have the same benefit if it provided workers with a means of voicing their concerns.

A second set of economic arguments in favour of worker participation is that it can improve the firm's productivity and performance. The White Paper *Fairness at Work* contains a useful summary of these ideas:

> ...the returns from effective partnership to the business and its employees are real whether it operates in local or global markets:
>
> – where they have an understanding of the business, employees recognise the importance of responding quickly to changing customer and market requirements;
> – where they are taken seriously, employees at every level come forward with ways to help the business innovate, for example by developing new products; and
> – where they are well-prepared for change, employees can help the company to introduce and operate new technologies and processes, helping to secure employment within the business.[20]

The idea is that the employer can use either consultation or collective bargaining to build close relationships with worker representatives. The representatives can then act as an important channel of communication between management and the workforce. They can inform management about workers' ideas for improving the firm's performance. And the representatives can inform workers about management's plans for the future of the business. The firm's productivity should improve both as a direct result of workers' suggestions, and indirectly because of workers' co-operation and enthusiasm.

If worker participation is as beneficial as the literature suggests, both in reducing turnover and improving productivity, it might be expected that firms would introduce it voluntarily out of self-interested motives. But it is often argued that legislation does have an essential role to play even when participation would benefit firms. First, legislation may educate employers. Economic theory assumes that employers always act rationally in order to maximise their profits. In the real world, employers may not realise the benefits of certain types of behaviour. Employers who are used to a hierarchical model of organisation may not be aware of what can be achieved through partnership. Thus, by requiring employers to respond to trade union requests for recognition or to set up consultation mechanisms, the law may trigger an interest in new ways of working. Second, legislation may help firms which are considering adopting a partnership approach but feel nervous about doing so. Partnership may require a considerable investment of time and effort over the short term in order to change the culture of the workplace. Firms may perceive the long-term benefits, but they may be afraid of being undercut by their competitors while

---

19 The terminology is from A.O. Hirschman, *Exit, Voice and Loyalty* (1970).
20 *Fairness at Work* (Cm. 3968, 1998), p. 12.

they incur the short-term costs. Legislation may assist here by imposing some set-up costs on all firms and making it easier to adopt the long-term view.

But there are some problems with legally mandated bargaining or consultation. A recent study of firms which had implemented a 'partnership' approach found that 'achieving partnership at work is often difficult, requires high levels of commitment from all concerned, and can take a significant length of time to achieve'.[21] This suggests that the key to achieving lower labour turnover or higher productivity through worker participation lies in the attitudes of those involved. Although legislation may encourage positive attitudes in some firms, it may also provoke resentment. Where consultation or collective bargaining is grudgingly implemented by a reluctant employer, it seems unlikely to have many benefits.

The law on collective bargaining

Around 45% of all workplaces have collective bargaining in respect of at least some employees. Collective bargaining is more likely in larger workplaces, and in the public sector.[22] We will look at the various ways in which the law supports collective bargaining before examining the provisions from the rights and economics perspectives.

When an employer has agreed to engage in collective bargaining with a union, we say that the union has been 'recognised'. The recognition agreement will usually specify which aspects of the employment relationship the parties have opened up for bargaining. The law offers certain advantages to recognised trade unions, some of which will be discussed below. Under the traditional theory of collective *laissez-faire*, it is up to the union to secure recognition for itself. The union's main mechanism for doing this is to engage in, or threaten to engage in, industrial action. The impact of such action depends on factors such as the employer's ability to withstand the strike and the state of the labour market. These matters will be considered in detail in chapter 12.

Recently, the government has reintroduced a statutory procedure to assist trade unions to obtain recognition where they are unable or unwilling to secure it through their industrial muscle alone.[23] The details of the procedure are set out in a new Sch. A1 to TULRCA 1992.[24] A union can obtain automatic recognition if 50% of the employees in a particular bargaining unit are members of the union.[25] It can

---

21 J. Knell, *Parnership at Work* (DTI URN 99/1078) (1999), p. 27.
22 M. Cully *et al.*, *Britain at Work* (1999), pp. 90–4.
23 The Industrial Relations Act 1971, ss. 44–50, first introduced a recognition procedure into English law. A revised procedure was contained in the Employment Protection Act 1975, ss. 11–6. This was repealed in 1980.
24 Inserted by ERA 1999, s. 1. For discussion, see B. Simpson, 'Trade union recognition and the law, a new approach – Parts I and II of Schedule A1 to TULRCA 1992' (2000) 29 *ILJ* 193; A.L. Bogg, 'The political theory of trade union recognition campaigns – legislating for democratic competitiveness' (2001) 64 *MLR* 875; T. Novitz and P. Skidmore, *Fairness at Work: a Critical Analysis of the Employment Relations Act 1999 and its Treatment of Collective Rights* (2001), chapter 4.
25 Schedule A1, para. 22.

also obtain recognition if a majority of those voting and at least 40% of those eligible to vote have supported recognition in a secret ballot.[26] Once recognition has been achieved, the parties may conduct negotiations as to how they will conduct collective bargaining, and if they fail to agree, the Central Arbitration Committee (CAC) may specify a procedure (called a 'method') for them.[27] The method takes effect as a legally binding contract which a court may enforce through an order for specific performance.[28] The bargaining must cover pay, hours and holidays, though the parties may add other matters by agreement.[29] Some evidence is now emerging as to the operation of the new procedure.[30] So far there have been 175 applications for recognition, of which 63 have reached the balloting stage. Many of those which dropped out along the way did so because the union and the employer reached a voluntary agreement. Of the 29 ballots concluded so far, unions won in 20 cases. In the majority of successful cases, the parties have agreed a method for collective bargaining, though the CAC has had to impose a method in one case.

Once recognition has been obtained, whether by agreement or through the statutory procedure, the union must then try to persuade the employer of the merits of its claims. Again, much will depend on the industrial muscle of the union, but the law does offer some indirect assistance to facilitate the bargaining process. Trade union representatives are entitled to a reasonable amount of paid time off work to prepare for and participate in collective bargaining,[31] and trade union members are entitled to a reasonable amount of unpaid time off for trade union activities, such as voting on the outcome of collective bargaining.[32]

The law also supports the collective bargaining process by giving recognised unions a statutory right of access to the employer's information. A strong union may be able to get information by negotiating for it, but where the union is weak, the employer may be able to frustrate collective bargaining by concealing relevant facts. Under TULRCA 1992, s. 181(2), the employer is under a duty to disclose information:

(a) without which the trade union representatives would be to a material extent impeded in carrying on collective bargaining with him, and
(b) which it would be in accordance with good industrial relations practice that he should disclose to them for the purposes of collective bargaining.

---

26 Schedule A1, paras. 23–9.
27 Schedule A1, para. 30; Trade Union Recognition (Method of Collective Bargaining) Order 2000 (SI 2000/1300). The CAC is a statutory body with responsibility for arbitration in various areas of collective labour law, including recognition and disclosure of information for collective bargaining (discussed below).
28 Schedule A1, para. 30(4) and (6).
29 Schedule A1, para. 1(3) and (4).
30 CAC, *Annual Report 2001/2* (2002), pp. 18–20.
31 TULRCA 1992, ss. 168–9.
32 TULRCA 1992, s. 170.

However, this offers limited guidance as to what information the employer is obliged to disclose.[33] The employer may also be able to rely on exceptions, for example, where the information is confidential or where its disclosure might damage the business.[34] The procedure for enforcement is through a complaint to the CAC,[35] but unions may be reluctant to invoke this for fear that to do so might damage their future relations with the employer. Research by Gospel and Lockwood, which found that relatively few claims had been made under s. 181, seems to bear this theory out.[36] As the authors argue, however, the statutory right to information may have significant indirect effects. In other words, unions may be able to extract information from employers simply by threatening to invoke the statutory procedure.

The process of collective bargaining usually results in a collective agreement. Most collective agreements are not legally binding.[37] Employers and unions generally prefer to keep their agreements informal and flexible. If certain conditions are met, the terms of a collective agreement may be incorporated into the contracts of employment of the employees to whom it applies.[38]

From a rights perspective, much of this legislation is uncontroversial. The statutory procedure for obtaining information is an obvious way in which the state could comply with the obligation to promote voluntary collective bargaining. But the recognition procedure is more difficult to assess. On one view, it is also a means of complying with ILO and other international standards. Collective bargaining is usually requested by the trade union, rather than by management. Many employers resist collective bargaining because it involves agreeing to *share* the power to determine terms and conditions of employment. Where the union has a high level of support but cannot persuade the employer to bargain, the law should intervene. This would not contradict the inherent voluntariness of negotiations because the law only forces the employer to take part in the procedure, not to reach a particular agreement. On another view, however, the recognition procedure is wholly inappropriate. The right to bargain collectively is a right for employers as well as unions. The employer's right to negotiate should include a right not to negotiate. The statutory recognition procedure conflicts with the very notion of voluntary collective bargaining and is forbidden – not required – by the right to collective bargaining.

In order to examine the law from an economics perspective, it is helpful to begin by looking at whether or not there is any empirical evidence to support the

---

33 Some detail is provided in ACAS Code of Practice 2, *Disclosure of information to trade unions for collective bargaining purposes* (1997), to which CAC must have regard by virtue of TULRCA 1992, s. 181(4).
34 TULRCA 1992, s. 182.
35 TULRCA 1992, s. 183.
36 H. Gospel and G. Lockwood, 'Disclosure of information for collective bargaining: the CAC approach revisited' (1999) 28 *ILJ* 233.
37 TULRCA 1992, s. 179, contains a presumption that this is the case unless the parties expressly agree otherwise.
38 See S. Deakin and G.S. Morris, *Labour Law* (3rd edn., 2001), pp. 259–66, for detail.

neoclassical theorists' claims about the union wage effect. Many of the UK studies have looked at the impact of unionisation on workplace profitability: if unionised firms show lower profitability than non-unionised firms, this suggests that unions are indeed able to extract rents from employers. In 1984, Machin and Stewart found that establishments with manual union recognition were 12.6% less likely to report above-average financial performance and 4.6% more likely to report below-average financial performance than non-unionised firms.[39] This suggests a significant union wage effect. By 1990, however, the effect had halved: workplaces with recognition were 6% less likely to report above-average performance and 2.5% more likely to report below-average performance.[40] By 1998, Addison and Belfield found no evidence that collective bargaining affected workplace profitability.[41] Bryson and Wilkinson confirm this finding even for workplaces with strong unions.[42]

Although the neoclassical theorists' fears are not being realised at present, this does not mean that they would regard the current law as satisfactory. First, the law enhances unions' bargaining power by helping them to gain access to information and, more seriously, by compelling employers to bargain with them. The recognition procedure obliges employers to listen to unions' demands. It is, however, important not to exaggerate its likely impact: it does not require the employer to reach an agreement with the union, or even to bargain in good faith. The procedure may not change the employer's decisions at all where it is determined to resist. Second, the law may impose significant costs on employers. For example, when a trade union representative is given paid time off to prepare for negotiations, the employer must find some other way of covering that person's work, whilst continuing to pay his or her wages.

But what about the argument that unions might have the beneficial effect of reducing labour turnover? The evidence indicates that unions do play a role in 'voicing' employees' grievances. Data from a recent survey show that union representatives spend a considerable amount of their time dealing with concerns about the treatment of employees and with disputes between employees and employers.[43] However, there is no evidence as to whether or not this reduces labour turnover. Moreover, unions may not play this role where they have achieved recognition through the statutory procedure, because the employer is only required to bargain on pay, hours and holidays and (if hostile to unions) may refuse to set up a grievance procedure. Another piece of indirect evidence for the UK is the effect of unions on employees' perceptions of the atmosphere at work. Bryson and Wilkinson found

---

39 S. Machin and M. Stewart, 'Trade unions and financial performance' (1996) 48 *Oxford Economic Papers* 213.

40 Machin and Stewart, above n. 39.

41 J. T. Addison and C. R. Belfield, 'The impact of financial participation and employee involvement on financial performance: a re-estimation using the 1998 WERS' (2000) 47 *Scottish Journal of Political Economy* 571.

42 A. Bryson and D. Wilkinson, *Collective Bargaining and Workplace Performance* (DTI URN 01/1224) (2001).

43 M. Cully *et al.*, above n. 22, p. 201.

that employees were happier when they believed that their union was effective and when they regarded management attitudes towards the union as favourable.[44] It seems reasonable to suppose that labour turnover would be reduced in these workplaces.

The subject-matter of bargaining is also relevant to the other advantage claimed for trade unions: that their presence may improve productivity. Voluntary collective bargaining could be used as a forum for receiving employees' suggestions and communicating the firm's plans because its scope is a matter for agreement between the parties. Compulsory collective bargaining seems less valuable because it is confined to discussion of pay, hours and holidays. During a discussion of pay, the employer could communicate information about the state of the business. But it is hard to see how employees could voice their suggestions for improving productivity. Of course, the employer and the union could agree to add this to their discussions, but since the employer has *ex hypothesi* resisted unionisation, it seems unlikely that this would happen.

The law on consultation

The law on consultation is largely derived from European Directives[45] and has developed in a piecemeal fashion, starting with obligations to consult on particular issues (collective redundancies,[46] health and safety,[47] and transfers of ownership of a business[48]), and turning more recently to obligations to consult more generally on the state of the employer's business. We will begin by looking briefly at the redundancy consultation provisions as an example of the former approach, before looking at provisions of the latter type.

Under TULRCA 1992, s. 188(1), the obligation to consult on collective redundancies arises when the employer is 'proposing to dismiss as redundant 20 or more employees at one establishment within a period of 90 days or less'. The scope of the consultation is defined in s. 188(2):

---

44 Above n. 42, chapter 5.
45 There are two purely domestic duties to consult. One is to consult a recognised trade union where the employer proposes to contract out of the state earnings-related pensions scheme, under the Occupational Pension Schemes (Contracting-Out) Regulations 1996 (SI 1996/1172), as amended. The other is to consult a union which has been recognised under the statutory procedure on training issues, under TULRCA 1992, s. 70B.
46 TULRCA 1992, ss. 188–92 (as amended). These provisions implement Directive 75/129/EEC as amended by Directive 92/56/EEC. These Directives have recently been consolidated in Directive 98/59/EC. For a detailed discussion of the ways in which national law may not fully implement EC law, see Deakin and Morris, above n. 38, pp. 796–815.
47 See the Health and Safety at Work etc Act 1974, the Safety Representatives and Safety Committees Regulations 1977 (SI 1977/500), and the Health and Safety (Consultation with Employees) Regulations 1996 (SI 1996/1513), and Directive 89/391/EEC. The law here is domestic in origin but has been amended in response to the Directive.
48 Transfer of Undertakings (Protection of Employment) Regulations 1981 (SI 1981/1794), regs. 10–11A (as amended). The Regulations implement Directive 77/187/EEC, as amended by Directive 98/50/EC. Both Directives have now been consolidated in Directive 2001/23/EC.

The consultation shall include consultation about ways of—

(a) avoiding the dismissals,
(b) reducing the numbers of employees to be dismissed, and
(c) mitigating the consequences of the dismissals,

and shall be undertaken by the employer with a view to reaching agreement with the appropriate representatives.

This uses a 'strong' definition of consultation – 'with a view to reaching agreement' – which suggests a process of negotiation similar to collective bargaining.

The selection of workforce representatives is governed by s. 188(1B).[49] Where the employer recognises a trade union in respect of the employees who may be made redundant, the employer must consult the union representatives. Where no trade union is recognised, the employer may choose one of two options. One is to arrange for the affected employees to elect representatives. The other is to use representatives who have already been elected by the affected employees for another purpose (for example, where the employer has a consultative committee or works council already in place). These arrangements ensure that employers cannot bypass a recognised union, and at the same time, that consultation can take place in non-unionised workplaces.

The consultation process can be enforced through a complaint to an employment tribunal under TULRCA 1992, s. 189. Where the employer has breached a duty owed to the union or employee representatives (for example, by failing to disclose information in accordance with the provisions described below), they have the right to bring a claim. The affected employees may only claim where the employer has failed to comply with the election requirements. The burden of proof is placed on the employer to show that the chosen representative was appropriate[50] and that the election requirements set out in s. 188A were complied with.[51] If the tribunal finds that the employer has breached the consultation requirements, it may make a 'protective award' of remuneration to the employees who have been dismissed or whose dismissal is proposed.[52] This remuneration must be such as the tribunal considers just and equitable, up to a maximum of 90 days' payment.

The information to which the representatives must have access is set out in some detail in TULRCA 1992, s. 188(4). Among other things, the employer must disclose the reasons for the proposed redundancies, the numbers and descriptions of employees who may be dismissed, the proposed method of redundancy selection, and the proposed method of calculating the redundancy payments. However, recognised trade unions cannot use their right of access to information for collective bargaining in order to obtain information for consultation.[53]

49 For the history of this provision, see Deakin and Morris, above n. 38, pp. 793–5.
50 TULRCA 1992, s. 189(1A).
51 TULRCA 1992, s. 189(1B).
52 TULRCA 1992, s. 189(2)–(4).
53 *R v CAC, ex p. BTP Tioxide Ltd* [1981] ICR 843.

More recent European Directives have adopted a new approach. Instead of requiring consultation on specific issues, they require employers to create a mechanism for the consultation of workforce representatives (a 'works council') on a regular basis. The Transnational Information and Consultation of Employees Regulations 1999[54] require 'Community-scale undertakings' to set up a European Works Council (EWC) or equivalent consultation procedure. A Community-scale undertaking must have at least 1000 employees within the Member States and at least 150 employees in each of at least two Member States.[55] A new 'Framework Directive'[56] will extend the obligation to create a works council or equivalent to firms operating on the national level. The Directive is to be implemented by 2005.[57] Member States can choose whether to implement the Directive for firms employing at least 50 employees or workplaces employing at least 20 employees.[58] However, the UK government has secured concessions which allow it to implement the Directive gradually. Under Article 10, the UK may confine the Directive to firms employing at least 150 or workplaces employing at least 100 until 2007, and to firms employing at least 100 or workplaces employing at least 50 until 2008. The government argued that the Directive would be more difficult to implement in the UK because, in contrast to other Member States, there was no tradition of routine consultation.[59] The government is currently consulting on how best to implement this Directive,[60] so we will take the existing EWC provisions as our example.

The role of the EWC is a matter for agreement between the employer and the workforce representatives.[61] If no agreement is reached, the parties must use the default model set out in the Regulations.[62] This limits the competence of the EWC to transnational questions: those concerning the Community-scale undertaking as a whole or those which concern at least two establishments situated in different Member States.[63] The model provides for two types of meeting. One is an annual meeting at which the management reports on the state of the business, and issues which might affect employees, such as possible plant closures or the introduction of new working methods.[64] The other is an exceptional meeting which can be called by the EWC where particular issues arise affecting employees, for example, where

---

54 SI 1999/3323, implementing the European Works Councils Directive (Directive 94/45/EC). For discussion, see M. Carley and M. Hall, 'The implementation of the European Works Councils Directive' (2000) 29 *ILJ* 103.
55 SI 1999/3323, regs. 2 and 4.
56 Directive 2002/14/EC establishing a general framework for informing and consulting employees in the EC.
57 Directive 2002/14/EC, Article 11.
58 Directive 2002/14/EC, Article 3.
59 For an excellent discussion of the Directive and the negotiating process, see B. Bercusson, 'The European social model comes to Britain' (2002) 31 *ILJ* 209.
60 DTI, *High Performance Workplaces – Informing and Consulting Employees* (2003).
61 SI 1999/3323, reg. 17.
62 SI 1999/3323, reg. 18 and Schedule.
63 SI 1999/3323, Schedule, para. 6.
64 SI 1999/3323, Schedule, para. 7.

the management proposes to close an establishment.[65] Again, this meeting must take place on the basis of a report prepared by management. Similar obligations arise under the Framework Directive, Article 4(2):

Information and consultation shall cover:

(a) information on the recent and probable development of the undertaking's or the establishment's activities and economic situation

(b) information and consultation on the situation, structure and probable development of employment within the undertaking or establishment and on any anticipatory measures envisaged, in particular where there is a threat to employment

(c) information and consultation on decisions likely to lead to substantial changes in work organisation or in contractual relations . . .

Although the matters to be covered by consultation are defined relatively broadly in both pieces of legislation, the concept of 'consultation' itself is limited to 'the exchange of views and establishment of dialogue'.[66] This means that the employer must listen to the representatives' views but need not try to reach agreement with them. The strong definition of consultation ('with a view to reaching an agreement') is used only once, in relation to Article 4(2)(c) above,[67] presumably because this obligation may overlap with the collective redundancy consultation provisions, discussed above.

The creation and enforcement of the EWC is a complex business. The employer is obliged to initiate negotiations for the establishment of an EWC where it receives a request by 100 employees or their representatives in at least two establishments in at least two Member States.[68] It may also start negotiations on its own initiative. The negotiations are conducted between management and a 'special negotiating body' (SNB), consisting of representatives of the various establishments in the different Member States.[69] The management and the SNB must negotiate 'in a spirit of co-operation with a view to reaching a written agreement' on the consultation of employees,[70] whether through an EWC or other arrangements. If the parties fail to agree or management refuses to negotiate, a Schedule to the Regulations sets out a standard form for the EWC which must be implemented as the default model.[71] If management fails to implement either its agreement with the SNB or the default model, a complaint may be made to the Employment Appeal Tribunal.[72] The EAT may order the central management to set up an EWC in accordance with the agreement or the schedule, and to pay a penalty to the

65 SI 1999/3323, Schedule, para. 8.
66 SI 1999/3323, reg. 2; Directive 2002/14/EC, Article 2(g).
67 Directive 2002/14/EC, Article 4(4)(e).
68 SI 1999/3323, reg. 9.
69 SI 1999/3323, regs. 11–8.
70 SI 1999/3323, reg. 17(1).
71 SI 1999/3323, reg. 18.
72 SI 1999/3323, regs. 20–2.

Secretary of State. Under the Framework Directive, the detail of how the consultation is to take place is left to the Member States to determine. Under Article 1(2), 'the practical arrangements for information and consultation shall be defined and implemented in accordance with national law and industrial relations practices in individual Member States in such a way as to ensure their effectiveness'. Article 8 obliges Member States to provide adequate remedies if consultation does not take place.

Where the EWC or information and consultation procedure is established voluntarily, access to information is largely a matter for agreement between the parties. Management is not obliged to disclose to the EWC any information where this would seriously harm the functioning of the undertaking.[73] But this must be on objective grounds, and an application may be made to the CAC to determine whether or not the management's refusal to disclose the information is within the exception. The Framework Directive specifies that information shall be given in such a way as to enable representatives to prepare for the consultation.[74] National legislation will presumably give further detail on this.

From a rights perspective, one apparent weakness of English law might lie in the scope of the consultation rights it affords. At present, routine consultation is only required for pan-European firms which are subject to the requirement to create an EWC. It will be introduced for national firms when the Framework Directive is implemented, but even when the law is brought into full compliance with this Directive, duties to consult will be confined to larger firms employing at least 50 workers or workplaces of at least 20. Similarly, the obligation to consult on collective redundancies only applies when the employer proposes to make at least 20 people redundant, so it is inherently unlikely to be relevant to smaller firms. If the right to be consulted is fundamental, should it not be available to all workers? The arguments against such an extension are usually practical ones: that smaller firms are run on a more personal level anyway, so duties to consult would be unduly clumsy, formal and costly. But it may not be correct to assume that smaller firms always communicate effectively with their staff.

Another concern for many rights theorists is the relationship between consultation and trade union recognition. Their concern is that workers' right to be represented by a trade union will be undermined by consultation, which they regard as a weaker form of participation than collective bargaining. The redundancy consultation provisions address this worry by providing that the employer must consult with trade union representatives where a union is recognised in the workplace. This prevents the employer from undermining the union by consulting with other representatives instead, an approach which was permitted until the law was amended in 1999. But the EWC provisions do not give any special status to union representatives. It remains to be seen whether this will disadvantage unions. It is possible that unions will, in practice, benefit from the provisions because workers will regard union

---

73 SI 1999/3323, reg. 24.
74 Directive 2002/14/EC, Article 4(3).

representatives as more expert than non-union representatives at negotiating with the employer.

Neoclassical economists are concerned about the ability of worker participation mechanisms to extract concessions from the employer which would not occur under normal market conditions. It is not possible simply to ask whether there is a 'consultation wage effect' comparable to the union wage effect because English law does not at present require consultation on wage rates. However, consultation does take place on issues which may require the employer to spend more money on the workforce, for example, by giving more generous redundancy payments. So it is still relevant to ask whether consultation enables worker representatives to extract concessions from the employer.

The answer depends in part on how consultation is defined. Consultation with the EWC is defined as 'the exchange of views and establishment of dialogue'. This is a relatively weak obligation which simply requires the employer to provide information and to listen to the representatives' comments. The final decision is left firmly in the hands of the employer. Of course, the employer may decide to implement this obligation in a way which allows the representatives a significant degree of influence over its decisions, but such action is not strictly required by the law. The position is rather different for the stronger form of consultation required for collective redundancies. Here, the employer is obliged to consult 'with a view to reaching agreement'. This model creates a greater expectation of joint governance by the employer and the representatives and can be more readily compared with collective bargaining.

As we saw above, the ability of a union to extract concessions from an employer through collective bargaining depends on its bargaining power, which in turn depends on a multiplicity of legal and non-legal factors. It seems likely that the effect of consultation 'with a view to reaching an agreement' would vary in a similar way. Some of the factors discussed above in relation to collective bargaining are equally relevant to consultation, such as the state of the employer's business. For example, in a redundancy consultation, representatives may decide not to challenge the need for redundancies if the future of the firm is under threat. Other factors are unique to consultation. One is the legal obligation to consult 'with a view to reaching an agreement' itself. If the employer does not approach the negotiations sincerely, with an open mind, it may be possible to argue that it is in breach of its legal obligations. However, such a point would be extremely difficult to prove, unless the employer made an obvious mistake such as giving the managers earplugs to wear to consultation meetings. Another factor unique to consultation is whether or not a trade union is present to represent the workers. In the absence of a trade union, it is unlikely that the workers will be able to enhance their bargaining power by making a credible threat to go on strike.

Whatever the substantive impact of consultation, simply putting a consultation procedure in place costs money. One of the most expensive mechanisms is the EWC. The EWC may involve substantial travel and interpreting costs, because representatives are drawn from different Member States of the EU and may not share a common language. A recent study of UK firms found that the average annual cost of an EWC (usually involving just one meeting) was £53,000.[75] Thus, neoclassical economists are unlikely to be enthusiastic about consultation mechanisms even if they have no adverse impact on employers' decision-making.

What about the new institutionalists' argument that consultation might reduce labour turnover? Consultation does have some potential to resolve employees' grievances. Health and safety consultation might be able to address workers' concerns about safety measures in their workplace. Redundancy consultation representatives might be able to voice employees' concerns about the fairness of the employer's proposed mechanism for redundancy selection. But consultation does not seem to provide a means for *any* grievance to be aired. Another issue is the role of unions in consultation. Freeman and Medoff were sceptical about grievance procedures in non-unionised firms.[76] They argued that in the absence of a strong union to protect them, employees would be reluctant to voice their grievances for fear of reprisals. However, in a recent study, Knell found that firms with 'partnership' policies were able to reduce their labour turnover to levels which were believed to be below average for the relevant industry, regardless of whether or not they were unionised.[77] All the firms studied provided a supportive environment for employee 'voice', both in terms of providing formal structures for consultation and in terms of 'dealing with problems and issues as they arise, informally, through talking'.[78]

The new institutionalists also claim that consultation may help to improve productivity. The presence of a works council does seem likely to improve employees' understanding of the state of the business and their preparedness for change. The employer is obliged to discuss these matters with worker representatives. Redundancy consultation may also require the employer to provide this kind of information in order to explain to the representatives why redundancies are needed. Again, however, opportunities for employees to make suggestions for improving production processes seem limited. Employees might make such suggestions in order to stave off redundancies or plant closures. But the consultation procedures are not designed with productivity in mind.

Further reading

For a detailed account of English law on consultation and collective bargaining, see S. Deakin and G. Morris, *Labour Law* (3rd edn., 2001), chapter 9; or H. Collins, K.D. Ewing and A. McColgan, *Labour Law: Text and Materials* (2001), chapter 8. The UK is unusual in not having a strong tradition of consultation, so you may

---

75 T. Weber *et al.*, *Costs and Benefits of the European Works Councils Directive* (DTI URN 00/630) (2000), chapter 4.
76 Above n. 15, pp. 107–9.
77 Above n. 21, p. 29.
78 Above n. 21, p. 21.

find it helpful to look at some comparative material: M. Biagi, 'Forms of employee representational participation', in R. Blanpain and C. Engels (eds.), *Comparative Labour Law and Industrial Relations in Industrialized Market Economies* (8th edn., 2001).

To understand the debate about collective bargaining today, you need to have a more general appreciation of the challenges facing trade unionism. Like firms and governments, unions must respond to globalisation: see K. Klare, 'Countervailing workers' power as a regulatory strategy', in H. Collins *et al.* (eds.), *Legal Regulation of the Employment Relation* (2000). Others blame hostile governments for unions' decline: see F. Raday, 'The decline of union power – structural inevitability or policy choice?' in J. Conaghan *et al.* (eds.), *Labour Law in an Era of Globalization* (2002). Are unions still relevant today? Are they more under threat from changes in the economy or from the failure of governments to enact supportive legislation? Might there be a connection between governments' attitudes and economic factors? What strategies could unions adopt in order to reverse the decline? Chapters 11 and 12 will give you more ideas on these issues.

Unions have traditionally regarded consultation as an unwelcome development: P. Davies, 'A challenge to single channel' (1994) 23 *ILJ* 2725. Unions' attitudes have changed, but commentators remain sceptical. See, for example, W. McCarthy, 'Representative consultations with specified employees – or the future of rung two', in H. Collins *et al.* (eds.), *Legal Regulation of the Employment Relation* (2000); or T. Novitz and P. Skidmore, *Fairness at Work: a Critical Analysis of the Employment Relations Act 1999 and its Treatment of Collective Rights* (2001), chapter 6. Does consultation help unions to get a foothold in the workplace? Or does it help management to satisfy employees' demands for participation without involving unions? Where do the rights of those who are not union members fit in to these debates? Are they to blame for not joining a union? Or do they have a right to be heard which the law should uphold?

The neoclassical argument against collective bargaining is best captured in F.A. Hayek, *The Constitution of Liberty* (1960), chapter 18; or R.A. Posner, *Economic Analysis of Law* (5th edn., 1998), pp. 349–56. But do these accounts oversimplify the aims of trade unions? For some ideas, see A. Flanders 'Collective Bargaining: A Theoretical Analysis' (1968) 6 *British Journal of Industrial Relations* 1.

The classic work on the economic benefits of collective bargaining is R.B. Freeman and J.L. Medoff, *What Do Unions Do?* (1984), especially chapters 6 and 11. For a more modern statement of the economic benefits of worker participation, try DTI, *High Performance Workplaces – Informing and Consulting Employees* (2003), chapter 2. What are the conditions for effective 'partnership' between workers and employees? For some ideas, see J. Knell, *Partnership at Work* (DTI URN 99/1078) (1999). Are these various conditions likely to be realised when firms comply with the recognition procedure or with legislation on consultation? How important are the parties' attitudes? Does it matter what topics they are required to discuss? Do unions help or hinder the creation of effective partnerships? And what is an *effective* partnership from the perspective of the firm? Or from the perspective of the employees? For a critique of partnership from a rights perspective, see T. Novitz and P. Skidmore, *Fairness at Work: a Critical Analysis of the Employment Relations Act 1999 and its Treatment of Collective Rights* (2001), chapter 1.

11

Trade union membership

In chapter 10, we looked at what trade unions did: at the relationship between the trade union and the employer. In this chapter, we will examine the substantial body of law surrounding trade union membership. The law governs the relationship between the trade union member and the employer, and between the trade union member and the union itself. Although trade union membership has been declining since the 1970s, the issues to be discussed still affect many workers. In 2002, 26.6% of UK workers – some 7.3 million individuals – were members of a trade union.[1] Moreover, both pro- and anti-union writers acknowledge that the law on membership plays an important role in encouraging – or discouraging – unionism.

A rights theorist would give this chapter the title 'freedom of association'. This denotes the right to form and join trade unions which features in civil and political rights instruments as well as economic and social ones. Rights theorists agree that the right is highly important, and they also agree on some aspects of its interpretation. For example, the right means that employers may not discriminate against workers on the grounds that they are members of a trade union, and that workers should be free to join a trade union if they want to. But other aspects of interpretation are much more controversial. Should employers be obliged to help unions by providing trade union officials with an office at the workplace? Can an individual be compelled to join a particular union? Can a union force its members to obey its instructions?

Economists tend not to write specifically about trade union membership. But, as we saw in chapter 10, they are concerned about the role of trade unions. The law on trade union membership may strengthen – or weaken – the unions. For example, if a union is allowed to discipline its members for failing to obey an instruction to go on strike, the union will be stronger. Its members will be more likely to comply with its orders, and its strike threats will be more credible as a result. The employer will be more likely to make concessions during collective bargaining. Thus, those economists who are hostile to collective bargaining are likely to be hostile

---

1 DTI, 'Labour Market Spotlight: Trade Union Membership', *Labour Market Trends* (July 2003), p. 338.

towards any laws which help trade unions to increase their bargaining power. Those who argue that trade unions are beneficial will welcome laws which make them stronger.

Rights perspectives

Freedom of association is a right common to instruments on civil and political rights and to those concerned with economic and social rights. Article 22(1) of the ICCPR is typical:

> Everyone shall have the right to freedom of association with others, including the right to form and join trade unions for the protection of his interests.

The right can be restricted on various grounds, including national security, public safety, public order and the protection of the rights and freedoms of others. Economic and social rights instruments tend to focus solely on freedom of association in trade unions, but the language used is surprisingly similar. Article 8(1)(a) of the ICESCR protects:

> The right of everyone to form trade unions and join the trade union of his choice, subject only to the rules of the organisation concerned, for the promotion and protection of his economic and social interests. No restrictions may be placed on the exercise of this right other than those prescribed by law and which are necessary in a democratic society in the interests of national security or public order or for the protection of the rights and freedoms of others.

We will look first at the implications of freedom of association for trade union members' relationships with their employers, before turning to the issues surrounding trade union members' relationships with their unions.

Freedom of association and employers

Imagine that the state allows workers to create trade unions, but hostile employers refuse to employ anyone who is a trade union member. This would render the workers' freedom to associate useless. Therefore, at a minimum, freedom of association implies that employers must be forbidden from discriminating against trade union members. This is confirmed by Article 1 of the ILO Convention 98:

> 1. Workers shall enjoy adequate protection against acts of anti-union discrimination in respect of their employment.
> 2. Such protection shall apply more particularly in respect of acts calculated to—
>
> (a) make the employment of a worker subject to the condition that he shall not join a union or shall relinquish trade union membership;

(b) cause the dismissal of or otherwise prejudice a worker by reason of union membership or because of participation in union activities outside working hours or, with the consent of the employer, within working hours.[2]

Thus, trade union members should be protected against discriminatory dismissal and hiring decisions, and against detrimental treatment during the employment relationship. Paragraph (b) makes clear that workers are protected not just against discrimination on grounds of membership, but also on the grounds of participation in trade union activities. Taking part in a strike is not covered by this provision because strikes, by their very nature, occur during working hours without the employer's consent. But other activities such as attending meetings or voting in elections are protected.

Most unions are run by a combination of full-time officials, who are employed by the union itself, and part-time officials. These part-time officials – often known as shop stewards – do an ordinary job for the employer but also devote some of their time to representing the trade union in the workplace. Part-time officials deal with most of the day-to-day issues which arise in the workplace, with advice and assistance from full-time union officials on more important matters.[3] They are particularly vulnerable to discriminatory treatment by employers. Those employers who are hostile to trade unions may regard part-time trade union officials as 'trouble-makers' who stir up discontent among ordinary trade union members. This is acknowledged in the international human rights instruments. The ESC 1996[4] and the ILO's Workers' Representatives Convention[5] both provide that states should take steps to protect representatives from dismissal or other detrimental treatment. These protections apply to worker representatives who are not trade union members too.

Many rights theorists would argue that while non-discrimination rights are necessary to protect freedom of association, they are by no means sufficient. They take the view that workers join trade unions not just because they want to be part of an organisation, but because they want that organisation to bargain on their behalf with the employer. If unions are to bargain effectively, they need legal support. In chapter 10, we saw that economic and social rights instruments fit in with this view because they include various explicit obligations on the state to help trade unions, particularly by promoting collective bargaining. Civil and political rights can be interpreted in this way too, but not everyone agrees: the ECtHR has been quite cautious, for example.

If we accept that employers should be obliged to help trade unions, this has important implications for the treatment of trade union members and representatives.

2 ILO, Right to Organise and Collective Bargaining Convention (Convention No. 98, 1949). This Convention has been ratified by the UK.
3 For empirical information about workplace representatives, see M. Cully *et al.*, *Britain at Work* (1999), chapter 9.
4 Article 28. The ESC 1996 has not been ratified by the UK.
5 ILO, Workers' Representatives Convention (Convention No. 135, 1971), Article 1. This Convention has been ratified by the UK.

Instead of just refraining from discriminating against them, employers could be obliged to support their activities. For example, trade union members could be given time off work to attend meetings. In fact, the international instruments focus mainly on facilities for trade union representatives. According to the ILO Workers' Representatives Convention, Article 2:

> 1. Such facilities in the undertaking shall be afforded to workers' representatives as may be appropriate in order to enable them to carry out their functions promptly and efficiently.
>
> 2. In this connection account shall be taken of the characteristics of the industrial relations system of the country and the needs, size and capabilities of the undertaking concerned.
>
> 3. The granting of such facilities shall not impair the efficient operation of the undertaking concerned.[6]

Facilities could include use of an office or meeting room and a telephone, or use of a notice-board in order to communicate with union members. The drafting of the right reflects the need to take account of the interests of the firm and of the different conditions faced by different firms. States have a considerable degree of discretion as to its implementation.

Freedom of association and unions

Three main controversies arise in interpreting the right to freedom of association as between individual trade union members and their unions. First, can an individual be compelled to join a particular union? Second, to what extent can unions set their own rules on who can and cannot become a member? And third, once a person has joined a union, can he or she be compelled to take part in the union's activities?

Very broadly, rights theorists adopt different views on these questions according to whether they are 'individualists' or 'collectivists'. Individualists believe that individuals are more important than groups.[7] They see freedom of association as a right for the individual to use as he or she chooses. The wishes of the group – to force the individual to join or to take part in a strike, or to exclude the individual from membership – are less important than the individual's choices. They argue that if we do not protect individuals' choices, they will be vulnerable to oppression by powerful groups. Collectivists believe that the interests of the group are more important than those of individuals.[8] They argue that groups are stronger if they are able to exercise some control over individuals: by forcing them to join or to go on strike, for example. And a powerful union will be better placed than a weak one to bargain with the employer. So although individuals may have to sacrifice their short-term choices, they should be better off in the long term.

---

6 Above n. 5. Article 28 of the ESC 1996 is in similar terms.
7 For an extreme example, see F.A. Hayek, *The Constitution of Liberty* (1960), chapter 18.
8 Lord Wedderburn, *The Worker and the Law* (3rd edn., 1986), chapter 1.

Can an individual be compelled to join a union?

On a collectivist view, the decision to join a union need not be a matter of individual choice at all. If there is a strong union presence in the workplace, and if the employer agrees, it should be possible to have a 'closed shop' in which having a job is conditional on being a member of the trade union. The justification for the closed shop is that it preserves the strength of the union.[9] Although the individual may not want to join the union,[10] his or her best interests are ultimately served by doing so, because a strong union will be able to secure better terms and conditions of employment. Moreover, the closed shop helps to deal with the problem of 'free riders', workers who take the benefit of the terms and conditions negotiated by the union (because these are usually extended to all workers by the employer) but do not contribute to the union's work by paying union dues or participating in union action.

On an individualist view, by contrast, the very notion of *freedom* of association suggests that joining a trade union should be voluntary. Individuals should not be forced to join an organisation when they might not support its industrial relations goals or political views.[11] The union strength argument, although important, is not sufficient to justify so great a potential violation of individual freedom. If an individual is refused a job or dismissed because he or she is not a trade union member, the employer's action should be viewed as a form of discrimination which is just as unwarranted as discrimination against a person who is a trade union member. The right to join and the right not to join should carry equal weight. And this does not mean that unions will inevitably be weak. If they bring genuine benefits, people will join of their own volition.

The closed shop has caused some difficulty for international human rights instruments. This is because states' practices on this issue vary widely, with some outlawing the closed shop and others positively encouraging it. The clearest stance is that taken by the Universal Declaration, which simply states in Article 20(2) that 'no-one may be compelled to belong to an association'. But this provision was omitted from the ICCPR and ICESCR. Article 5 of the ICESCR has been held to contain a right not to join a union.[12]

ILO Convention No. 87 is also silent on the question of the closed shop.[13] This has been interpreted to mean that states have a discretion to prohibit or permit the

---

9 W.E.J. McCarthy, *The Closed Shop in Britain* (1964), especially chapter 11.
10 Systems which permit closed shops do sometimes provide narrow exceptions for those with a conscientious objection to joining a trade union, for example, where their religion does not permit it.
11 C.S. Hanson, S. Jackson and D. Miller, *The Closed Shop* (1982), chapter 1.
12 See, for example, ESC Committee, *Conclusions XII-1* (1992), pp. 114–6. For a review of the limited jurisprudence on Article 22 of the ICCPR, see K.D. Ewing, 'Freedom of association and trade unions', in D. Harris and S. Joseph (eds.), *The International Convention on Civil and Political Rights and UK Law* (1995).
13 ILO, Freedom of Association and Protection of the Right to Organise Convention (Convention No. 87, 1948).

closed shop as they choose.[14] The ILO Committee of Experts has stated that 'systems which prohibit union security practices in order to guarantee the right not to join an organisation, as well as systems which authorise such practices, are compatible with the Convention'.[15] The main qualification to this is that a closed shop will only be permitted where it results from a voluntary agreement between unions and employers. States are not allowed to impose closed shops through legislation.

The position of the ECtHR on this issue is of particular interest for our purposes, since English courts are obliged to uphold Article 11 of the Convention by virtue of the HRA 1998. There is some evidence from the *travaux préparatoires* that the drafters intended to adopt a neutral approach like that taken by the ILO:

> On account of the difficulties raised by the 'closed-shop system' in certain countries, the Conference in this connection considered that it was undesirable to introduce into the Convention a rule under which 'no one may be compelled to belong to an association' which features in [Article 20, para. 2 of] the United Nations Universal Declaration.[16]

However, this stance has not found favour with the ECtHR. In *Young, James and Webster v UK*, the Court refused to decide whether or not the Convention protected the right not to associate.[17] Assuming that it did not, the Court went on to state that not every form of compulsion to join a trade union could be compatible with Article 11, since 'freedom' of association implied an element of choice. The claimants had been employed by British Rail for some years prior to the introduction of the closed shop agreement, and the sanction for their refusal to join a union was dismissal. The Court found a breach of Article 11 on these facts because of the degree of compulsion faced by the applicants.

In the later case of *Sigurour A Sigurjonsson v Iceland*, the Court became rather more bold in its protection of the right not to join.[18] It pointed out that a number of states protected the right not to join, as did international instruments such as the ESC and the Community Charter of the Fundamental Social Rights of Workers 1989. The Court then held that:

> Article 11 must be viewed as encompassing a negative right of association. It is not necessary for the Court to determine in this instance whether this right is to be considered on an equal footing with the positive right.[19]

The full implications of the judgment remain unclear. First, the closed shop to which Sigurjonsson objected had been imposed by law, rather than by agreement between workers and employers, so it would have been considered

---

14 International Labour Conference, 43rd Session, 1959, Report of the Committee of Experts, Report III (Part IV), para. 36.
15 ILO, *General Survey on Freedom of Association and Collective Bargaining* (1994), para. 100.
16 'Report of 19 June 1950 of the Conference of Senior Officials', in Council of Europe, *Collected Edition of the 'Travaux Préparatoires'* (1975–85), vol. IV, p. 262.
17 [1981] 4 EHRR 38. See M. Forde, 'The 'closed shop' case' (1982) 11 *ILJ* 1.
18 [1993] 16 EHRR 462.
19 [1993] 16 EHRR 462 at 479.

objectionable even by the ILO. Uncertainty still surrounds the status of a closed shop agreed by the union and the employer, given the narrowness of the judgment in *Young, James and Webster*. Second, like the applicants in *Young*, Sigurjonsson's livelihood was at stake and he had taken up his occupation before the closed shop had been imposed. The status of a closed shop which was a condition of employment only for new hires is uncertain. Third, the Court's refusal to decide the status of the right not to join a union is highly problematic. If the negative and positive rights have equal status, workers should have a free choice as to whether or not to join a union. If the negative right plays a subsidiary role, the closed shop might still be permitted if there were safeguards for those who had strong objections to joining.

Can unions set their own membership criteria?

In a system of voluntary trade union membership, should the individual be able to choose which union to join, or should the union be able to set rules on who is eligible to join? In other words, should the individual be able to force a union to admit him or her even if the union does not want to do so? The idea that membership of a particular union is a matter of choice for the individual – an 'extreme individualist' view – can be supported by arguing that unions are not simply private associations but have a quasi-public role. Because of their importance in the workplace, individuals should have a positive right to join the union of their choice, unless the union specialises in representing a particular job category or region to which the worker does not belong.[20] The government should protect this choice by regulating union rules.

The more moderate view is that union membership should be voluntary for unions as well as individuals. 'Freedom' of association implies some element of mutuality, so that individuals should not have a right to associate with people who are unwilling to associate with them.[21] On this view, unions are private associations which should be free to set their own membership rules without government interference. This would enable them to exclude – for example – those who did not undertake to uphold the objectives of the trade union. Some controls might be imposed on public policy grounds – it is hard to justify exempting unions from discrimination law, for instance – but these should be kept to a minimum.

International human rights instruments place considerable emphasis on the autonomy of trade unions and on protecting them from interference by the state. This suggests that it should be up to unions to decide who they want to admit to membership. ILO Convention 87 addresses this issue directly.[22] Article 2 provides that:

---

20 For an account of the government's reasoning in introducing the section, see B. Simpson, 'Individualism versus collectivism: an evaluation of section 14 of the Trade Union Reform and Employment Rights Act 1993' (1993) 22 *ILJ* 181 at 182.

21 See *Cheall v APEX* [1983] ICR 398 at 405, per Lord Diplock.

22 Above n. 13.

Workers and employers, without distinction whatsoever, shall have the right to establish and, subject only to the rules of the organisation concerned, to join organisations of their own choosing without previous authorisation.

This emphasises individuals' freedom to choose which organisation to join, whilst at the same time making clear that it is acceptable for unions to restrict membership through their rules. The process of drafting union rules is governed by Article 3, which is also worth setting out in full:

1. Workers' and employers' organisations shall have the right to draw up their constitutions and rules, to elect their representatives in full freedom, to organise their administration and activities and to formulate their programmes.
2. The public authorities shall refrain from any interference which would restrict this right or impede the lawful exercise thereof.

It is therefore inappropriate for the government to interfere in the setting of union membership rules. There is, however, one important limitation on union autonomy. According to Article 8, workers and unions must 'respect the law of the land' in exercising their rights. For example, a government could prohibit union rules which discriminated on grounds of sex, race, disability and so on in the selection of members.

Civil and political rights instruments do not contain any detail on the internal affairs of trade unions. Interestingly, Article 5 of the ESC does not offer any assistance on this issue either. The ICESCR adopts language which is very similar to that used by the ILO, referring to a person's right to 'join the trade union of his choice, subject only to the rules of the organisation concerned', and the 'right of trade unions to function freely'.[23] Both rights are qualified. They can be subject to limitations which are 'prescribed by law and which are necessary in a democratic society in the interests of national security or public order or for the protection of the rights and freedoms of others'. Again, this opens up the possibility of some limitations on trade union autonomy, for example, to protect the right of others not to be subjected to discrimination. But the overall message is that unions should be free to set their own rules, and that individuals should be free to join subject to those rules.

Can unions compel their members to participate in union activities?
Once the individual has joined a union, a further set of issues arises concerning his or her freedom to choose whether or not to take part in union activities, such as strike action. On an individualistic interpretation, the individual should be able to decide his or her level of participation in any given situation.[24] An individual might have conscientious objections to a strike: for example, he or she might think that the employer's offer is reasonable and that the strike is unwarranted. Or the individual might have personal objections: workers are not paid during a strike, so he or she

23 Article 8(1)(a) and (c).
24 Department of Employment, *Trade Unions and their Members* (Cm. 95, 1987), pp. 7–8.

might feel that the economic sacrifice is too great. It might be argued that either or both of these excuses should be permitted, even if union members as a group have voted to support the strike.

On a collectivist view, the union should be able to compel its members to participate in lawful activities which have majority support,[25] by subjecting them to disciplinary action if they refuse.[26] Industrial action is, inevitably, much stronger if it has the full involvement of the workforce. Individuals who participate are much less exposed to victimisation by the employer if they do not have the option of continuing to work. And compulsion would address the problem of free riders: those who take the benefit of concessions secured by industrial action whilst refusing to participate in the action themselves.

The issue of participation cannot be entirely separated from the issue of membership. On an extreme collectivist view, compulsion would be present at both stages: an individual could be forced to join the union and forced to go on strike. On an extreme individualist view, individual choice would prevail at both stages: the individual could choose whether or not to join and whether or not to go on strike. But middle positions are also possible. One option would be to allow unions to compel individuals to join, but then to give union members the choice of how much to participate in union activities. This solution combines the collectivist advantage of high levels of union membership with the individualist advantage that this would not entail anything more than carrying a union card unless the member chose to play a more active role. But it has the disadvantages of compulsion to join (for individualists) and of creating large numbers of passive members (for collectivists). The other option would be to allow individuals to choose whether or not to join a union, and then to subject them to compulsion once they had done so. The element of compulsion can be justified by arguing that the union member has chosen to join in the knowledge that this might involve participation in industrial action with which he or she does not fully agree. Moreover, it remains open to the individual to resign from the union if he or she feels sufficiently strongly opposed to the union's policies.

The human rights issues raised here are very similar to those considered above, since they again raise the question of the extent to which unions are free to set their own internal rules. Articles 3 and 8 of ILO Convention 87 allow unions complete autonomy in this regard provided that they respect the law of the land.[27] This suggests that it would be perfectly appropriate for unions to require their members to participate in lawful union activities. Some instruments, such as the ESC, provide an explicit right to take industrial action, including strike action, but they remain silent as to whether a union can make this compulsory.[28] On one view, a 'right'

---

25 E. McKendrick, 'The rights of trade union members – Part I of the Employment Act 1988' (1988) 17 *ILJ* 141 at 147–50.

26 Of course, the individual would always retain the option of resigning from the union (though in a closed shop situation this would lead to the loss of his or her job).

27 Above n. 13.

28 Article 6(4), in both the 1961 version (ratified by the UK) and the revised 1996 version.

to strike inherently includes a choice as to whether or not to exercise the right. This would make 'compulsory' industrial action problematic. On another view, the right to strike should not be viewed as a matter of *individual* choice at all. Industrial action only makes sense when it is taken by unions or groups of workers. Thus, once workers as a group have decided in favour of industrial action – by a majority vote – then all members of the group should abide by that vote and should participate in the exercise of the right.

Economics perspectives

As we saw in chapter 10, economists disagree quite radically about the impact of trade unions on the labour market. Some take the view that unions are damaging to the economy because they artificially inflate the wages of their members above the market rate.[29] This leads to unemployment, and inefficiency in the allocation of labour. Others argue that unions can benefit firms by providing an important channel of communication between management and the workforce.[30] This can be used to improve productivity and to reduce labour turnover. Economists tend not to focus on the detailed law on trade union membership, but it has important implications for their analysis of the role of unions. This is because it influences unions' *bargaining power*.

The law on freedom of association as against employers may have an impact on union membership and on union activities. If workers are not protected against discrimination, they are unlikely to join a trade union. But if the law imposes sanctions on employers who discriminate against trade unionists, workers will feel more confident about joining. The level of protection afforded to trade union activists is particularly important because of the role they play in organising other workers. If they are not protected, it may be difficult for a union to start organising a workplace for the first time or to bargain with the employer once it has got some support. The facilities granted to trade union officials may also play a role in determining the union's impact in the workplace. For example, if union officials have time off to prepare for negotiations, they may be better placed to secure concessions from the employer. If they have no facilities, they may prove to be ineffective at bargaining, and ordinary workers may decide that it is not worth supporting the union any more.

The union's relationship with its own members is also very important in determining its bargaining power as against the employer. The closed shop is the most obvious example of this. If the law allows the closed shop, the union can maintain 100% membership in the workplace by insisting that the employer only hires union members. This obviously enhances the union's bargaining power because it is difficult for the employer to ignore an organisation which represents all the workers in a

29 See, for example, R.A. Posner, *Economic Analysis of Law* (5th edn., 1998), pp. 349–56.
30 See, for example, R.B. Freeman and J.L. Medoff, *What Do Unions Do?* (1984).

particular category or even in the firm as a whole. Moreover, if the union threatens to call a strike, it is able to threaten severe disruption because of its high level of membership. The employer cannot rely on a few non-members to come to work and keep the business running during the strike. If the law prohibits the closed shop, the union may still be able to achieve 100% membership but it is less likely to do so. Some people may decide not to join, whether through opposition or indifference. And the smaller the proportion of union members in the workplace, the weaker the union is likely to be.

A similar analysis applies to the issue of whether unions should be free to set their own rules on membership and discipline. If they can set their own rules, they can discipline those who refuse to support the union's activities, particularly strikes. Again, this increases the value of the union's strike threat. If the employer knows that the union can pressurise all its members into taking part, the prospect of a strike may seem more worrying. It could lead to major disruption of the employer's business. This might prompt the employer to make concessions during bargaining. If the union cannot discipline its members, the employer might decide to take the chance that a strike would not be well supported and would not have much impact on the business.

As chapter 10 explained, unions' bargaining power is affected by a number of factors, including the state of the employer's product market and the overall level of unemployment. But the law can play a role too. Those economists who are hostile to trade unions would argue that – for example – unions should have no power to discipline their members for refusing to go on strike. This would lessen the power of the trade unions and limit the economic damage they can cause. Those who identify benefits in trade unionism would obviously support a greater degree of protection. For example, they would argue that unions cannot play a constructive role in negotiations with the employer unless they have time to prepare and suitable facilities in the workplace.

Freedom of association as against employers

Freedom of association as against employers has been a topic of some controversy in recent years. Although the law appears to protect the right not to be discriminated against, there are various loopholes in the provisions. Economics arguments have played an important role in limiting the scope of trade unionists' rights.

Discrimination against trade unionists

Access to employment
TULRCA 1992, s. 137 tackles the employer's first opportunity to discriminate, at the hiring stage, by making it unlawful to refuse to employ a person on the grounds of his or her trade union membership. However, the section refers only to membership and not to activities. This omission was intended to allow firms to exclude people who had a history of working as union officials or organisers from the workplace.

The government took the view that an employer which did not want to engage in collective bargaining should be able to prevent a union from getting the opportunity to organise the workforce.[31] But rights theorists are strongly critical of this provision, arguing that trade union activists are particularly vulnerable to discrimination and that instruments such as the ESC and relevant ILO Conventions, discussed above, demand that they be given more, not less, protection than ordinary trade unionists.

How do employers find out about people's trade union activities? One possibility is that the employer might have access to a 'blacklist'. This term refers to a list of known union activists, perhaps shared among a group of employers, or drawn up by a firm or individual and sold to employers for profit. In ERA 1999, s. 3, the government took power to make regulations to prohibit the compilation, circulation and use of blacklists.[32] Draft regulations were issued in February 2003.[33] Among other things, the regulations would make it unlawful to refuse a person employment on the grounds that his or her name was included in a blacklist. From a rights perspective, this would go some way towards mitigating the narrowness of TULRCA 1992, s. 137. However, two limitations remain. First, the government argues that there is, at present, no evidence that blacklists are in use. It therefore proposes to refrain from enacting the regulations until there is proof that they are needed.[34] Second, even if the regulations were enacted, TULRCA 1992, s. 137 would still permit an employer to exclude a trade union activist from the workplace provided that the employer had found out about the person's union activities from a source other than a blacklist.

During employment
Discrimination during employment is addressed by TULRCA 1992, s. 146. Subsection (1) provides that:

An employee has the right not to be subjected to any detriment as an individual by any act, or any deliberate failure to act, by his employer if the act or failure takes place for the purpose of—

(a) preventing or deterring him from being or seeking to become a member of an independent trade union, or penalising him for doing so,
(b) preventing or deterring him from taking part in the activities of an independent trade union at an appropriate time, or penalising him for doing so ...

A preliminary point to note about this provision is that it only protects employees. Workers do not benefit from protection against discrimination on the grounds of

---

31 See comments by Patrick Nicholls, Parliamentary Under-Secretary of State for Employment, House of Commons, Official Report of Standing Committee D, col. 27, 8 February 1990.
32 For discussion, see K.D. Ewing, 'Freedom of association and the Employment Relations Act 1999' (1999) 28 *ILJ* 283.
33 DTI, *Draft Regulations to Prohibit the Blacklisting of Trade Unionists: a Consultation Document* (URN 03/648) (2003).
34 DTI, *Review of the Employment Relations Act 1999* (2003), paras. 3.18–3.20.

their trade union membership. From a rights perspective, this technical distinction is difficult to justify given the universal nature of the right to freedom of association set out in Article 11 of the ECHR and elsewhere.

Although s. 146 appears to conform to the ILO's requirements, discussed above, litigation has exposed some loopholes in the protection. In *Associated Newspapers Ltd v Wilson*, the employer decided to 'derecognise' the union: in other words, to decide workers' terms and conditions for itself without bargaining with the union.[35] In order to achieve this end, the employer offered a pay rise to workers who signed 'personal contracts' not bargained by the union. Rights theorists argued that this amounted to discrimination against trade union members. The employer was paying less to those who wanted to retain their collectively bargained contracts. But an economist hostile to unions might argue that employers should have the flexibility to abandon collective bargaining because of the damage it causes to the business. How did the courts approach the case?

The House of Lords held that no discrimination had taken place. First, the judges accepted the employer's argument that there was a distinction between trade union membership and using the services of the union. Mr Wilson's desire to have his contract determined by collective bargaining was an example of using the services of the union. Since s. 146(1)(a) refers only to membership, Mr Wilson was not protected. Second, the judges accepted the employer's argument that it had not sought to deter Mr Wilson and others from being members of the union. Lord Bridge pointed out that those giving evidence on behalf of the employer had stated that although they wished to derecognise the union, they were happy for employees to retain their union membership.[36]

Rights theorists have strongly criticised this decision. They argue that the House of Lords took an unduly narrow approach to the definition of membership.[37] As we saw in chapter 10, it is commonly argued that people join unions because they want collective bargaining, not just because they want to join an organisation. On this view, collective bargaining is an inherent part of trade union membership, not just an additional 'service' provided by unions. If this broader view of membership had been accepted, it would have been more difficult for the House of Lords to have held that the employer was not seeking to deter the employees from membership. It could have been argued that the employer was trying to make membership worthless by taking away its main advantage, collective bargaining.

Before the House of Lords heard the *Wilson* case, the government decided to change the law to ensure that employers would be able to derecognise unions without being held to have discriminated against union members. The government feared that the House of Lords might uphold the Court of Appeal's finding that

---

35 [1995] 2 AC 454.
36 [1995] 2 AC 454 at 476.
37 For a critique, see B. Simpson, 'Freedom of association and the right to organize: the failure of an individual rights strategy' (1995) 24 *ILJ* 235.

discrimination had taken place.[38] The Trade Union Reform and Employment Rights Bill happened to be before Parliament at the time, so an amendment was put forward.[39] As a result, TULRCA 1992, s. 148(3) now reads:

In determining what was the purpose for which the employer acted or failed to act in a case where—

(a) there is evidence that the employer's purpose was to further a change in his relationship with all or any class of his employees, and
(b) there is also evidence that his purpose was one falling within section 146,

the tribunal shall regard the purpose mentioned in paragraph (a) (and not the purpose mentioned in paragraph (b)) as the purpose for which the employer acted or failed to act, unless it considers that no reasonable employer would act or fail to act in the way concerned having regard to the purpose mentioned in paragraph (a).

This subsection requires the tribunal to ignore any evidence that the employer is seeking to deter employees from being members of a trade union. This is so even if it is clear on the facts that the employer has simply disguised an attack on the union as a desire to change employment relationships. The tribunal may take evidence of an anti-union purpose into account only where no reasonable employer would have acted as it did in order to persuade its employees to sign new contracts. It seems unlikely that this high standard would often be satisfied in practice. The subsection makes it virtually impossible to establish discrimination against trade union members in cases like *Wilson*.

Not surprisingly, the decision in *Wilson* and the new s. 148(3) have been subjected to considerable criticism.[40] The ILO Committee of Experts has condemned the narrow definition of membership given by the House of Lords, arguing that it should include use of the essential services of the union in order to comply with Convention 98.[41] It criticised s. 148(3), holding that this breached the government's obligations under the same Convention to protect individuals against anti-union discrimination and to promote collective bargaining. The TUC also brought a successful complaint before the ILO Freedom of Association Committee, based on the *Wilson* case.[42]

However, no action was taken to remedy the situation until the *Wilson* case was heard by the ECtHR.[43] The Court accepted a broader definition of trade union

---

38 *Associated Newspapers Ltd v Wilson* [1994] ICR 97 (CA). For discussion, see K.D. Ewing, 'Trade union derecognition and personal contracts: a note on recent developments' (1993) 22 *ILJ* 297.
39 Sometimes referred to as the Ullswater amendment because it was introduced by Viscount Ullswater in the House of Lords.
40 See also condemnation by the ESC Committee, *Conclusions – XIII-3* (1996), pp. 127–9.
41 The Committee's most recent statement on this issue is its *Individual Observation on Convention 98*, in 2002.
42 Freedom of Association Committee, *Complaint against the Government of the United Kingdom presented by the TUC, Case No. 1730*, Report No. 294 (1994), para. 202.
43 *Wilson v UK* [2002] 35 EHRR 20. For discussion of the implications of this decision for English law, see K.D. Ewing, 'The implications of *Wilson and Palmer*' (2003) 32 *ILJ* 1.

membership than that which had found favour with the House of Lords. The Court stated that:

> ... it is of the essence of the right to join a trade union for the protection of their interests that employees should be free to instruct or permit the union to make representations to their employer or to take action in support of their interests on their behalf. If workers are prevented from so doing, their freedom to belong to a trade union, for the protection of their interests, becomes illusory.[44]

Article 11 had been violated because English law permitted employers to discriminate against employees who refused to give up this essential part of their union membership.

Under the HRA 1998, it would be possible for a claimant to rely on *Wilson v UK* in order to argue for a fresh interpretation of the statutory provisions on discrimination or for a declaration that they are incompatible with Article 11 of the ECHR.[45] But this may not be necessary because, at the time of writing, the government is planning to change the law to bring it into compliance with the ECtHR's findings.[46] The most significant proposal is the repeal of s. 148(3). This will allow tribunals to determine whether the employer's purpose is an anti-union purpose on the facts before them, without having recourse to artificial statutory presumptions. The government also plans to introduce a specific statutory right for trade union members to make use of their union's services. This would address the gap in protection created by the House of Lords' view that trade union membership does not include using the union's services.

Nevertheless, rights theorists may not be entirely satisfied with the government's plans. Economics arguments continue to play an important role in the government's reasoning. The government still believes that employers should be free to offer personal contracts to trade union members without laying themselves open to discrimination claims. It argues that employers need 'flexibility ... to reward and retain key staff, and to shape working patterns to specific or particular circumstances'.[47] It therefore plans to legislate to the effect that offering personal contracts is not unlawful where there is no requirement or inducement for the individual to give up union representation. From a rights perspective, the danger is that employers will be able to exploit this provision in order to derecognise unions, for example, by covertly offering inducements. The provision will need to be carefully drafted and implemented to prevent this.

Dismissal
So far, we have considered discrimination at the hiring stage and during the employment relationship. English law also addresses the possibility of discrimination when

---

44 Above n. 43, at 539.
45 HRA 1998, ss. 3 and 4.
46 DTI, above n. 34, paras. 3.3–3.17.
47 DTI, above n. 34, para. 3.12.

an employee is dismissed (TULRCA 1992, s. 152) or selected for redundancy (TULRCA 1992, s. 153). In line with the general law on unfair dismissal and redundancy, only employees – not workers – are eligible for this protection. The prohibited grounds of discrimination are union membership and taking part in the activities of an independent trade union 'at an appropriate time'. The narrow interpretations of membership referred to above are also applicable in this area.

Although these rights are limited in scope, they do offer advantages over and above ordinary unfair dismissal claims for those able to invoke them. First, employees are eligible to claim from the moment they start work. They do not have to complete a year of qualifying service. Second, a dismissal on trade union grounds is automatically unfair. Third, the remedies are slightly enhanced. Under TULRCA 1992, s. 161, the employee may apply for interim relief. With the employer's consent, the employee may be reinstated or re-engaged pending the hearing of the claim. If the employer does not consent, the tribunal may make an order for the continuation of the contract of employment, which means that the employee will at least continue to get paid pending the hearing of the claim. Under TULRCA 1992, s. 156, if the claim is successful, the employee is entitled to a minimum basic award currently set at £3600, regardless of his or her length of service. In contrast to claims for unfair dismissal on grounds of sex or race discrimination, however, trade union discrimination claims remain subject to the upper limit of around £55,000 on the compensatory award.

Duties to support union activities

Perhaps surprisingly, the rights perspective is more in evidence when we consider the law on employers' duties to support trade union activities. Employers are obliged to provide union members and officials with time off for union activities, provided that certain conditions are met. And as we saw in chapter 10, employers may be obliged to bargain with unions under the statutory recognition procedure.

Under TULRCA 1992, s. 168, employees (not workers) who are union representatives are entitled to time off for negotiations with the employer about matters within the statutory definition of 'collective bargaining', for performing functions in relation to employees as agreed with the employer (such as informing them of the outcome of negotiations), and for training in connection with these roles. The representatives must be paid during these periods. Under s. 170, employees (not workers) who are trade union members are entitled to time off to take part in union activities (such as voting on the outcome of negotiations) or to act as union representatives. This time off need not be paid.

In both cases, the entitlement is to 'reasonable' time off with the employer's permission. This makes good economic sense. It allows the employer to control when and for how long union representatives and members can take time off, in the light of the needs of the business. It would be difficult to give effect to a more precise right (such as a right to a fixed amount of time off per week) given that negotiations may vary considerably in duration and complexity. However, the current right can be frustrated by a recalcitrant employer. If time off is refused, the affected representative or member must take a case to the Employment Tribunal to obtain a declaration or an award of compensation. This remedy is cumbersome and although it may act as a deterrent, it does not help employees to secure time off when they need it.

The most significant limitation on these rights is that they are only available to members and officials of *recognised* trade unions. This means that the employer only comes under an obligation to provide time off once it has agreed to engage in collective bargaining with the relevant union. From a new institutionalist perspective, there is much to be said for providing time off in this situation, since the bargaining process is likely to operate more smoothly if union representatives are well prepared and union members well informed. But these rights would also be of benefit to unrecognised unions which were seeking to recruit new members or to persuade the employer to negotiate with them.[48]

The ILO standards, quoted above, also refer to the provision of 'facilities' for trade union representatives. This is not addressed in TULRCA 1992 itself, but it is discussed in the ACAS Code of Practice issued under the Act.[49] Paragraph 28 suggests that employers should 'consider' providing meeting rooms, notice boards, use of a telephone and even office space, taking into account the firm's resources and the amount of work carried out by trade union officials. These facilities may be just as important as the provision of time off to the ability of union officials to represent workers effectively. Rights theorists might prefer to see them enshrined in a precise legal right, but such a right would be difficult to draft given the need to take account of employers' specific circumstances.

To conclude, it can be seen that English law's concept of freedom of association as against employers is somewhat confused. On the one hand, the law follows a strongly rights-based approach in placing employers under some duties to facilitate trade union activities and (through the recognition procedure) to engage in collective bargaining. On the other hand, the law is narrow in its interpretation of what it means to discriminate against someone on trade union grounds. The government's proposed reforms will strengthen the anti-discrimination provisions, but some gaps – such as the lack of protection for union activists at the hiring stage – will remain.

Freedom of association between workers and trade unions

English law provides trade union members with a number of rights against their unions. It reflects the 'individualistic' view of freedom of association, discussed above, which emphasises individual choice over the needs of the group. The law is likely to be welcomed by those economists who are hostile to trade unions, because

---

48 If an unrecognised union invokes the statutory recognition procedure, it has a right of access to the workers at the balloting stage: TULRCA 1992, Sch. A1, para. 26.
49 ACAS Code of Practice 3, *Time off for Trade Union Duties and Activities* (1997), issued under TULRCA 1992, s. 201.

it does much to limit their powers. But it is heavily criticised by rights theorists in the collectivist tradition. They argue that individual rights weaken unions and harm individuals' interests in the long term.

Compulsory trade union membership

English law does not permit employers and unions to enforce the closed shop. It is no longer possible to insist that an individual be a member of a particular trade union in order to work for a particular firm. To understand how the law achieves this result, you need to understand how a closed shop is enforced. Although the closed shop involves compulsory trade union membership, it is enforced by the *employer*, acting at the union's request. In a pre-entry closed shop, the employer agrees to consider only those applicants who are already members of the union. In a post-entry closed shop, non-union candidates may apply for jobs but must join the union if they are successful. The employer undertakes to dismiss any who refuse to join.

We saw above that the law forbids any discrimination against trade union members in recruitment, during the life of the contract and at dismissal.[50] These protections are symmetrical. In other words, they apply not only to trade union members but also to those who are not members. This means that it is unlawful for the employer to refuse to employ or to dismiss someone on the grounds that he or she is *not* a member of a trade union. As a result, the employer would be acting unlawfully if it tried to enforce the closed shop. Moreover, because non-membership is much easier to define than membership, the provisions are much more effective in their protection of non-members.

From a neoclassical economics perspective, these provisions are to be welcomed. They limit unions' ability to get into a powerful position in the workplace and to extract significant rents from employers as a consequence. From a collectivist rights perspective, they are harmful for precisely the same reasons. From an individualistic rights perspective, they play an important role in protecting individuals' choice of whether or not to join a union. Theorists in this tradition receive the most support from international human rights instruments.

Trade union rules on membership

The human rights instruments discussed above set out relatively clearly the principle that trade unions should have the freedom to set their own membership rules, subject to basic controls such as anti-discrimination law. English law takes a much more individualistic approach. TULRCA 1992 controls unions' decisions on membership applications by setting out lists of permitted and prohibited criteria for membership.[51] Section 174 lists the four permitted grounds of exclusion: failure to satisfy an

---

50 TULRCA 1992, ss. 137, 146 and 152–3.
51 At common law, the courts intervened only in exceptional circumstances. Compare *Faramus v Film Artistes' Association* [1964] AC 925, with *Nagle v Feilden* [1966] 2 QB 633.

'enforceable membership requirement'; where the union is regional, failure to work in the relevant part of the UK; where the union is employer-specific, failure to work for that employer; and conduct. Membership requirements are deemed enforceable under s. 174(3) if they relate to the occupation or qualifications of the applicant, thus allowing unions to focus on representing workers with specific skills.

The fourth permitted ground of exclusion, 'conduct', appears to give unions a wide discretion to reject applicants on the basis of union rules, but in fact this is not the case. By virtue of s. 174(4), unions are not allowed to consider certain types of 'conduct'. One is that the applicant is or has been a member of another union. This was intended as an attack on the Bridlington Principles, an agreement amongst TUC-affiliated unions that they would not 'poach' each other's members. Although the Principles still exist, they cannot be enforced by requiring unions to exclude 'poached' members.[52] Another type of conduct which cannot be taken into account is membership of a political party. This prevents unions from requiring applicants to join a party they favour or to resign from a party which is hostile to the union. Finally, the union cannot take into account any 'conduct' which would amount to 'unjustifiable discipline' within TULRCA 1992, s. 65. This provision is discussed in more detail below, but it includes bringing proceedings against the union or refusing to take part in industrial action. Thus, if someone who had been a member of the union in the past sought to join again, he or she could not be excluded because of these activities during his or her previous period of membership.

An individual who feels that he or she has been wrongly excluded from the union can apply to the Employment Tribunal for a declaration.[53] The union is then given four weeks in which to decide whether or not to admit the applicant to membership. If the individual is admitted to the union, he or she may nevertheless apply to the Employment Tribunal for compensation, and may be given an award such as the tribunal considers 'just and equitable' of up to £63,100. If the individual is not admitted, he or she must apply to the Employment Appeal Tribunal for compensation. The same maximum award applies, but the individual must receive a *minimum* award of £5900. These remedies (which are in some respects stronger than those for unfair dismissal) clearly reinforce the principle that it is for individuals to choose their union, rather than for unions to choose their members. Very little space is left for unions to act autonomously in setting their membership rules. This aspect of English law is in breach of ILO Convention 87 and Article 5 ESC.[54]

Union discipline and expulsion

So far, we have seen that the law is strongly individualistic: effectively outlaw-ing the closed shop and giving applicants for union membership what amounts to a right to join the union of their choice. At this point, it might be expected

---

52 For a critique of the provisions with particular reference to their impact on the Bridlington Principles, see Simpson, above n. 20.
53 TULRCA 1992, s. 176.
54 ESC Committee, *Conclusions XIII-3* (1996), pp. 107–11.

that the law would switch to a collectivist mode, thereby putting in place one of the compromise positions set out above. Because individuals have made a free choice to join, they should accept the obligations that go with membership, and should obey the lawful orders of the union. However, English law remains strongly individualistic. Initially, protection for union members developed at common law through the courts' construction of the contract of membership. Now, the grounds on which unions can discipline or expel their members are governed by TULRCA 1992.

At common law, the courts were heavily influenced by the consequences of union disciplinary action for members. In particular, if the union decided to expel a member in a closed shop situation, that member would lose his or her job.[55] The courts therefore held that they had jurisdiction to construe the contract of membership between the individual and the union. Various techniques were adopted which ensured that the court's interpretation would protect the individual.[56] Perhaps the least controversial technique was to imply the rules of natural justice into the contract of membership. This served to ensure that members could not be disciplined or dismissed without proper notice of the charges against them and an opportunity to state their case. An example of this is *Edwards v SOGAT*.[57] The union's rules provided that membership would terminate automatically if any member fell into arrears of more than six weeks with his or her subscriptions. The Court of Appeal held that this was a breach of natural justice since it did not give the member the opportunity of putting forward any arguments as to why he or she should not be expelled. The position was exacerbated by the fact that the union rules did not allow Edwards to appeal against the decision of the union's branch committee, a clear breach of natural justice.

More controversially, the courts have intervened in unions' substantive disciplinary decisions. Union rules commonly contain a general offence of 'unfitness to be a member', in addition to more specific offences such as falling behind with subscriptions. The general offence is often framed in a subjective manner: it is seen as a matter of opinion for the relevant committee of the union. Just such an offence was before the court in *Esterman v NALGO*.[58] The relevant union rule provided for the expulsion of a member who was 'guilty of conduct which, in the opinion of the executive committee, renders him unfit for membership'. Instead of relying on the opinion of the committee, the court looked at whether or not there was sufficient evidence to support the committee's findings. In other words, the court construed the apparently subjective term objectively. Ms Esterman had refused to obey a union order because she doubted whether the union had power to issue it. The court held that this did not render her unfit to be a member of the union.

---

55 See *Lee v Showmen's Guild of Great Britain* [1952] 2 QB 329 at 343, per Denning LJ.
56 For a detailed discussion, see P. Elias and K. Ewing, *Trade Union Democracy: Members' Rights and the Law* (1987), chapter 6.
57 [1971] Ch 354.
58 [1974] ICR 625.

Nowadays, union discipline and expulsion is extensively regulated by statute.[59] Expulsion from a trade union is dealt with under TULRCA 1992, s. 174, in just the same way that exclusion, discussed above, is addressed. Thus, a member can be expelled if he or she ceases to work in the relevant trade or in the relevant part of the UK, but cannot be expelled for joining a political party. Nor can he or she be expelled for conduct amounting to 'unjustifiable discipline' under s. 65.

Where the penalty imposed on the individual is a lesser one than expulsion, such as being made to pay a fine or being denied access to union facilities, the case is governed by s. 64, which grants trade union members a right not to be unjustifiably disciplined. This last phrase is defined in s. 65, which thus serves a three-fold role of regulating exclusion, expulsion and discipline of trade union members. Some of the requirements in s. 65 are relatively straightforward. For example, s. 65(2)(j) protects a member who asserts his or her statutory rights against the union. This is analogous to provisions protecting employees from being victimised by their employers for bringing legal proceedings against them. Others illustrate the individualistic tenor of this area of the law. Under s. 65(2)(a), a member cannot be disciplined for 'failing to participate in or support a strike or other industrial action (whether by members of the union or by others), or indicating opposition to or a lack of support for such action'.

The ILO has condemned the UK for the 'unjustifiable discipline' provisions in particular.[60] In 2002, the Committee of Experts reiterated its long-held view that:

> Unions should have the right to draw up their rules without interference from public authorities and so to determine whether or not it should be possible to discipline members who refuse to comply with democratic decisions to take lawful industrial action.[61]

In 1998, the Committee justified its view by pointing out that individuals in the UK had a free choice as to whether or not to join a union.[62] This meant that they could take into account any element of compulsion contained in union rules when making their decision about membership. Collectivists would also argue that individuals' long-term interests are best served by strong unions which can make credible strike threats to employers. But individualists would point to the unfairness of forcing the individual to choose between striking and resigning from the union, particularly when he or she might have a good reason for not wanting to strike, such as not being able to manage without pay. Neoclassicists would agree, but on

---

59 Some claimants might still invoke the common law where necessary, for example, in the event of a breach of natural justice. But the courts might be slightly less sympathetic now that the closed shop is no longer lawful and the consequences of expulsion are less serious.

60 As has the ESC Committee. See above n. 54.

61 ILO Committee of Experts on the Application of Conventions and Recommendations, *Observation* (on UK and Convention No. 87) (73rd Session) (2002).

62 ILO Committee of Experts on the Application of Conventions and Recommendations, *Observation* (on UK and Convention No. 87) (69th Session) (1998).

different grounds: strong unions are bad for the economy, firms and individual workers, so the law should discourage them.

Further reading

For detailed textbook accounts of this topic, see S. Deakin and G. Morris, *Labour Law* (3rd edn., 2001), chapters 8 and 10; or H. Collins, K.D. Ewing and A. McColgan, *Labour Law: Text and Materials* (2001), chapters 7 and 8.

Much of the modern law was enacted during the 1980s by a government which was hostile to trade unions. It used both the arguments of neoclassical economics and the individualistic rights approach. For an excellent account of the development of the law, see P. Davies and M. Freedland, *Labour Legislation and Public Policy* (1993), chapter 9. Do you think that individuals are vulnerable to oppression by trade unions? Was the government's concern with individual rights 'genuine', or did it serve to conceal other motives?

New institutionalist economists focus on the advantages of trade unions. It was suggested in this chapter that they would support some basic aspects of freedom of association, such as a duty on employers not to discriminate. But how strong do unions need to be in order to have a positive impact in the workplace? For example, would a closed shop have more impact on productivity than a mere union presence? Or would a union which could choose and discipline its members in accordance with its own rules have more influence over labour turnover than one which could not? You may find it helpful to revisit R.B. Freeman and J.L. Medoff, *What Do Unions Do?* (1984), when thinking about these questions.

For a detailed account and critique of recent developments from a (collectivist) rights perspective, see K.D. Ewing, 'Freedom of association and the Employment Relations Act 1999' (1999) 28 *ILJ* 283; 'The implications of *Wilson and Palmer*' (2003) 32 *ILJ* 1; and B. Simpson, 'Individualism versus collectivism: an evaluation of section 14 of the Trade Union Reform and Employment Rights Act 1993' (1993) 22 *ILJ* 181. What rights should union members have against their employers? Why? Are there any costs associated with these rights? (On the last question, see P. Todd, 'Action short of dismissal', in H. Collins *et al.* (eds.), *Legal Regulation of the Employment Relation* (2000).) What rights, if any, should union members have against their union? Why should individuals' interests be sacrificed for the good of the group? Why should unions be given autonomy to set their own rules? When thinking about union autonomy, you may like to consider the law on union elections and political funds (discussed in the textbooks, cited above, and excluded from this chapter on grounds of space) and industrial action ballots (to be considered in chapter 12).

12

Industrial action

Strikes are not very common in the UK. The 'strike rate' is defined by statisticians as the number of working days lost through strike action per 1000 employees. The most recent figure for the UK is for the year 2000, in which 20 working days per 1000 employees were lost.[1] In general, the strike rate for the UK has been falling, from 34 in 1991 to 10 in 1999, though there are occasional 'blips': a large dispute in 1996 took the average up to 55. It is not yet clear whether the figure of 20 for 2000 is a similar 'blip', or the start of a new upward trend. Further proof that the UK's strike rate has declined to a very low level is provided by the WERS.[2] This study collects data by asking managers whether or not any industrial action has taken place in their workplace during the last year. In 1980, a quarter of workplaces reported some kind of industrial action (including non-strike action). In 1990, the figure had fallen to 13% and by 1998 it was just 2%. The figures for strike action were 11% in 1990 falling to 1% in 1998. Nevertheless, industrial action is probably the most controversial topic in labour law. Most people have experienced the disruption industrial action can cause: perhaps your travel plans have been affected by a strike of train drivers or air traffic controllers, for example. And it provokes very different reactions from rights theorists and economists.

It is clear that industrial action does not bring any economic benefits in itself. A strike damages the employer's business and may have substantial indirect effects on other firms, consumers and the public. However, as we shall see, industrial action plays an important role in collective bargaining. Economists' views on strikes are therefore closely linked to their views on collective bargaining. Those who see collective bargaining as damaging to firms because it enables workers to extract excessive pay rises are opposed to industrial action. Those who see collective bargaining as beneficial are more tolerant of industrial action.

Rights theorists take a very different starting point. They view industrial action either as a fundamental human right or at least as a very important labour right. Those who take the fundamental human rights standpoint link the right to strike

---

1 The statistics in this paragraph are from J. Monger, 'International comparisons of labour disputes in 2000' (2003) 111 *Labour Market Trends* 19, available at http://www.statistics.gov.uk/cci/article.asp?id=371.
2 M. Cully *et al.*, *Britain at Work* (1999), p. 245.

to civil and political rights such as the right not to be subjected to forced labour. Those who take the labour rights standpoint focus on the role of strike action in a system of collective bargaining. They see the right to strike as an essential means of equalising the bargaining power of workers as against employers.

These competing views present legislators with a difficult set of choices. Most legal systems opt for some kind of middle position in which strikes are lawful provided that certain conditions are met. These conditions might relate to the subject-matter or purpose of the strike or to the procedure to be followed by the union before organising the strike, for example. Middle positions are easier to justify than extreme ones – they protect a version of the right to strike whilst minimising the disruption to the economy – but they can be quite difficult to operate in practice. Someone has to decide whether or not the conditions for the legality of the strike have been met in any particular case, a job which usually falls to the courts. And as we shall see, they may not be well equipped to perform so politically controversial a task.

Rights perspectives

The right to strike is expressly granted in many economic and social rights instruments. The ICESCR provides, in Article 8(1)(d), that states should protect 'the right to strike, provided that it is exercised in conformity with the laws of the particular country'. Some instruments link the right quite clearly with collective bargaining. Article 6 of the ESC is headed 'the right to bargain collectively' and includes an obligation on states to protect the right to strike alongside the obligation to promote collective bargaining. The EU Charter makes a similar link. Article 28 provides that:

> Workers and employers, or their respective organisations, have, in accordance with Community law and national laws and practices, the right to negotiate and conclude collective agreements at the appropriate levels and, in cases of conflicts of interest, to take collective action to defend their interests, including strike action.

Strikes play an important role in collective bargaining because they increase the bargaining power of workers as against their employer. Workers and their representatives need to have some way of persuading the employer to listen to their demands. If they have a right to strike, they are able to threaten the employer with disruption to the business. This should at least make the employer take notice, even if it does not make the employer agree to their demands: the employer might decide to take the chance that the workers will not strike or that the strike will not be very disruptive. In the absence of a right to strike, the employer can simply refuse to hear the workers without even having to make these calculations.

However, if we choose to justify the right to strike in terms of its role in collective bargaining, this has implications for the *scope* of the right. First, a legitimate strike would have to be related to the issues which were the subject of collective bargaining. Thus, if the union and the employer were bargaining about pay, a strike could take place if the workers rejected the employer's final offer in the negotiations. But a strike could not be used as a means of protesting about government policy in general. ILO jurisprudence does allow some political strikes but only where they are protesting about government policy on the economic and social interests of workers (the minimum wage rate, for example).[3] Second, if the right to strike is linked to collective bargaining, it should be regarded as a collective rather than an individual right. This means that the right to strike is not a right which can be exercised by one individual on his or her own. Instead, it must be exercised by a trade union, or by workers acting on the instructions of their trade union. This is because collective bargaining by its very definition involves bargaining by a union or group of workers rather than by an individual.

Some rights theorists have sought alternative justifications for the right to strike which treat it as a civil and political right rather than a socio-economic one. Often, this is because they dislike the limitations which attach to the right to strike when it is viewed as an aspect of collective bargaining. Moreover, as we saw in chapter 3, civil and political rights tend to attract higher levels of support and more effective legal protection than do economic and social rights. A preliminary difficulty, however, is that civil and political rights instruments simply do not mention the right to strike. Commentators have therefore tried to include the right to strike in at least three of the well-established civil and political rights: freedom of association, freedom from forced labour, and freedom of expression. We will examine each in turn.

Perhaps rather surprisingly, freedom of association is the underlying basis of the right to strike in ILO jurisprudence. For political reasons, the ILO has never reached agreement on a Convention containing an express right to strike.[4] However, for some years now the right has been accepted as an essential part of the right to freedom of association protected by Conventions 87 and 98. The Freedom of Association Committee has stated that:

> Freedom of association implies not only the right of workers and employers to form freely organizations of their own choosing, but also the right for the organizations themselves to pursue lawful activities for the defence of their occupational interests.[5]

The right to strike is the main weapon in trade unions' efforts to defend their members' interests. But theorists have been more interested in including the right to strike in the freedom of association rights contained in the major civil and political rights instruments, such as the ECHR and ICCPR. Article 11 of the ECHR provides that:

> Everyone has the right ... to freedom of association with others, including the right to form and to join trade unions for the protection of his interests.

---

3 ILO, *Digest of Decisions and Principles of the Freedom of Association Committee* (1996), para. 482.
4 See T. Novitz, *International and European Protection of the Right to Strike* (2003), chapter 5.
5 ILO, above n. 3, para. 447.

Article 22 of the ICCPR is framed in similar terms. The argument that this right should be understood as including a right to strike relies on the phrase 'for the protection of his interests'.[6] It is argued that workers join trade unions not just because they want to be a member of an organisation but because they want the benefit of collective bargaining by that organisation on their behalf, to protect their interests. And if a link can be made from freedom of association to collective bargaining, it is relatively easy to make the further link to a right to strike, by arguing that collective bargaining does not make sense without a right to strike. In fact, this set of arguments is very similar to the economic and social rights approach of linking the right to strike to the right to engage in collective bargaining. As a result, it suffers from the same limitations: strikes must relate to the subject-matter of bargaining, and must be collective rather than individual. However, a right to strike protected through civil and political rights instruments might attain a higher level of support and legal protection.

Some attempts have been made to persuade the ECtHR to include a right to strike in Article 11. This jurisprudence is of particular interest because it could be relied on in the English courts under the HRA 1998. In the *National Union of Belgian Police* case, the ECtHR appeared to take the view that governments were under some obligation to provide rights for trade unions as part of their protection of freedom of association: 'what the Convention requires is that under national law trade unions should be enabled ... to strive for the protection of their members' interests'.[7] However, in *Schmidt and Dahlströhm v Sweden*, the Court was unenthusiastic about the right to strike.[8] It emphasised the discretion states had in promoting trade union action, and held that while the 'right to strike represents without any doubt one of the most important of these means ... there are others'.[9] Similarly, in *Wilson v UK*, the Court appeared to treat the right to strike and the right of a trade union to be recognised by the employer as *alternative* ways in which a state could choose to assist trade unions in their task of representing their members.[10] Thus, a state which protected the right to strike could rely on this as a partial fulfilment of its Article 11 obligations, but a state which chose not to protect the right to strike could comply with Article 11 in some other way. However, *Unison v UK* does offer some hope.[11] In this case, the union had not been able to strike, and the ECtHR held that the state had to justify this under Article 11(2) even though Article 11(1) does not require protection of the right to strike. Ewing suggests that although the right to strike remains formally unprotected, it now has a 'twilight status'.[12]

---

6 See, for example, J. Hendy, 'The Human Rights Act, Article 11, and the Right to Strike' (1998) 5 EHRLR 582.
7 *National Union of Belgian Police v Belgium* [1979–80] 1 EHRR 578 at 591.
8 [1979–80] 1 EHRR 632.
9 [1979–80] 1 EHRR 637 at 644.
10 [2002] 35 EHRR 20.
11 [2002] IRLR 497.
12 K.D. Ewing, 'The Implications of *Wilson and Palmer*' (2003) 32 *ILJ* 1 at 18.

Some commentators have tried to advance the right to strike using civil and political rights other than freedom of association. One possibility is the right to be free from forced labour.[13] This right has a particularly high level of support. The connection with industrial action is that if a country operates a strike ban, then it is in effect forcing workers to do their jobs even when they do not want to. However, the argument suffers from a number of flaws. First, even if a strike ban was in operation, workers could still resign their jobs. This makes it difficult to claim that they are being forced to work. Second, workers usually expect a strike to be a temporary measure, after which they will return to work. Even if the right to be free from forced labour justifies allowing the workers to stop work, it is difficult to see how it can be used to allow them to return to work at a time of their choice.[14]

Finally, some writers use freedom of expression as the basis of the right to strike.[15] Freedom of expression does not just protect speech. It also protects various 'acts' which are designed to express ideas, such as works of art. Strikes could be viewed as a 'speech act', in which workers are trying to convey their demands to the employer and to the wider public. This justification is particularly relevant to picketing: when striking workers stand outside the workplace in order to protest about the employer's behaviour and to make sure that others (customers, non-striking employees, suppliers and so on) are aware of the strike and its aims. However, the main difficulty with this right is that – like most human rights – it is qualified. This means that the right can be limited where it causes significant harm to others. Strikes obviously cause significant harm to the employer and may have damaging effects on customers and the wider public. If a strike was seen as an aspect of freedom of expression it would have to be justified by comparison with other modes of *expressing* workers' demands. The problem is that other types of expression – such as posters or leaflets or public meetings – are much less harmful. This makes it quite difficult to justify industrial action in this way.

The discussion so far has shown that the most plausible justification for strike action is that it helps to equalise the bargaining power of workers and the employer during collective bargaining. A right to strike is usually expressly mentioned in economic and social rights instruments in the context of the state's obligation to support collective bargaining. It may also be implied into civil and political rights instruments, *if* freedom of association is interpreted so as to include rights for trade unions.

Whichever method is adopted, however, it is important to remember that the right to strike is likely to be qualified. This means that states will be able to restrict the right in order to protect other important interests. The ICESCR and the EU Charter of Fundamental Rights both provide that the right to strike is to be exercised in accordance with national laws. This gives each state a substantial degree of discretion

13 R. Ben-Israel, *International Labour Standards: the Case of Freedom to Strike* (1988), pp. 24–5.
14 For a counter-argument, see Ben-Israel, above n. 13, p. 25.
15 For example, S. Kupferberg, 'Political Strikes, Labor Law and Democratic Rights' (1985) 71 *Virginia Law Review* 685.

to place limits on the right. The ILO's Freedom of Association Committee has held that:

> The conditions that have to be fulfilled under the law in order to render a strike lawful should be reasonable and in any event not such as to place a substantial limitation on the means of action open to trade union organizations.[16]

Article 11 of the ECHR (assuming now that it could include a right to strike) is qualified in the following terms:

> No restrictions shall be placed on the exercise of these rights other than such as are prescribed by law and are necessary in a democratic society in the interests of national security or public safety, for the prevention of disorder or crime, for the protection of health or morals or for the protection of the rights and freedoms of others. This article shall not prevent the imposition of lawful restrictions on the exercise of these rights by members of the armed forces, of the police or of the administration of the state.

Put very broadly, there are three main justifications for limiting the right to strike. First, strikes may be restricted to prevent 'disorder or crime'. Picketing and other demonstrations organised during a strike may involve the commission of criminal offences if violence or serious disruption ensues. Second, certain groups of workers may be barred from taking industrial action. The practice varies from country to country but may include the police, army, prison officers, fire-fighters and so on.[17] The justification is that strikes by these workers could cause serious damage to the safety of the public or the security of the state. It is usual for the state to provide some mechanism for the arbitration of pay claims so that workers are not disadvantaged by the strike ban. Third, there is the need to protect the 'rights and freedoms of others'. Novitz identifies a number of groups who may be harmed by a strike, including employers, other workers, consumers and the public at large.[18] The protection of these groups will be explored more fully in our discussion of the economic impact of strikes, below. Any limitations on the right to strike must be carefully scrutinised in order to ascertain whether they fit within one of these justifications and whether they are proportionate to the goal being pursued.

Economics perspectives

It is virtually impossible to identify any positive economic benefits flowing directly from industrial action. Most obviously, strikes cause harm to the employer. Depending on the extent of the strike, the employer's ability to trade may be reduced or removed altogether. The business may even be damaged over the longer term, as previously loyal customers discover other suppliers and do not return once the strike is over. Strikes may harm workers too: if the employer's business is damaged, some

16 ILO, above n. 3, para. 498.
17 For ILO jurisprudence on this, see above n. 3, paras. 526–53.
18 Above n. 4, chapter 4.

may have to be laid off. Jobs may also be lost in firms which supply to, or buy from, the affected employer. If the strike is successful, the ensuing rise in wages may lead to redundancies to enable the employer to keep costs down, and may make it more difficult for the unemployed to find work. Strikes may injure consumers where they are unable to obtain the goods or services they want. Finally, strikes may damage the economy as a whole by reducing productivity.

Rights theorists have argued that some of these claims may be exaggerated.[19] A rational trade union would not conduct a strike which would lead to substantial job losses. This would harm its members much more than missing out on a pay rise. Unions must therefore take into account the need to safeguard jobs as well as the need to improve workers' terms and conditions when formulating their demands at the negotiating table. Similarly, while it is important to balance the right to strike against the interests of consumers, much of what consumers will suffer during a strike is inconvenience rather than positive harm. A one-day train strike might be a nuisance but it is unlikely to be overwhelmingly damaging. The only strikes which have a real potential for causing harm are those in essential services, such as the police or fire brigade. Most rights theorists would accept the need to limit strikes by these workers.

Nevertheless, the role that strikes play in collective bargaining *depends* on the fact that they cause harm to the employer. When a union bargains with an employer, it does not want to take strike action. Instead, it wants to persuade the employer to agree to its demands by threatening to take strike action. Let us imagine a simple negotiation in which the union asks for a 4% pay rise and the employer responds by saying that it can only afford 2%. Each side has to calculate what to do next.[20] The employer must calculate the union's bargaining power. It can do this by comparing the cost of disagreeing with the union's demands to the cost of agreeing with the union's demands. The cost of agreeing with the union's demands is relatively simple: it is the loss of profit which will occur if the firm has to give a 4% pay rise to the employees. The cost of disagreeing is more complex. Management must work out how likely it is that a strike might take place, how long it might last, and how much profit would be lost as a result. Similarly, the union can calculate the bargaining power of management by comparing its cost of disagreeing with its cost of agreeing. The cost of agreeing is the difference between the 2% pay rise the employees will get and the 4% they were hoping for. The cost of disagreeing is the loss of wages union members would suffer if they were on strike. The union will have superior bargaining power – and will get the desired pay rise – if it can make a credible threat of a strike and if the employer does not want to risk the disruption.

Inevitably, the parties do not always reach agreement. Both sides may decide that the cost of disagreeing is insufficient to outweigh the cost of agreeing. Economists

---

19 Novitz, above n. 4, chapter 4.
20 The model of bargaining used here is drawn from N.W. Chamberlain, *A General Theory of Economic Process* (1955), chapters 6–8.

have tried to identify some of the reasons why negotiations fail. One problem is incomplete or asymmetric information.[21] In other words, disagreements may arise because each party does not know what the other would be willing to agree to. Imagine that, in our scenario, the firm would in fact be willing to offer 3% in order to prevent a strike. The union would be willing to accept this but believes that management can be persuaded to give 4%. In theory, the parties could reach agreement on 3%. But this would not happen in practice because the union would hold out for the 4% it thinks it can achieve. The negotiations would end in deadlock and a strike would ensue. Once the strike is in progress, the parties may return to the negotiating table. Management's decision to tolerate the strike signals to the union that management's highest possible offer is something less than 4%. Once the union has realised its 'mistake', it will lower its demand and the parties may then be able to reach agreement.

Another reason for strikes identified by some economists is the problem of 'commitments'.[22] Unions and employers may commit themselves to particular principles before the negotiations begin, making it difficult to retreat when it becomes clear that these principles will lead to conflict. In our example, perhaps managers have told the firm's shareholders that they will not agree to pay rises above 2% because this is the current rate of inflation. And perhaps the union is seeking a 4% pay rise because this would bring wages into line with those at other firms in the same industry. Two main problems arise from these commitments. First, management and the union may 'lose face' with each other if they step back from their publicly proclaimed positions. The parties are 'repeat players' in the negotiations: they will have to go through the same process in future years. The parties will not want to sacrifice their credibility over the longer term in order to solve the current dispute. For example, if the union drops its 4% claim, management may not believe its arguments next year. Second, the firm and the union may 'lose face' with other people outside the negotiations. Management may fear the wrath of shareholders and union leaders may fear the wrath of union members. Thus, although the parties could reach agreement at 3%, they may be impeded from doing so by the public commitments they have made.

Ultimately, economists' views of industrial action depend heavily on their views of collective bargaining, since the two are inextricably linked. As we saw in chapter 10, collective bargaining is a matter of considerable controversy. Neoclassical economists focus on the ability of unions to secure pay for their members over and above the 'market rate' for the job.[23] Although these 'rents' are beneficial for union members, they have a number of harmful consequences. They make it more expensive for the firm to employ labour, leading to job losses and making it more difficult

---

21 See, for example, M.J. Mauro, 'Strikes as a result of imperfect information' (1982) 35 *Industrial and Labor Relations Review* 522.

22 See, for example, C.M. Stevens, *Strategy and Collective Bargaining Negotiations* (1963), chapter 5.

23 See F.A. Hayek, *The Constitution of Liberty* (1960), chapter 18; R.A. Posner, *Economic Analysis of Law* (5th edn., 1998), pp. 349–56.

for the unemployed to find work. And they contribute to inefficiency in the economy as a whole, since the firm will not be able to achieve optimal productivity when labour is too expensive. Pro-union economists accept some of these arguments but believe that they are outweighed by the other benefits unions can bring.[24] One such benefit is a reduction in labour turnover. Because unions give 'voice' to employees' grievances, those employees are likely to remain with the firm instead of seeking new jobs elsewhere. This reduces the firm's hiring and training costs. Another claimed benefit is that unions improve productivity by helping management to explain its needs to the workers and by helping workers to convey their ideas to management. Of course, these economists would not advocate the widespread use of strike action, but they would be prepared to tolerate it as an essential part of collective bargaining.

In recent years, a new school of thought has emerged which emphasises the idea of 'partnership' between employers and workers, including unions. The idea of partnership is supported by the TUC[25] and the government. It formed an important part of the *Fairness at Work* White Paper[26] and the government has set up a fund to support partnership projects.[27] Thus, although partnership approaches are not currently very widespread among firms,[28] they are likely to become more popular in the future. The concept of partnership is closely linked to the argument that the UK should concentrate on producing innovative goods and services which require highly skilled workers in order to compete under conditions of globalisation. Firms need:

> Employees with multiple competencies, who will work diligently and thoughtfully without close supervision, use their knowledge and experience to find more efficient and effective ways of doing things, and are committed to the objectives of the firm ... Participative company cultures that incorporate high-trust and non-adversarial relationships are seen as the most appropriate to motivate people to work in these ways.[29]

Where a trade union is present in the workplace, management should build a close relationship with union leaders in order to improve communication with the workforce. Union leaders can provide managers with information about workers' ideas for improving productivity; managers can use union leaders to help explain the firm's goals and plans to the workers. Unions and employers are portrayed as having the same interest in creating a profitable firm. Strikes have no place in a partnership firm.

---

24 See, generally, R.B. Freeman and J.L. Medoff, *What Do Unions Do?* (1984).
25 The TUC has created a Partnership Institute to help unions and employers develop partnerships: for more information see http://www.tuc.org.uk/theme/index.cfm?theme=partnership.
26 DTI, *Fairness at Work* (Cm. 3968, 1998), especially chapter 1.
27 DTI, above n. 26, para. 2.7; ERA 1999, s. 30; and see http://www.dti.gov.uk/partnershipfund/index.html.
28 J. Knell, *Partnership at Work* (DTI URN 99/1078) (1999), pp. 23–5.
29 S. Hill 'How Do You Manage A Flexible Firm? The Total Quality Model' (1991) 5 *Work, Employment and Society* 397 at 397–8, quoted in Knell, above n. 28.

Rights theorists are sceptical of the partnership approach, arguing that it downplays the existence of genuine conflicts between management and unions. At a very general level, it is obviously true that unions have an interest in a profitable firm. There is no point in making a pay claim which would drive the firm out of business. But conflicts may still arise: over redundancies, new working methods, pay rises and so on. The partnership concept may be dangerous for unions because it may undermine the legitimacy of expressing opposition to management's ideas and acting on that opposition by exercising the right to strike. It is easy to see how a union's attempt to represent the concerns of workers could be portrayed as 'old-fashioned adversarialism'.[30]

The law on trade unions and strike organisers

Now that we have examined the various rights and economics perspectives on industrial action, we are in a position to consider the underlying policy of English law. In this section, we will examine the law relating to trade unions and others who organise strikes. The next section will consider the position of individual workers who go on strike.

English law does not grant a right to strike in express terms. Indeed, those who organise a strike generally commit one or more of the economic torts. For example, by persuading an employee to go on strike, a strike organiser commits the tort of inducing breach of contract (because employees will be in breach of contract if they strike) and probably the tort of interfering with trade or business by unlawful means (because the unlawful act of inducing employees to breach their contracts of employment will prevent the employer from fulfilling its commercial contracts with customers).[31] Thus, the law's starting-point is that it is unlawful to organise a strike. However, statute offers trade unions and strike organisers the possibility of an immunity against liability in tort if certain conditions are fulfilled. The immunity applies to the torts of inducing breach of contract or interfering with the performance of a contract, intimidation and simple conspiracy.[32] The immunity also applies where one of these torts is relied upon as the 'unlawful means' element of another tort, such as interfering with trade or business by unlawful means.[33] This extends the protection quite considerably.

On one view, it does not matter that English law does not grant an explicit right to strike. A legal right is no guarantee of effective protection, since it could be hedged about with exceptions and limitations. And rights can be protected by indirect means, such as a system of immunities against legal liability, provided that the immunities are strong enough. However, most rights theorists are critical of

---

30 For example, DTI, above n. 26, para. 2.2.
31 Space precludes a full discussion of the economic torts. For more detail see S. Deakin and G.S. Morris, *Labour Law* (3rd edn., 2001), chapter 11.4.
32 TULRCA 1992, s. 219(1) and (2).
33 *Hadmor Productions Ltd v Hamilton* [1982] IRLR 102.

the law's approach, for two reasons. First, the common law is in a constant state of development. This means that the economic torts can be expanded by the courts to cover new situations. The case of *Rookes v Barnard* is an illustration of this.[34] If the immunity is to remain effective, new torts must be added to the list in TULRCA 1992, s. 219. But many rights theorists fear that nowadays, the government would not intervene because it would not want to be seen to support industrial action. As a result, the immunity might gradually be eroded by judicial creativity. Second, it is often argued that the concept of 'immunity' does not have the same rhetorical force as the term 'right', and may even have negative connotations. It is difficult to deny someone their rights without a good justification. But an immunity sounds like a privilege rather than an entitlement. Hayek describes unions as 'uniquely privileged institutions to which the general rules of law do not apply'.[35] This may have implications for the way in which the judges construe the immunities.[36] Rights would be construed generously; privileges are construed narrowly.

The immunity applies to acts 'done by a person in contemplation or further- ance of a trade dispute'.[37] A 'trade dispute' is defined in TULRCA 1992, s. 218, and includes the main areas which are likely to be the subject of disagreement, such as terms and conditions of employment, facilities for union officials, and machinery for negotiation. One matter which is not mentioned is a protest by workers against government policy. Workers cannot lawfully use a strike as an avenue of politi- cal action unrelated to their employment. This can create particular problems for workers in the public sector who must be sure to present their dispute as one about terms and conditions of employment even though it may be closely related to their concerns about government policy.[38]

The definition of a trade dispute helps to illustrate the underlying basis of the right to strike in English law. A right to strike based on freedom of expression would probably include political strikes. Political speech is regarded as particularly deserving of protection and it would be difficult to justify restrictions on the content of the views workers could express through strike action. Instead, English law only permits strikes relating to matters in the control of the employer. The topics listed in s. 218 relate either to the process of collective bargaining or to topics about which bargaining could take place. This suggests that – to the extent that English law protects a right to strike at all – it does so on the grounds that a strike is a weapon to be used in collective bargaining.

English law also prohibits 'secondary action'.[39] This occurs where workers who are not in dispute with their own employer, B, take action to support workers

---

34 [1964] AC 1129, and see the government's response: Trade Disputes Act 1965, s. 1.
35 Hayek, above n. 23, p. 267.
36 For an example, see *McShane and Ashton v Express Newspapers Ltd* [1980] AC 672 at 687.
37 TULRCA 1992, s. 219(1), sometimes referred to as the 'golden formula'. See B. Simpson, 'Trade disputes and industrial action ballots in the twenty-first century' (2002) 31 *ILJ* 270.
38 See, for example, *Mercury Communications Ltd v Scott-Garner* [1983] IRLR 494.
39 TULRCA 1992, s. 224.

who are in dispute with their employer, A. This type of action may occur for a variety of different reasons. One possibility is that B's workers simply wish to show their support for A's workers. Another perhaps more likely scenario occurs where employer B decides to help employer A to withstand the strike by fulfilling employer A's commercial contracts. B's workers may decide that they do not want to harm A's workers in this way. Whatever the motivation, TULRCA 1992, s. 224, ensures that secondary action does not benefit from the statutory immunity provided by s. 219.

This is a topic of considerable controversy. Rights theorists argue that secondary action is a legitimate exercise of the right to strike. English law's ban on this type of action has been condemned by the ILO. The Committee of Experts in a 2003 report recalled its earlier comments that:

> Workers should be able to participate in sympathy strikes provided the initial strike they are supporting is itself lawful ... this principle is particularly important in the light of earlier TUC comments that employers commonly avoid the adverse effects of disputes by transferring work to associated employers and that companies have restructured their businesses in order to make primary action secondary.[40]

This highlights one of the major arguments in favour of allowing secondary action. Employers are able to structure their businesses in any way they choose. One large firm can be broken up into a set of smaller firms which appear to be separate but in fact have close links. This makes it difficult for unions to cause disruption. If only one firm is affected by a strike, the others in the group can easily take over its work. The union is unlikely to be able to call all the workers out on strike across the enterprise as a whole, because it would be difficult to show a dispute between each of the small firms and its workers. However, from an economics perspective, the ban on secondary action can be viewed as a sensible measure to limit the disruption a strike can cause.[41] If secondary action is permitted, a strike can extend beyond the firm in dispute to associated firms or even to other firms in the same industry. These firms suffer damage to their business even though they are not responsible for the dispute and can do nothing to resolve it. The level of productivity in the economy as a whole is reduced, and multinational firms may be deterred from investing in Britain as a result.

The criteria for securing immunity from tort liability that we have considered so far apply both to trade unions and to individuals who organise strikes. But if a trade union is responsible for a strike (if the action is 'official'), there are some additional conditions which must be fulfilled if the strike is to be immune.[42] The union must ensure that the action has the support of a ballot. The balloting requirements are

---

40 Committee of Experts on the Application of Conventions and Recommendations, *Individual Observation concerning Convention No. 87, Freedom of Association and Protection of the Right to Organise, 1948, United Kingdom* (2003), para. 2. See also ILO, above n. 3, para. 486.

41 Department of Employment, *Removing Barriers to Employment* (Cm. 655, 1989), para. 3.10.

42 Whether or not a union is responsible for the action is determined by TULRCA 1992, ss. 20–1 for the torts therein listed, and by *Heatons Transport (St Helens) Ltd v TGWU* [1972] ICR 308, for other torts.

set out in considerable detail in TULRCA 1992, ss. 226–34A. The employer must be given seven days' notice of the ballot and must be sent a sample voting paper.[43] The notice need not name the employees who are eligible to vote[44] but the union must give the employer any information it has which would enable the employer to make contingency plans, such as information about the number and category of employees who are affected.[45] The ballot must be conducted by postal vote[46] and TULRCA 1992, s. 229 specifies exactly what must appear on the ballot paper, including a warning that a strike is a breach of the contract of employment. The union must take particular care to ensure that ballot papers are sent to all those who it reasonably believes will be called on to take action, and to no others,[47] although accidental failures which do not affect the outcome of the ballot may be disregarded under s. 232B. The employer must be given notice of the result of the ballot[48] and at least seven days' notice of any industrial action to be taken on the basis of the ballot.[49] The ballot remains effective for four weeks (or up to eight weeks if the employer agrees).[50] If the union does not begin the industrial action during this time, for example, because it is continuing to negotiate with the employer, it must conduct the ballot again.

From an economics perspective, the balloting requirement can be regarded as a useful tool in the negotiating process. One of the difficulties faced by employers is calculating the cost of disagreeing with the union's demands. The employer must predict the likelihood of a strike taking place and its probable duration before it can work out the loss of profits the strike would entail. Both the employer and the union are faced with the risk that the employer will underestimate the probability of a strike. This might lead the employer to think that it is not worth agreeing with the union's demands. The union will then be put to the expense of calling a strike in order to show its sincerity. This will also impose costs on the employer until a settlement is reached. The law can address this problem by providing the union with a mechanism for signalling to the employer that it is sincere about a strike threat. The balloting provisions perform this function. Once the union has conducted a strike ballot and obtained a majority in favour of the action, the employer's cost of disagreeing can be calculated with a greater degree of certainty. This might well prompt the parties to reach a settlement. Moreover, the strike ballot is only effective for four weeks (or eight weeks if the employer and the union agree to extend it).[51] As this deadline nears, the likelihood that a strike will take place increases. This

---

43 TULRCA 1992, s. 226A.
44 TULRCA 1992, s. 226A(3A)(b).
45 TULRCA 1992, s. 226A(2) and (3A)(a); and see *London Underground Ltd v RMT* [2001] IRLR 228. In practice this information may nevertheless enable the employer to identify the relevant employees.
46 TULRCA 1992, s. 230.
47 TULRCA 1992, s. 227(1).
48 TULRCA 1992, s. 231A.
49 TULRCA 1992, s. 234A.
50 TULRCA 1992, s. 234.
51 TULRCA 1992, s. 234.

gradually raises the cost of disagreeing for both the employer and the union. At some point before the deadline, one or both parties might decide that it would be cheaper to reach an agreement.

From a rights perspective, an obligation to conduct a ballot could, in principle, be a legitimate control on industrial action.[52] It is consistent with unions' status as democratic organisations that they should consult their members before calling a strike and act on the majority view. However, the current English law on strike ballots is difficult to justify on these terms. The government which introduced the legal provisions was hostile to trade unions and had an overriding concern to discourage strike action. This motivation was carried through into the substance of the legislation in several different ways. First, the legislation sought to discourage workers from voting in favour of a strike. For example, instead of allowing the union to determine the content of the ballot paper, the government prescribed the content and placed particular emphasis on the fact that strikers would be in breach of their contract of employment.[53] This sounds quite frightening but does nothing to explain to workers what the practical consequences of doing so might be. Second, the legislation is highly complex.[54] Even if a union is trying to comply, it may fail to do so. This does not seem consistent with a simple requirement of a democratic vote before industrial action. For example, under TULRCA 1992, s. 227(1):

> Entitlement to vote in the ballot must be accorded equally to all the members of the trade union who it is reasonable at the time of the ballot for the union to believe will be induced to take part . . . and to no others.

On basic democratic principles it is clearly important to ensure that the affected workers all get a vote, and that the result is not skewed by the inclusion of voters who will not in fact be called upon to strike. But it can be extremely difficult for a union to keep track of its members, particularly when they change jobs or places of work frequently. Under s. 232B, an accidental failure to comply with this provision which would not have affected the result of the ballot is to be disregarded. However, in *Midland Mainline Ltd v RMT*, the court construed this provision narrowly.[55] The government has recently proposed further amendments to the law on balloting,[56] though it claims that 'there is only limited scope to simplify this complex body of legislation further'.[57]

If the conditions for obtaining the immunity are not met, and the action goes ahead, the union or strike organiser will be exposed to liability in tort. Under TULRCA 1992, s. 22, there are limits on the damages which trade unions may be

---

52 ILO, above n. 3, para. 503, indicates that balloting requirements are acceptable.
53 TULRCA 1992, s. 229(4), amended in 1999 to include a reference to strikers' unfair dismissal rights, discussed below.
54 For discussion of recent cases, see Simpson, above n. 37.
55 [2001] IRLR 813. See also *P v NASUWT* [2003] 1 All ER 993.
56 DTI, *Review of the Employment Relations Act 1999* (2003), paras. 3.21–3.33.
57 DTI, above n. 56, para. 3.32.

required to pay, varying according to the size of the union. In practice, however, most employers would prefer to stop the strike taking place instead of suffering the damage and seeking compensation afterwards. This can be done by seeking an interim injunction, so called because it stops the strike from taking place until there has been a trial to determine its legality. To obtain an injunction, the employer must fulfil the *American Cyanamid* test,[58] by showing that there is a serious issue to be tried as to the lawfulness of the strike, and by showing that damages would not be an adequate remedy. Under TULRCA 1992, s. 221(2), the court is supposed to have regard to the likelihood that the union or strike organiser could establish the immunity when considering whether or not to grant the injunction. Despite this provision, both elements of the *American Cyanamid* test are easy to satisfy. The employer can usually persuade the court that the action may not be immune, and that damages would not fully compensate for all the harm which might be caused by the strike. Moreover, in urgent cases, an injunction can be granted by a court which has only heard argument from the party seeking the injunction. Under TULRCA 1992, s. 221(1), in a case involving trade dispute immunities, the court should only handle the case in this way if it is satisfied that reasonable steps have been taken to inform the union or strike organiser that an injunction is being sought. This is designed to give the union or organiser a chance to put its side of the case. However, critics argue that in practice, courts are too often willing to find that this provision has been satisfied.

The employer obviously has the greatest interest in taking legal action when a strike is taking place. But the employer is not the only party with a possibility of intervening. Under TULRCA 1992, s. 62, a member of the trade union may seek an injunction to prevent the action going ahead if it does not have the support of a validly conducted ballot. This allows union members to force the union to comply with internal democracy provisions. However, union members are not allowed to challenge industrial action on the ground that it is unlawful for some other reason, for example, that there is no 'trade dispute' within TULRCA 1992, s. 244. A broader right to seek an injunction is granted to individual members of the public who can show that the strike is unlawful (in any respect) and that it will 'prevent or delay the supply of goods or services' to them.[59] So far, there have been no successful actions under this provision.[60] However, it raises the possibility that even if the employer chose not to use legal means to tackle the dispute, a member of the public could intervene.

Strikes can and do take place in Britain. But trade unions and strike organisers must comply with substantive limitations (on the types of strike which are allowed) and procedural controls (on the procedures they must follow before calling a strike). These restrictions can be viewed in different ways: as the inevitable result of the link

---

58 From the case of *American Cyanamid v Ethicon Ltd* [1975] 1 All ER 504.
59 TULRCA 1992, s. 235A.
60 Though it has been invoked: *P v NASUWT* [2003] 1 All ER 993.

between strikes and collective bargaining; as legitimate attempts to limit the economic damage caused by strikes; or as illegitimate attempts to undermine workers' rights. But before you draw your conclusions, we need to examine the position of individual workers who go on strike.

The law on individual strikers

Individual strikers are almost always in breach of their contract, whether it is a contract of employment or a worker's contract. This is because they are refusing to perform some or all of the obligations set out in the contract. So the law on individual strikers starts from the same premise as the law on strike organisers: a strike is in principle unlawful but those involved may receive some degree of statutory protection. From a rights perspective, the difficulty with this is that strike action may be viewed by commentators and judges as a privilege rather than an entitlement. Moreover, workers may feel deterred from participating because they do not want to act unlawfully. The warning on strike ballot papers that strike action may be a breach of contract was intended to have exactly this effect. Some countries treat a strike as a suspension of the contract of employment in order to avoid this problem.[61]

The main consequence to follow from the fact that a strike is a breach of the contract of employment is that the employer is under no obligation to pay strikers' wages. This is uncontroversial: it is accepted by the ILO[62] and it is the position adopted by the legal systems of most other industrialised countries.[63] If strikers were paid, there would be very little incentive on their part to end the dispute whilst the pressure on the employer would be overwhelming. For the same reason, most countries (including the UK) do not give social security payments to strikers.[64] Some rights commentators have argued that this amounts to the state intervening to help the employer break the strike.[65] But if the state did support strikers financially, it is easy to see how this could be characterised as state intervention to help the union. Traditionally, unions help their members who are on strike by giving them 'strike pay', but this tends to be a relatively small sum of money.

More controversially, the employer may be allowed to withhold pay in full even when the employees are performing some of their duties. In *Sim v Rotherham MBC*, the court held that it was lawful for the employer to calculate the value of the services the employees were refusing to provide and to deduct this amount from their pay.[66] In *Wiluszynski v Tower Hamlets LBC* the employer sought to improve on

---

61 A.T.J.M. Jacobs, 'The law of strikes and lockouts', in R. Blanpain and C. Engels (eds.), *Comparative Labour Law and Industrial Relations in Industrialized Market Economies* (8th edn., 2001).
62 Above n. 3, para. 588.
63 Jacobs, above n. 61.
64 N. Wikeley, A.I. Ogus and E.M. Barendt, *The Law of Social Security* (5th edn., 2002), pp. 379–81 and 505–14.
65 K.D. Ewing, *The Right to Strike* (1991), chapters 5 and 6.
66 [1986] IRLR 391.

this remedy.[67] The council's employees took industrial action by refusing to answer queries from elected councillors whilst continuing to perform their other duties as normal. Over a five-week period this amounted to some three hours of missed work. However, the employer told the employees that if they refused to perform part of their duties, they would not be paid at all, and any work they did would be regarded as voluntary. The court accepted that because the employer had made its position clear, it was entitled to withhold the employees' pay in full for the period of the industrial action.

From an economics perspective, this decision is a curious one. It gives employees no incentive to use a less disruptive form of action like refusing to perform some of their duties. If they are not going to be paid at all, they might as well cause maximum disruption by going on strike. Of course, there are still reasons why union members might vote for a less disruptive form of industrial action. Strikers generally want to secure the support of the public, and in sectors such as transport or education, continuous action would quickly become unpopular. And there might be some justification for restricting action short of a continuous strike. If Mr Wiluszynski had won his case, he would have been able to continue his industrial action for a considerable period of time because he would have been liable to lose only a small proportion of his salary. The employer would suffer disruption, but perhaps not enough to outweigh its perceived cost of agreeing with the union's demands. Thus, the dispute could have rumbled on for years – souring relations in the workplace – without ever reaching a satisfactory resolution.

Strikers are also vulnerable to being dismissed. Workers do not receive the protection of unfair dismissal law (as chapter 9 explained) so their dismissal is governed by the ordinary principles of contract law. Since taking strike action is likely to amount to a repudiatory breach of contract, the employer will usually be entitled to terminate a worker's contract without notice. Employees fare rather better because they may be able to secure some unfair dismissal protection. However, this depends on whether or not the action has been organised by a trade union and on whether or not the action is lawful. If the action has not been organised by a trade union – in other words, the workers have simply walked out of their own accord – the action will be deemed to be 'unofficial'. It is automatically *fair* for the employer to dismiss unofficial strikers.[68]

If the action has been organised by a trade union, it counts as 'official' action. The employer can dismiss official strikers provided that it dismisses all of them and does not re-engage any of them within three months of the dismissals.[69] This is intended to prevent the employer from victimising those who are thought to have organised or encouraged the strike. The level of protection it affords depends on what proportion of the employer's workers are on strike and how easily new recruits

67 [1989] IRLR 259.
68 TULRCA 1992, s. 237.
69 TULRCA 1992, s. 238.

could be trained. If a large proportion of a highly skilled workforce is on strike, they are relatively well protected by this provision.

If the industrial action has been organised by a trade union (so that it is official) and is lawful, the action counts as 'protected'. The requirements for industrial action to be immune from tort liability and therefore lawful were discussed above. If the action is protected, it is automatically *unfair* for the employer to dismiss the striking employees within eight weeks of the start of the action.[70] After the end of the eight weeks, it may still be automatically unfair to dismiss the strikers if the employer has not taken reasonable steps to resolve the dispute. If the employer has taken such steps, the action ceases to be protected and the employees move into the category of official strikers with protection against selective dismissal only.

The dismissal provisions offer another insight into the underlying basis of the right to strike in English law. As we have seen, individual strikers are only protected against unfair dismissal if the action is organised by a trade union. This means that the right to strike is most unlikely to be based on the right to be free from forced labour. This would surely permit any worker to withdraw their labour, regardless of whether or not a trade union had authorised the action. The link with trade union activities suggests that, once again, the right to engage in collective bargaining is the basis for the right to strike. The strike is seen as a weapon for trade unions to deploy as part of the bargaining process, rather than as a weapon for individual workers.[71]

Perhaps the most controversial aspect of the dismissal provisions is the fact that protection is generally limited to eight weeks. From an economics perspective, this can be justified as a means of controlling the disruption caused by strikes by limiting their likely duration. Once a strike starts, the union's cost of disagreeing gradually increases as the workers lose more and more money in wages. Towards the end of the eight weeks, the union's cost of disagreeing may increase substantially if it believes that the employer is likely to dismiss the striking workers. This may be enough to outweigh the union's cost of agreeing and may therefore lead to a settlement. From the employer's perspective, the cost of disagreeing also increases as the strike goes on because it loses more and more in profits. But the employer knows that the expiry of eight weeks (coupled with a plausible threat to dismiss all the strikers) is likely to alter the union's calculations. If the employer thinks that the cost of an eight-week strike is greater than the cost of agreeing with the union, it is likely to try to settle the dispute at an early stage. If the employer thinks that the cost of an eight-week strike is less than the cost of agreeing with the union, it is likely to hold out for eight weeks in the hope that the union will be more willing to make concessions at the end of that period. The law helps to ensure that strikes do not go on longer than eight weeks.

However, the eight-week limit has been criticised. An economist might regard it as counter-productive – rather like the *Wiluszynski* decision – in that it discourages

---

70 TULRCA 1992, s. 238A. For discussion, see DTI, above n. 56, paras. 3.34–3.40.
71 This approach is accepted by the ILO (above n. 3, para. 477).

workers from taking less disruptive forms of action. The eight-week protected period of industrial action runs continuously from the first day of action.[72] If employees opt for a one-day strike each week, they will only be able to take eight days of action before their unfair dismissal protection runs out. This makes a continuous strike seem more attractive. More fundamentally, many rights theorists regard the eight-week limit as an illegitimate restriction on the right to strike. According to the ILO's Freedom of Association Committee, allowing employers to dismiss workers for taking part in a strike puts the state in breach of Convention 98 and is a serious instance of discrimination against trade unionists.[73] However, the government argues that the provision does offer effective protection to strikers (because in recent years few strikes have lasted longer than eight weeks) and that it acts as an incentive to settle disputes.[74]

Further reading

For a detailed account of English law on industrial action, see S. Deakin and G. Morris, *Labour Law* (3rd edn., 2001), chapter 11; or H. Collins, K.D. Ewing and A. McColgan, *Labour Law: Text and Materials* (2001), chapter 9. For a comparative perspective, see A.T.J.M. Jacobs, 'The law of strikes and lockouts', in R. Blanpain and C. Engels (eds.), *Comparative Labour Law and Industrial Relations in Industrialized Market Economies* (8th edn., 2001). Statistical data on strikes is available from the ILO at http://laborsta.ilo.org and (for the UK) from the Office of National Statistics at http://www.statistics.gov.uk/CCI/nscl.asp?ID=6625.

For an excellent general account of the reasons for protecting and for restricting the right to strike, see T. Novitz, *International and European Protection of the Right to Strike* (2003), chapters 2–4. The book is a comprehensive study of ILO, ECHR and ESC standards so it is a valuable source of further information on these topics too. For a critique of English law from a rights perspective, see K.D. Ewing, *The Right to Strike* (1991), chapter 8; and T. Novitz and P. Skidmore, *Fairness at Work: a Critical Analysis of the Employment Relations Act 1999 and its Treatment of Collective Rights* (2001), chapter 5. What is the best justification for the right to strike? Is it linked to the right to engage in collective bargaining or to some other right? What restrictions can legitimately be imposed on the right in order to protect other people? How can we distinguish between a legitimate restriction on, and an interference with, the right?

The real question from an economics perspective is whether or not the benefits of collective bargaining are sufficient to outweigh the damage done by the occasional strike, so you should revisit the literature on the economic impact of collective

---

72 According to s. 238A(3), the protection applies to a dismissal 'if it takes place within the period of eight weeks beginning with the day on which the employee started to take protected industrial action'.
73 Above n. 3, para. 591.
74 DTI, above n. 56, para. 3.37.

bargaining listed in the further reading section in chapter 10. The role of strike action in a 'partnership' model of industrial relations is particularly controversial. Does partnership make strikes illegitimate? Or just unnecessary? Could a strike serve a useful purpose within a partnership model?

The incidence of industrial action depends not just on the laws about strikes, but also on the laws regulating trade union activities more generally. What is the relationship between the recognition procedure discussed in chapter 10 and strike action? Is the possibility of legally enforced collective bargaining likely to increase or reduce the incidence of strikes? And what about the relationship between strike action and the controls on the closed shop and union discipline explored in chapter 11?

What next?

This postscript is not intended to draw any conclusions from our discussions. The purpose of this book has been to present you with a variety of – often conflicting – perspectives on labour law, and to leave you to draw your own conclusions about which arguments you find most persuasive. Instead, this postscript looks towards the future. Labour law is in a constant state of flux. Sometimes policy-makers may be more heavily influenced by rights arguments; sometimes they may act on economic imperatives. And as we saw in chapter 4, labour law is regulated in many different layers: international, regional and domestic. So the competing arguments may carry different weight at these various levels, leading to conflicts between them. How is labour law likely to develop in the next few years?

The economic and social context

At many points in this book, we have referred to the process of globalisation. Multi-national enterprises are able to locate their management, research and production activities virtually anywhere in the world. Cost is a major factor in their decisions. The fear is that a state like the UK will seem unattractive because of its high labour costs, and that this will lead to substantial job losses. National governments will lose control over labour law because they are beholden to the multinationals. Many fear that this will lead to a 'race to the bottom' as governments seek to reduce their labour standards to the lowest possible level. What is the future of globalisation?

Those who are strongly opposed to multinational enterprises and their activities argue that globalisation can, and should, be stopped. The job losses would end and governments would get control over labour law again. But there are at least two reasons for thinking that this view is too simplistic. First, in our capacity as consumers rather than workers, we usually welcome globalisation. It means that we can buy products such as clothing or electrical goods at a much lower cost. Some consumers might be prepared to pay extra in order to get a guarantee that the workers who made the goods were well paid, but not all consumers are concerned about these issues. Second, although jobs might be lost in developed countries as a result of globalisation, new jobs are being created in developing countries. Globalisation produces winners as well as losers. And these winners are often countries which have high levels of poverty and unemployment. They are in desperate need of foreign investment so that they can improve their health care and education systems, transport infrastructure and so on. Of course, the benefits of globalisation might not be distributed fairly in some countries. Perhaps the ruling elite might take a big chunk of the profits, leaving ordinary workers with very low wages. But this is not a reason to stop the process of globalisation altogether.

Most economists believe that globalisation is an inevitable process which could not be stopped even if this was what we wanted to do. This suggests that the debates we have been having in this book will remain highly relevant in the future. It will still be necessary to ask whether developed countries should adopt the neoclassical or new institutional prescriptions for survival. And rights theorists will still need to be able to defend their claims against arguments that rights are too costly and create too much of a burden on businesses in the globalising world economy.

The ILO

One way to deal with some of the problems of globalisation might be to address them at the international level. Globalisation forces governments to compete with each other in order to attract multinational corporations to their countries. But there would no longer be competition on labour standards if they could be agreed by all states. The ILO is the obvious forum in which this could take place. However, although globalisation makes international agreements seem more necessary, it also makes them more difficult to achieve. Developing countries suspect that developed countries are trying to take away their competitive advantage by imposing impossibly high labour standards on them. And developed countries suspect developing countries of exploiting their own workers in order to maintain that advantage.

In 1998, the ILO gave a renewed impetus to its activities through the *Declaration on Fundamental Principles and Rights at Work*. This document was intended to do two main things. One was to require all ILO member states to respect a set of very basic and (relatively) uncontroversial labour rights. The other was to address developing countries' economic concerns by making it clear that labour standards would not be used to protect developed countries from competitive pressures.[1] The Declaration seems to have succeeded in giving the ILO more focus. The rights themselves have widespread support and the ILO produces a powerful report on one of the rights each year, 'naming and shaming' countries which are in breach. But the Declaration also raises several key questions for the future. Many commentators are concerned that instead of being a floor – a basic set of standards from which countries can improve – the Declaration will become a ceiling – the maximum which can be expected from a country. Will the ILO be able to add new rights to the Declaration? How will it deal with persistent offenders? And will it be able to persuade countries to focus not just on complying with the fundamental rights referred to in the

---

1 ILO, *Declaration on Fundamental Principles and Rights at Work* (1998), para. 5.

Declaration, but also on complying with the more detailed standards set out in the ILO's other Conventions?

Another area of interest is the relationship between the ILO and the World Trade Organisation (WTO).[2] The WTO is responsible for managing and enforcing the General Agreement on Tariffs and Trade (GATT), which governs the conditions for trade between different countries. Many commentators have compared the effectiveness of the two organisations and have found the ILO to be sadly lacking. If a country is found to be in breach of the GATT, its victim may be allowed to impose trade sanctions on that country until the violation is rectified. This gives states a powerful incentive to comply with the rules. The ILO, in contrast, usually tries to shame states into complying with labour standards. As a result, it has been argued that WTO mechanisms should be used to uphold labour standards. States should be allowed to impose trade sanctions on other states which breach certain obligations, such as those contained in the ILO Declaration. In the Singapore Declaration, the WTO rejected this idea, stating that the ILO should retain responsibility for enforcing its own norms.[3] But this clear-cut distinction between the two organisations may not last forever. If a state tries to enforce labour standards using trade sanctions, it may find itself in breach of WTO rules. This will force the WTO to judge on labour issues. At present, a case is before the WTO challenging the EU's policy of giving preferential treatment in trade to countries which comply with certain labour standards.[4] The ILO may benefit by having access to better enforcement of its norms. But it may also find that its rights-based approach comes under considerable challenge in the WTO, an organisation based on free-market economics.

The EU

The UK might also look to the EU for some protection against globalisation. Not all firms will want to consider locating their factories anywhere in the world. If they face significant transport costs, for example, they might want to produce goods nearer to their main markets. In these cases, the UK is competing not with the rest of the world, but with the rest of the EU. Much of the EU's social and labour legislation, particularly in the early years, was motivated by a desire to prevent Member States from undercutting each other by lowering standards. So what does the future hold for the EU? It will be suggested here that although the EU is becoming increasingly rights-focused, it faces significant deregulatory pressures from a variety of sources.

As we saw in chapter 4, the EU has become increasingly conscious of the need to legitimise its activities in terms of human rights. At first, this task fell largely to the

---

2　See, generally, C. McCrudden and A.C.L. Davies, 'A perspective on trade and labor rights' (2000) 3 *JIEL* 43.

3　WTO, *Singapore Ministerial Declaration* (1996), para. 4.

4　DS 242, brought by Thailand against the EC. In DS 246, brought by India, the EC was found to be in breach of the GATT for giving preferential treatment to countries which complied with its requirements to combat drug trafficking.

ECJ, which developed a doctrine of fundamental rights to constrain the Community institutions and the Member States when they were implementing Community law.[5] In 2000, the Member States 'proclaimed' the EU Charter of Fundamental Rights, a comprehensive statement of both civil and political and economic and social rights. At the moment, the Charter is a soft law measure, but it is highly likely to be incorporated into the EU's new Constitution which is currently under negotiation. This will strengthen the EU's human rights focus more than ever before. The Charter rights will play the same role as they do in the ECJ jurisprudence at present: as a control on the activities of the Community institutions and the Member States. It will not be possible to bring a claim that the EU should act to protect one of the rights. Nevertheless, the institutions will still be forced to review their actions for their compatibility with human rights. And once the rights are in the Constitution, their role might develop in future so that they supplement or expand the EU's competences.

Perhaps the strongest deregulatory pressure facing the EU is globalisation itself. Although the EU can prevent damaging competition between the Member States, it must still compete with the rest of the world. Part of the EU's response is new institutionalist: it is seeking to create a highly skilled and adaptable workforce made up of loyal and productive workers whose rights are respected. But some aspects of EU policy are more protectionist in character and may have to be dismantled. Perhaps the most significant example of this is the Common Agricultural Policy (CAP). Many developing countries have agriculture as a major component of their economies. They would like to export their goods to the EU. But they find it difficult to do so because the EU places prohibitive tariffs in the way of imported agricultural products, and because the EU subsidises its own farmers through the CAP. The latest round of trade negotiations in the WTO is, in part, concerned to liberate the market in agricultural products – in other words, to allow globalisation to take place – in order to help developing countries. It seems likely that the EU will eventually have to make some concessions on this issue. When it does so, there are bound to be job losses in the agricultural sector. It will be interesting to see how the EU deals with these job losses.

Within the EU, the process of 'enlargement' may also create deregulatory pressure. In 2004, 10 countries from Eastern Europe will join the EU. Enlargement can be regarded as an economically motivated process. The firm in our example, above, which wanted to keep its transportation and labour costs down could, prior to enlargement, have chosen to locate in a country on the EU's borders which was not bound by EU labour legislation. As more countries join the EU, the possibility of this kind of competition is reduced. Of course, enlargement has other motivations too, notably achieving greater political unity and stability across the continent. The implications of enlargement for labour standards are difficult to predict. One

---

5 See, generally, P. Craig and G. de Búrca, *EU Law: Text, Cases and Materials* (3rd edn., 2003), chapter 8.

problem is that enlargement makes the EU's decision-making processes more unwieldy. Some efforts have been made to reform voting procedures so that fewer measures will require unanimous agreement among Member States. But even where a measure only requires a qualified majority, it may still be more difficult to reach agreement. Moreover, the new Member States may be reluctant to accept new labour legislation in the first few years after joining. In order to satisfy the criteria for EU membership, these states have had to ensure that their legislation conforms to EU standards. This has involved a steep learning curve and, in many cases, dramatic changes to national legislation. Further changes are unlikely to be welcomed until these initial reforms have settled into place.

Another important trend in EU policy is the increasing emphasis on flexibility. Although flexibility does not necessarily denote deregulation, it does suggest that in future, the EU will be less concerned to require the Member States to comply with detailed standards. Flexibility manifests itself in two main ways in the labour law context. First, there is slightly less emphasis on harmonising the laws of the Member States by enacting 'hard law' measures such as directives. Instead, Member States are being encouraged to pursue common goals through non-binding 'soft law' strategies. The main example of this is the 'open method of co-ordination' used as part of the European Employment Strategy (EES).[6] The EES is an important part of the EU's response to globalisation. Its aim is to help Member States reduce unemployment by developing a well-trained and flexible workforce. The 'open method of co-ordination' involves agreeing a set of objectives for the EU as a whole and translating them into objectives for each Member State. Then, Member States are given targets to achieve. There are no penalties for failing to meet the targets but Member States are 'named and shamed' if they fall short. The important point is that Member States are given *flexibility* as to how they go about achieving the targets.

A second area in which flexibility has been given greater emphasis is in the drafting of 'hard law' measures themselves. Barnard explains that hard law measures can cause problems when they are too prescriptive: in other words, when they try to lay down very precise rights and obligations.[7] This is because Member States have different traditions and cultures, so a measure which might fit well in one country could seem alien to another. Moreover, firms and employees in different sectors of the economy have different needs. Barnard uses the Working Time Directive as an example of this.[8] Some countries had a long tradition of regulation in this area; the UK had none at all. So the Directive's fixed limits on working time (the 11-hour rest period in 24 hours, and so on) might not have been appropriate for a particular country or for some firms within that country. She argues that European legislation should be less prescriptive. Member States should be given a greater degree of choice

---

6 For detail, see J. Kenner, *EU Employment Law: from Rome to Amsterdam and beyond* (2003), chapter 11.
7 C. Barnard, 'EC Social Policy' in P. P. Craig and G. de Búrca (eds.), *The Evolution of EU Law* (1999).
8 Directive 93/104/EC.

at the implementation stage. And firms should be allowed to reach agreements with the workforce to vary some obligations in the light of local conditions. Barnard uses the Parental Leave Directive as an illustration of a more effective piece of legislation which employs both these types of flexibility.[9]

The implications of flexibility for labour law are of considerable interest for the future. Some commentators argue that soft law measures are being used tactically by the Commission. Once Member States have agreed to soft law or flexible measures, this paves the way for the Commission to develop hard law or more precise obligations at a later date. Others welcome flexibility as a wise regulatory strategy. They point out that given the diversity of Europe – soon to be enhanced by enlargement – it is not sensible to use a 'one-size-fits-all' approach. Member States and firms are more likely to comply with legislation where it can be adapted to their circumstances. Yet others are suspicious. Flexibility could be used as an excuse to deny workers their rights. New European legislation appears to create binding obligations, but in practice, Member States or firms may be able to invoke flexibility provisions in order to set up very different arrangements. Workers are at a disadvantage because they often lack the knowledge and bargaining power to insist on their rights.

The UK

The issues we have considered so far – globalisation itself, and the role of international and regional organisations – are bound to influence what occurs in domestic law. But their influence is by no means straightforward. The domestic response to the pressures they create depends on a range of factors. One is the policy of the government of the day: whether it is pursuing a deregulatory strategy, or a high productivity or pro-rights approach. Another factor is the attitude of the various key actors in labour law, notably the trade unions and employers' organisations. Yet another is the role of the courts: for example, the HRA 1998 may affect labour law in unpredictable ways. These factors interact with the economic context and pressures from other organisations in the process of creating the labour law of the future.

As we have seen, the present government's policy is rarely couched in the language of rights. This creates some degree of conflict between the government's aims and those of international human rights instruments. The litigation surrounding the *Wilson* case, discussed in chapter 11, is an interesting example of this.[10] The ILO strongly condemned English law's position on transferring staff to so-called 'personal contracts'.[11] The government responded not by offering a competing interpretation of workers' rights, but instead by emphasising the impact a change in the

---

9 Directive 96/34/EC.
10 *Associated Newspapers Ltd v Wilson* [1995] 2 AC 454.
11 ILO Committee of Experts, *Individual Observation on Convention 98* (2002).

law would have on firms. The ECtHR upheld Mr Wilson's claim that his Article 11 rights had been breached, and although the government is now changing the law, it still plans to introduce a provision which will allow firms to transfer workers to personal contracts without being found to have discriminated on trade union grounds.[12] Again, the emphasis is on the needs of firms and there is a clear reluctance to consider rights-based justifications. From a strategic point of view, there is an important lesson here for those who want to advocate new labour legislation. It is that they should emphasise the business benefits of their proposals rather than the need to protect workers' rights. But this will not come easily to those labour lawyers who are used to viewing their subject from a rights perspective. Moreover, it may have some dangers for the future. The claim that a particular measure will benefit firms can be tested empirically. If it is found that a new piece of legislation has in fact been damaging to firms, there will be immediate calls for its repeal. It will be difficult to start arguing at this stage that the measure should be retained because it protects workers' rights.

As we have seen, both the government and the EU are drawn towards new institutionalist arguments because they offer a solution to the problems of globalisation. This solution is regarded as either more likely to succeed – or more politically acceptable – than the deregulatory solution prescribed by the neoclassical theorists. In the future, it will be possible to test whether or not the new institutionalist approach has worked. Will multinational firms invest in the UK? Will low-skilled jobs lost in manufacturing be replaced by high-skilled jobs in information technology? The new institutionalists assume that countries with lower wages cannot offer the same benefits in terms of worker attitudes and qualifications. But this might be regarded as a rather patronising assumption. India is a good example of a relatively low-wage country with a good education system whose workers can compete not only on cost but also on quality. So one question to ponder for the future is whether the high-skills strategy seems likely to succeed. And if not, what (if anything) is the alternative?

As well as evaluating these arguments at the more general, theoretical level, it is also important to assess the precise version being implemented by the government. We saw on many occasions in earlier chapters that the government is also concerned to ensure that employers do not face high costs as a result of regulation. This often limits the government's pursuit of new institutionalist arguments. For example, the decision to introduce *unpaid* parental leave was criticised by many commentators as a 'half-hearted' measure because it means that many families will not be able to afford to take up the new right.[13] The government also seeks to limit the EU's regulatory ambitions by putting forward the argument that new measures will be a burden on business, particularly when the measures being proposed are unfamiliar

---

12 *Wilson v UK* [2002] 35 EHRR 20; DTI, *Review of the Employment Relations Act 1999* (2003), paras. 3.3–3.17.
13 See chapter 6.

to UK firms.[14] The Framework Directive on Informing and Consulting Employees is an excellent example of this.[15] Of course, new institutionalist arguments must, and do, weigh the benefits of regulation against the costs. But some commentators believe that the government is failing to implement the new institutionalist approach because of its overriding concern with costs. Will the high-skills strategy bring benefits even if it is implemented only in part?

The government's focus on costs is explained in part at least by its desire to take into account the arguments put forward by firms, through employers' organisations such as the Confederation of British Industry (CBI). Although the CBI has accepted some elements of the high productivity approach, such as the emphasis on partnership in industrial relations and on providing training for the workforce, it retains a strongly deregulatory outlook.[16] It campaigns in particular about the burden of 'red tape' faced by businesses: in other words, against the costs of complying with the law. It argues that this is especially relevant for small businesses because they may not be able to afford legal advice and certainly cannot employ dedicated staff to deal with employment law issues. As one of the members of UNICE, the European employers' federation, the CBI is able to pursue these arguments on the EU level too, particularly when proposals are made to enact directives through the social dialogue procedure. UNICE has resisted directives on informing and consulting employees in particular.[17] The Member States were forced to enact the new Framework Directive through ordinary legislative procedures because it could not be agreed using the social dialogue. It seems that deregulation is still the policy of the Conservative Party, so if there were to be a change of government at some point in the future, we would be likely to see significant shifts in direction for labour law. Reducing the burdens on businesses would become the main focus of labour law policy, not just a factor to be taken into account when formulating that policy.

Recently, there has been considerable media interest in the increasing radicalism of trade unions, as evidenced by the strike action taken by fire-fighters and postal workers among others. It is argued that unions are frustrated by the present government's pro-business rhetoric and limited emphasis on labour rights. The government's decision to retain most of the industrial action legislation passed by previous Conservative governments has been a particular source of dissatisfaction. It is certainly true that trade unions are a force for rights-based regulation of the labour market. But industrial action is not their only strategy. Unions regard litigation as an important means of securing their objectives. The *Wilson* case, discussed above, illustrates the role of complaints to the ILO and the ECtHR.[18] The *BECTU* case,[19] in which a union successfully challenged the government's attempt to impose

---

14 See, for example, B. Bercusson, 'The European social model comes to Britain' (2002) 31 *ILJ* 209.
15 Directive 2002/14/EC.
16 The CBI's website is a useful source of information: http://www.cbi.org.uk/home.html.
17 See Bercusson, above n. 14.
18 Above nn. 11 and 12.
19 Case C-173/99 *R (on the application of BECTU) v Secretary of State for Trade and Industry* [2001] IRLR 559 (ECJ).

a qualifying period on those claiming their four weeks of paid annual leave under the Working Time Directive,[20] illustrates the role of litigation before the ECJ. Nevertheless, it would be too simplistic to portray unions as pursuing workers' rights at the expense of all other considerations. Unions have been given significant opportunities to participate in the legislative process, both at EU level through the social dialogue, and at national level through consultation with the government. This involves making concessions and reaching compromises as well as putting forward the case for workers' rights.

We saw in chapter 4 that the courts have long been regarded with suspicion by trade unions and by many labour lawyers. Their use of contract doctrine (and their emphasis on the ideology of freedom of contract) often leads to a perception that they are favouring employers over workers. And their emphasis on the individual makes it difficult for them to deal with collective interests such as the claims of trade unions. Are there signs of change? One important factor to consider is the impact of the HRA 1998. On the one hand, this may make the courts more focused on the needs of workers because they will have to consider cases explicitly in terms of workers' rights. They will also have to take into account the Strasbourg jurisprudence, some of which has favoured workers. On the other hand, many commentators are sceptical about the value of the Act. They point out that the rights themselves, particularly as interpreted by the Strasbourg court, are rights for individuals. There is virtually no emphasis on collective interests or on the role of trade unions. Moreover, the UK courts are regarded as having been so far relatively cautious in their use of the HRA 1998. Another important factor is the impact of EU law. The domestic courts are bound by the jurisprudence of the ECJ so they have less room to develop their own lines of reasoning. And much of that jurisprudence is quite strongly protective of workers' rights. Of course, there are exceptions – commentators have criticised the justification test in discrimination law as applied both domestically and by the ECJ – but on the whole, EU law does encourage the courts to favour workers. This is reflected in the litigation strategies of trade unions, discussed above.

Predicting the future is, of course, a dangerous game. Perhaps all that can be said with certainty is that labour law will continue to reflect compromises between the advocates of regulation (whether they are using rights or economics arguments) and the advocates of deregulation. Which camp will be able to claim victory on any particular issue will depend on a whole host of factors, such as the political complexion of the government of the day, the attitudes of employers, the Strasbourg jurisprudence and the litigation strategies of trade unions. The purpose of this chapter has been to show that the perspectives used throughout this book will help you not only to analyse today's labour law, but also to analyse the labour law of the future, whatever shape it may take.

---

20 Directive 93/104/EC.

Index